Born Colin Johnson at Narrogin in Western Australia in 1938, Mudrooroo left Perth for Melbourne in the 1950s. He studied at night while working in the Motor Registration Office and State Library. He wrote *Wild Cat Falling* (1965), which was welcomed as the first novel by an Aboriginal writer, then left Australia to travel in Asia, where he studied Buddhism and became a Buddhist monk.

Returning to Melbourne in 1976, he worked at the Aboriginal Research Centre at Monash University, studied at Melbourne University and taught at Koorie College. He has more recently been a lecturer on indigenous/black Australian writing at Murdoch University and the University of Queensland. His ground-breaking study of Aboriginal literature, *Writing from the Fringe* (1991) was short-listed for the WA Premier's Award and the Stanner Award in 1992.

He formally changed his name from Colin Johnson to Mudrooroo in 1988.

Mudrooroo is the author of over a dozen literary works, including the novel *Doctor Wooreddy's Prescription for Enduring the Ending of the World* (1983), which has been published around the world and is now regarded as a modern Australian classic. His poetry collection *The Garden of Gethsemane*, was double winner of the WA Premier's Award in 1992 and was also short-listed for the Victorian Premier's Awards.

He currently lives in Queensland.

By the same author

Novels
Wild Cat Falling (1965)
Long Live Sandawara (1979)
Doctor Wooreddy's Prescription for
    Enduring the Ending of the World (1983)
Doin Wildcat (1988)
Master of the Ghost Dreaming (1991)
Wildcat Screaming (1992)
The Kwinkan (1995)

Poetry
The Song Circle of Jacky and Selected Poems (1986)
Dalwurra: the Black Bittern (1988)
The Garden of Gethsemane: Poems from the Lost Decade
    (1992)
Pacific Highway Boo-Blooz (1996)

Criticism
Writing from the Fringe (1991)
Us Mob (1995)

MUDROOROO

Indigenous Literature of Australia

Milli Milli Wangka

HYLAND  HOUSE

First published in Australia in 1997 by
Hyland House Publishing Pty Ltd
Hyland House
387–389 Clarendon Street
South Melbourne
Victoria 3205

National Library of Australia
Cataloguing-in-publication data:

Mudrooroo, 1938- .
  The indigenous literature of Australia = Milli milli wangka.

  Bibliography.
  Includes index.
  ISBN 1 86447 014 3.

  1. Australian literature - Aboriginal authors - History and criticism. 2. Australian literature - 20th century - History and criticism. I. Title.

A820.989915

Edited by Raylee Singh
Index by Kerry Biram
Typeset in Caslon 11/12 by Hyland House
Printed in Australia by Australian Print Group

Contents

Acknowledgements

The author acknowledges permission to quote from the following works: *Songs of Central Australia* by T.G.H. Strehlow, published by Harper Collins; 'My Love' by Oodgeroo of the tribe Noonuccal (formerly know as Kath Walker) in *My People* 3rd Edition, 1990, published by Jacaranda Press; 'Free Our Dreams' by Lionel Fogarty in *New and Selected Poems*, 1995, published by Hyland House; Paddy Roe's and Butcher Joe Nangan's Djaringalong stories in *Gularabulu*, 1983, published by the Fremantle Arts Centre Press; 'Epitaph' by Kevin Gilbert in *Black from the Edge*, 1994, published by Hyland House; *The Cake Man*, 1978, by Robert Merritt, published by Currency Press. The author also wishes to thank Mark Bin Baker for quoting from 'Fly Away Pidgin', transcribed from the audio-cassette *Kimberley Legend* (n.d.), sung by Lucy Cox; and Ted Egan for quoting from 'Tjandamara' transcribed from the audio-cassette *Ted Egan Presents the Kimberely* (n.d.).

The author also acknowledges permission to reproduce the covers of the following books: *Don't Take Your Love to Town* by Ruby Langford, published by Penguin Books; *New and Selected Poems* by Lionel Fogarty, published by Hyland House; *Black from the Edge* by Kevin Gilbert, published by Hyland House; and *My People* 3rd Edition, by Oodgeroo of the tribe Noonuccal, 1990, published by Jacaranda Wiley.

Introduction

We're generally much better educated about Indigenous culture and history, much more aware of the existence of the civilisation which existed here before Europeans came, much more knowledge-able about what has happened since—and much more concerned about what is happening now.
(Paul Keating, then Prime Minister of Australia, at the inaugural meeting of the Council for Aboriginal Reconciliation, 21 February 1992)

THAT MEETING, AND HIS WORDS, SHOW HOW MUCH things have changed since *Writing from the Fringe*, the first edition of this work, appeared in 1990. The Council for Aboriginal Reconciliation is committed to bringing the Indigenous people of Australia into the mainstream, not only physically but culturally. It may be said that the political agenda behind Indigenous reconcili-ation is tied to the increasing push for a Republic of Australia, a new beginning to commence in 2001. Old crimes are to be forgiven and a new future forged. The Republic of Australia needs to be a united nation and with us Indigenous people it will have a past extending back into what we call 'The Dreaming', remote antiquity. We Indigenous people of Australia have never given up our sovereignty and so, with the throwing off of the shackles of the old colonial country, it may be said that we will resume our sovereignty when the Republic is declared. The Indigenous culture of Australia is increasingly seen as the culture of Australia and there is, as the Prime Minister declared, an increasing knowledge of this culture, even to the extent of appropriating some of its forms, or even discovering an Indigenous ancestry. The Dreaming is increasingly seen as the heritage of all Australians and the songlines of our Indigenous ancestors, the great epics singing the land, part of our common heritage.

It should not be forgotten that such an appropriation is not impossible, for the British empire in its heyday appropriated the Greek epics, the *Iliad* and the *Odyssey*, as inspiration for their imperial culture, though these epics emerged from a past every bit as foreign as that of pre-invasion Indigenous Australia as well as being in a foreign language which necessitated translation, adaptation and explanation. In the republican future Indigenous motifs and myths can provide the well-springs of a vibrant Australian culture resting on the land and the sense of national identity which can only come from our land. Thus, the great epics such as the *Djanggawul* might become as familiar to as many Australians as are the stories from ancient Greece, that is, if the process of reconciliation achieves some or all of its stated aims.

Although the reconciliation process is seen by many to be a government initiative foisted on the Indigenous people (and other Australians), it should not be forgotten that the Indigenous people have been crying out for some such process for many years now. In fact, it may be said that the beginnings and continuance of Indigenous literature in English is part of the process of reconciliation, for Indigenous literature begins as a cry from the heart directed at the invaders of our land. It is a cry for justice and for a better deal, a cry for understanding and an asking to be understood. Black writers, such as the late Kevin Gilbert and Oodgeroo Noonuccal, had a white Australian readership firmly in mind when they wrote and it was their aim to get across to as many people as possible the Indigenous predicament in Australia, a predicament which had resulted in many Indigenous persons becoming strangers in their own land, so alienated that sometimes they seemed to have lost the will to survive. Invasion, occupation and dispossession have resulted in the coming into being of a people without visible means of support, a lumpen proletariat objectified in these lines from my *Song Circle of Jacky* (1986, p. 31):

> The shuffling drunk the street derides,
> God staggers by in drunken rage.

Both white and black writers have written of the predicament and this has resulted in a strong literature which is evergrowing. It may be said that over the last decades conditions have improved and with this improvement Indigenous literature has begun to turn towards cultural and self introspection. Guilt and blame are not enough for the continuation of a literature and so histories from an Indigenous viewpoint are being constructed; life stories (often in collaboration), novels, short stories and poems are devoting their words to the Indigenous existential being in what is now said to be a 'multicultural' Australia and what in a few years time will be a republican Australia.

These topics are not new, though they are becoming of increasing concern to Indigenous writers. From the strong beginnings of Indigenous literature in English in the sixties and seventies, Kevin Gilbert, a major Indigenous writer, stated in *Living Black* (1984, p. 3) that the existential predicament of the modern Aborigine resides in 'a rape of the soul'. In his works, he consciously analyses the decay of Indigenous society which has occurred and is occurring all across Australia, seeing it as the result of a historical process rather than as a reality to be endured as Archie Weller describes in some of his stories, such as 'Pension Day' in his collection *Going Home* (1986, pp. 68–73):

> *They steal $20 from him with quick black fingers. They always do, every pension day. Where they had been afraid of his powers before, now they laugh and steal from him.*

Both writers are critical of the degradation often found within Indigenous communities. They do not romanticise this culture of poverty in which drunkenness plays too great a part, in which pensioners are robbed of their pensions by youngsters, in which cruel revenge is taken, in which parents gamble the day away while their children stumble around brain-damaged from sniffing petrol. The coarseness of life is painful to witness—in fact, it may seem that entire communities are deliberately attempting to wipe themselves out; but Indigenous writers refuse to see this as an inherent trait, or as a Social Darwinism based on an evolution which stresses that only the strong shall survive and that when a people is confronted by a different race equipped with strange and terrifying things, then everything is lost and those people unable to adapt become extinct. It would be easy to blame the *watjela* or *gubba* for all the ills of Indigenous communities, but Indigenous writers refuse to take this negative trail though they are fully cognisant of what happens to a people which has suffered a rape of the soul with continuing effects to the present.

Perhaps this picture is too white and it would be if Indigenous writers only concentrated on the evils which bedevil Indigenous society, but they also write of the bright things, the human warmth, the spontaneity and humour with which life and its problems are faced. Still, in a study of Indigenous literature, before we proceed to examine some of their texts and their presentation, the existential condition of Indigenous people and their historicity must be taken into account. Indigenous literature in English does not exist in an aesthetic vacuum, but within the context of Indigenous affairs. It must be seen holistically, within a cultural, historical and social context. To try and approach Indigenous writers and their literature as existing apart from their communities would be a falsity. Not only this, but contemporary Indigenous communities are the end result of 200 years of white history, and this past must never be forgotten.

Most, if not all, Indigenous writers may be labelled 'committed' writers. They are deeply concerned with the problems of their communities even to the extent that community is stressed at the expense of the individual. In writing about these problems, some of them become aware of similar situations facing minorities in other countries of the world and give their support to those communities fighting for a place under the sun, free from the domination of national majorities. Still, these writers acknowledge that their primary goal is to understand their own communities—the basis of their literature—and from there to create a literature which will not only be of use to their community, but will help to spread a knowledge about the Indigenous people of Australia and their unique culture. These are their aims, aims shared on occasion by some white academic and creative writers.

To have an understanding of this literature coming from the different communities—*Nangas, Nyungars, Yamadjis, Murris, Kooris, Yolngus*, and other regional and local groups making up the totality of people placed under the white term 'Indigenous'—there first must be a general schema of history which may be fleshed out from the works of the writers, storytellers and singers.

I will divide Indigenous history into a number of periods and it is these periods which not only go towards forming the styles of the writers, but also supply the contents of their works:

THE DIVISIONS OF INDIGENOUS LITERATURE HISTORY

1. **The Time of the Dreaming:** From the Beginning to 1788; Prehistory; Before the Coming of the Europeans.

2. **The Time of the Invasion(s):** A convenient cutoff date for this period might be 1901 and the coming into being of the federation of the Australian colonies.

3. **Punitive Expeditions and Protection:** The utter conquering and control of Indigenous peoples with the framing of restrictive legislation.

4. **The Colonial Period: Paternalism, then Assimilation:** A convenient cutoff date is 1967 when a referendum was conducted which made Indigenous people Australian citizens.

5. **The Period of Self-determination and Self-management:** The official policy from 1967 to 1988.

6. **The Period of Reconciliation:** Sharing cultures.

Indigenous being and history and the literature which helps to define it was until 1967 dominated by Anglo-Celts who held and hold the political power in Australia. 'The Time of the Dreaming', in line with European thought, was and still is called prehistory and a whole theoretical structure has been erected with little recourse to the Indigenous communities except as informants. Most Indigenous communities used the past, recorded in song-lines and stories, for all explanation of the present and future. This way of placing time and things in a continuum is called mythology by Europeans and is contrasted with the scientific way of thinking which seeks to explain the past from the present. Scientists and scholars prefer to work backwards from what is now to what was and tend to ignore any accounts found in the oral records and literature of the Indigenous communities, with the exception of anthropologists Ronald and Catherine Berndt who, in their *Arnhem Land: Its History and People* (1954), utilised Arnhem Land songlines. Other scholars defend theories from the evidence they collect and often their accounts and explanations seem more fantastic than the myths they seek to replace. Their investigations wander over and under the land. They measure and chart data from which they postulate things about Indigenous people, often based on race and evolutionary theories.

These theories are constructed and then discarded like European fashions and, as there is a history of fashion, so there is a history of racial theories and this is called 'anthropology'. One of its speculations concerns the origin of the Indigenous people. We have been said at different points of this genealogy of speculation to have been one of the lost tribes of the Hebrews; to once have been part of the ancient population of Gondwanaland; or to have floated here, either deliberately or accidentally, after walking across Indonesia when the seas froze during the last Ice Age and the islands became a single landmass except for one single stretch of water a hundred or so kilometres in width. This last speculation at the time I write is the one generally accepted. It achieved popular acceptance because of its political implications. The Indigenous peoples may be seen as the first immigrants and thus just like the other peoples in Australia though it is admitted that we arrived on the continent some tens of thousands of years before anyone else. This means politically that we were the original possessors of Australia. This genealogy of speculation may be contrasted with Indigenous history as contained in the oral records. There it is stated that some peoples have been here from the very beginning of humanity. Later arrivers, such as the *Djanggawul* of Arnhem Land and the *Three Brothers* of northern New South Wales, found Australia already inhabited.

It must be admitted that the beginnings of Indigenous occupation of Australia are lost in the mists of time. It is difficult, if not impossible, to place a definite date on when human beings first arrived. Often, 40 000 or 50 000 years ago is stated, but these figures have been arrived at by dating archaeological sites such as Keilor and Lake Mungo in eastern Australia. Scientifically, all that they say is that at that time people camped, or buried their dead, there.

Few if any peoples can date their origins with any certainty. Mythology only tells of the events happening when they were created, or when they arrived at a certain country. If dates are given, they often are found to have been added long afterwards. In Australia, many stories dealing with the origins of the different Indigenous communities have either been lost, or incorrectly recorded. This means that much of the oral literature of the Indigenous people is no longer available for examination and that it is impossible to deconstruct records dealing with each and every community. Some extant accounts describe events which happened thousands of years ago. These may provide dates when people were in a certain area. Thus there is an account which describes the eruption of volcanoes around Mount Gambier in South Australia which happened some 6,000 years ago.

Oral literature, apart from being important as the first literature of Australia, has an added importance in that it describes Indigenous life here before the invasion, though I must modify this to say that the formal oral literature as preserved in religious cults may be considered to have suffered less change and thus is more reliable for reconstituting pre-invasion Indigenous lifestyles. This oral literature, often detailing the early wanderings of the creative ancestors or ancestral beings in long songlines, has received some study. A theory postulated by Ronald Berndt is that the routes of these beings are early migratory trails along which groups of hunters and gatherers travelled as they settled the continent; but this is uncertain. The songlines which are still treasured do show that Australia was never a trackless wilderness, a *terra nullius*, as once stated by the invaders. In fact, if all these songlines remained intact, from them we might construct a detailed road map. This in many regions is no longer possible and those which remain, or have been written down, now may be seen as the classical literature of Australia and it is to them that present and future Australians may go for inspiration.

The Time of the Dreaming, or when the great epics were being created, lasted for many thousands of years. The first British settlement at Port Jackson marks the beginning of the end of this period with the steady erosion and breakage of many songlines. Examples of this literature may be found scattered throughout various books of ethnology and in the minds of elderly men and women. Some scholars, for example the anthropologists T.G.H. Strehlow and Ronald Berndt, have collected, translated and explained some of the songlines and stories from central and northern Australia, though, sadly, incompletely.

There also are collections of stories and legends which preserve examples of pre-invasion literature, though often these are heavily Europeanised. The uniqueness of the literature and the aesthetic use of language is lost in the translation. It is only recently that scholars are beginning to be concerned with narrative discourse, the way in which the story is told and structured, but in many areas it is too late to collect authentic structures of Indigenous narrative discourse in the original language. The languages have changed over time and often been replaced with an English of varying degrees of standardisation.

The Time of the Invasion(s) began when Europeans visited the shores of Australia. Dutch, French and British established initial aggressive relations which were not propitious for the future. William Dampier, supposedly the first European to land on the western coast of the continent, met Indigenous resistance which drove him back to his ship. In his journal, he made a number of assertions which for the next centuries, with a short interlude of the concept of the noble savage, were to be held by most European invaders. In his words, the people differed but little from brutes.

There are oral records of Indigenous people meeting Europeans for the first time, and there are also some written accounts. Walmatjarri writer and artist Peter Skipper, in his booklet *The Pushman* (n.d.), has given a short account of when he came in from the desert and of how he reacted to the *Gadiya* and their strange animals and objects. The scholars Luise Hercus and Peter Sutton (1986) have put together a number of accounts by Indigenous storytellers in their original languages, with an English translation of some initial meetings. These are in the main short accounts dealing with the lack of understanding on both sides and the brutal and bloody clashes which ended with Indigenous people being massacred. In some accounts, it is said that the lightskinned strangers were accepted at first as ghosts of the deceased returning. Indigenous writers in English, using oral and written sources, have reconstructed accounts of the initial contact.

One of these Indigenous writers, Eric Willmot, in his historical novel *Pemulwuy, the Rainbow Warrior* (1987), detailed Indigenous resistance around Port Jackson. Other writers, including Jack Davis, James Miller, Kevin Gilbert, Robert Merritt and myself, have dealt with this period in plays, histories and novels.

This oral and written literature coming from storytellers and writers from all the regions of Australia relates how once-strong Indigenous communities became weakened and demoralised as many of their number fell before the guns of the advancing colonists. They also tell of a more compassionate invader who came to soothe the pillows of what was coming to be seen as a dying race. These were the Christian missionaries who, although they saw Indigenous cultures as intrinsically pagan and thus evil, did bring with them a policy of education which in effect helped to foster the first Indigenous writings in English. One of the first

Indigenous writers, David Unaipon, was the product of a mission school. Some missionaries, for example the Germans C.G. Teichelmann and C.W. Schurmann in South Australia, even used the native language, but eventually English became the language of instruction. Often, it is written that the missionaries laboured to soften the coarse pioneering spirit of the first settlers, who often considered the Indigenous people vermin to be destroyed; but, for the Indigenous communities who came under their sway, the feelings were ambiguous.

Philip McLaren's 1993 novel, *Sweet Water—Stolen Land*, is a psychological study of one such missionary who emerges as a serial murderer. *Reaching Back*, edited by Judy Thompson (1989), is a collection of stories of Yarrabah Mission in Queensland and reveals the same ambiguity. In spite of this, it may be said that the missionaries accepted the Indigenous people as human beings, gave some of them an education of sorts, and eventually Christianised them. Their influence on Indigenous writing in English is enormous and this is apparent from the strong current of Christianity running through much of it. Also, it must be said that T.G.H. Strehlow, an ethnologist and missionary at Hermannsburg in Central Australia, was among the first to record and discuss Indigenous oral literature as a literature in its own right. His *Songs of Central Australia* (1971) is an important study of an Indigenous community's oral literature, as literature rather than as materials for anthropological study.

As soon as Indigenous resistance was crushed, there began a period of complete colonial subjugation. The peoples were herded into mission or government stations. Those outside on the vast cattle runs and farms which had been carved from their homelands were exploited for their labour value. In fact, punitive laws were enforced to prevent them from leaving these stations. They in effect became slaves, working for rations of tobacco, sugar and tea. While the men worked in the fields, the women worked as domestics in the homesteads of masters who were not averse to the soft feel of 'black velvet'. These liaisons resulted in the growth of a mixed-blood population, some of whom are related to the most-respected white Australian families. Indigenous people were outside the white law, or incarcerated under special Indigenous laws which prevented them from any assertion of rights. In fact, they were declared 'wards of the state' and had no rights. Any resistance was put down by the police or settlers. The result of this oppression is what is often accepted as the public face of Indigenous persons: shiftless, dirty, drunken natives, fighting and carrying on without hope for a future of grace and dignity. But it should be remembered that, until the sixties, Indigenous people were the mainstay of the cattle industry and their stories are now being told and written. Ann McGrath's *Born in the Saddle* (1987) is a history of those times; Jack Davis in his biography, *A Life Story*, edited by Keith Chesson (1988), speaks about those times and how it was seen from the Indigenous side. Other similar accounts can be found in such books as *Countrymen*, edited by Bruce Shaw (1986), *Wanamurraganya, the Story of Jack McPhee* as written down by Sally Morgan (1989), and the marvellous *Unbranded* by Herb Wharton (1992).

At first, there was slight mixing between the two races except during the course of work and for sexual intercourse between white men and black women. This led to the rise of a *mestizo* class, the coloured or half-caste who served as an intermediary between the two races and often given a decent wage. They might even find a place in the white township and be allowed to drink in the hotel. But public separation of the races was instituted from the beginning of the invasion, and at present the gap seems to have widened in spite of all the talk about reconciliation.

Separation and domination are strong in many rural areas of Australia and have resulted in the deaths of Indigenous people at the hands of the forces of law and order. In fact, so many Indigenous men died in police custody that a Royal Commission was called to investigate this appalling state of affairs. A number of Indigenous writers have written about this, including Jack Davis in his play, *Barungin (Smell the Wind)* (1988), based on the Indigenous (Nyungar) burial ceremony. The death of one young man, John Pat— allegedly kicked to death by the police in the streets of Roebourne, Western Australia, in 1983—has led to any number of poems. Indigenous literature also suffered a loss when the promising poet, Robert Walker, was brutally killed in Fremantle Prison, Western Australia, in 1984.

In Australia, the strengthening of the policy of separation, and economic conditions caused by the government enforcing the payment of a basic wage to Indigenous workers by their employers, resulted in mass sackings and eviction from the cattle stations carved from ancestral land. Many Indigenous people were forced into living on the fringes of country towns. This has been the subject of a play: *Coordah* (1989), by Richard Walley. In this work the gap between white and black is bridged by the *mestizo*, the do-gooder and the missionary, though these latter intermediaries were constantly under attack for seeking to educate the native. A.O. Neville, the Commissioner of Native Affairs in Western Australia earlier this century—and a character in two of Jack Davis' plays, *Kullark* (1982) and *No Sugar* (1986)—was no friend of the missionary or of education for Indigenous people. He described the Nyungar people thus:

> A *nameless, unclassified outcast race, increasing in numbers but decreasing in vitality and stamina, and largely unemployable ... They have very little in the way of education, but some of them have just enough to enable them to become defiant and unrestrained.*

Richard Walley in *Coordah* and Jack Davis in his drama, *No Sugar*, depict those days under this commissioner and the conditions and rules under which the Nyungar people had to live. Robert Bropho in his work, *Fringedweller* (1980), describes the conditions on the so-called native reserves and the problems faced in the search for decent living standards. These authors do not accept the explanation that Indigenous people are not used to proper houses and must make do with sub-standard housing, tin sheds for which they must appear grateful. Instead they demand adequate shelter, a sense of human dignity and fair play towards their community.

Much of the attitude of the invaders towards the Indigenous inhabitants of Australia came about because of the influence of Social Darwinism. This was an evolutionary theory stemming from the work of Charles Darwin, applied to the social systems of human beings. It came into vogue in the latter part of the nineteenth century and the early decades of the twentieth century. The Indigenous communities in Australia were found to have failed the test of evolution—the survival of the fittest—and were said to be on the verge of extinction. Thus a benign paternalism arose to ease the exit of our people. This attitude of paternalism lasted officially until 1937 when representatives of all the state governments came together to discuss the Indigenous problem. The problem was what to do with us. Victoria had almost solved the problem by genocide; New South Wales reported much the same success with only a miserable remnant living on reserves or mission stations and a growing body of people of Indigenous descent living in extreme poverty on the fringes of country towns; Western Australia and Queensland still had large populations of Indigenous people collected together in missions and stations and kept under control by stringent laws; while the Northern Territory had a huge problem in that the Indigenous population still outnumbered the white and if steps were not taken they might eventually take over the state.

Different states had formulated different policies to deal with the problem. Western Australia declared that it was going to merge the native race into its white community. Queensland decided that it was going to keep the Indigenous population under paternal care and control on special reserves. This was until recently their policy, though like an angry father the authorities could expel troublesome children from their homes, or even place them in special centres of detention such as Palm Island. The Northern Territory's policy was to keep the majority of the Indigenous population firmly under control in missions, except for those coloureds who might be bred into the European population.

It was declared outright that the reason behind this policy was fear: fear of a people of Indigenous descent eventually breeding into an underprivileged, angry, militant majority. A result of this policy has been the separation of so-called coloureds from blacks. In Western Australia the policy of assimilation was used as a tool of separation. A split developed between the assimilated and the unassimilated which is still seen today. Most Indigenous writers writing in English are a direct result of such divide-and-control policies. Assimilation did give them a limited education, though it must be admitted that the incarceration of the most militant Indigenous people in the prisons also helped the rise of Indigenous writing in English. Prison for many Indigenous people has been their college. One of these writers was the winner of the David Unaipon Award for Indigenous Literature in 1989, Graeme Dixon, whose *Holocaust Island* (1990) is a savage indictment of white Australia. The prison experience has often led to a literature of anger, though this is being submerged by the coming into being of a literature of reconciliation which is based on bringing all Australians together and stressing their connection rather than their separation. This is often written by Indigenous people who have had no grassroots experience and who were the beneficiaries of the assimilation period.

The Indigenous writers who arose in the sixties were the products of assimilation revolting against assimilation. Assimilation was a policy of division, of seeking to alienate individual Indigenous people from their communities and pushing them into European society. These individuals, it was hoped, would be completely estranged from their families and become like Europeans. Children were forcibly removed from their parents and placed in institutions which became the only homes they ever knew. It is a sadness of the policy that today some Indigenous people, knowing no other childhood, look back with fondness on these institutions.

In Western Australia many Indigenous people became completely institutionalised and made the trip down the Canning River, on which most of these institutions were located, to the port of Fremantle and the prison there. They could exist nowhere else but in an institution and the outer world was a frightening place to be deadened by grog until the inevitable happened and they found themselves safely inside again.

The policy of assimilation attempted to merge a dark

minority—the remnants of the victims of a brutal colonisation—into Anglo-Celtic life and culture without questioning
the right to do so. A first step was to make all Indigenous
people wards of the state without any rights of citizenship.
They were trainee citizens who had to earn their right to be
white; but in tandem with assimilation went a racism which
effectively broke the policy. Even when granted citizenship
rights, Indigenous people still found themselves discrimi-
nated against, still found that they were not accepted by the
white majority. They were caught in a no-man's-land
between black and white. To the whites they were considered black, and to the blacks they were considered quislings
or 'Jackies'. It was from these contradictions that there arose
the struggles for dignity in the mid-sixties when a benign
government came to power, and when there were enough
Indigenous people formally or informally trained to lead the
struggle. Indigenous writers such as Oodgeroo Noonuccal
and Kevin Gilbert were at the forefront of the struggle, and
remained there until their deaths.

At this time were developed the Indigenous political
struggles for justice, landrights and self-management. The
recognition of native title by the High Court of Australia
and the efforts at reconciliation by the Commonwealth
government have to a great extent put an end to any mili-
tancy based on a continent-wide programme. With
increased education and job opportunities, together with
an acceptance of what passes for Indigenous culture, there
is an impetus towards a merging of cultures. Some see this
as assimilation, but younger writers such as Sally Morgan
and Glenyse Ward accept it. They do not see themselves
as part of an active ongoing movement, but as individuals
either searching for their roots or seeking equal opportunity in a multicultural Australia.

This was clearly seen in 1988 when 200 years of white
rule was celebrated. Some Indigenous writers saw the year
as an opportunity to forge links between the Indigenous
minority and the white majority. The poster for the
Indigenous day (NAIDOC) celebrations bore the slogan
'Come and Share Our Culture'. Any separatist sentiments
were downplayed and there was a return to a call for under-

standing, such as we find in the poems of Oodgeroo Noonuccal dating from the rise of Indigenous literature in English in the early sixties.

Thus we have moved to what I call The Period of Reconciliation, which was signalled by the autobiography/biography of Sally Morgan, *My Place* (1987). Activist literature is being replaced by a literature of understanding, a literature not committed to educating individuals as to their place in Indigenous society, but to explaining Indigenous individuals to a predominantly white readership. It is significant that in 1988 creative writing was replaced in importance by the 'life story'. Three books published then continue to sell well and reflect this transition: *My Place* by Sally Morgan, *Don't Take Your Love to Town* by Ruby Langford Ginibi (1988), and *Wandering Girl* by Glenyse Ward (1988). A form of literature akin to biography and autobiography, often this is a heavily edited literature written and revised in conjunction with a European and its message is one of understanding and tolerance, which may be a good thing in regard to an Indigenous place in a multicultural Australia and with the stated aim of the Council for Aboriginal Reconciliation of bringing all people together in mutual understanding in what will be a new republic. As such, it is not concerned with the future aims and aspirations of the Indigenous people. The closing words of Glenyse Ward's *Wandering Girl* reveal the accommodation found in this literature:

> We will be making sure that our
> Kids will be given every opportunity
> In their lives to get a good education,
> So that they can take their place
> In today's society as Lawyers or Doctors,
> Or etc.—and be equal in the one human Race!

The Songlines

1

Sing in me, Muse, and through me tell the story
of that man skilled in all ways of contending,
the wanderer, harried for years on end,
after he plundered the stronghold
on the proud height of Troy.
(Odyssey)

MANY KNOW OF THE LONG EPIC POEMS, THE SONG-lines of the *Iliad* and the *Odyssey*, which mark the beginnings of European literature and which have been lovingly translated time after time, version after version, into the English language. To the ancient Greeks they became sources for tragedy and a practical guide to all aspects of life, and long after them they provided a literary form to be imitated, a seed-bed for the novel and for the film. They still serve for inspiration and have achieved a universality which will always be there.

But how many know of the long epic poems, the song-lines such as these verses from the *Djanggawul* epic, that belong to Australia?

Let us rest on our paddles, brother,
Let us rest, for I am tired.

What is happening there, brother,
My body aches with tiredness,
I worry because of our sacred emblems;
I am tired because we threw them away.
Now we are close to the shore;
Now our journey, our paddling is over.
We land on the beach at Port Bradshaw.
This is our country, plant our flag here,
We have arrived, O brother.

Terra nullius, terra nullius, a stark and unpeopled land which the brave British pioneers, some perhaps with a copy of the *Iliad* in their pockets, occupied with much bloodshed, capturing her as the ancient Greeks captured and took Troy. Who now knows the songs of Troy, or the epics which they might have sung? They are gone and forgotten, perhaps after being long ignored, or sung by the Trojans in captivity until a new generation knew them not. So to the victors belong the spoils and this is what has happened in Australia. Our epics in many places have disappeared and those that survive survive in obscurity, the fodder of anthropologists and ethnomusicologists. It is a shame that our epics are ignored, as they are truly Australian and arrive at the land or come from the land and move over the land. They in effect removed the stigma of *terra nullius* from this continent long before the British invaders arrived and thus were political because they civilised the land and made it known.

I may declare that these are the world's forgotten epics and are hidden in a darkness of obscurity from which they should emerge. Of course, like the *Iliad* and the *Odyssey*, they cannot be dated or given single authors, although it is said that they were first sung by our ancestors who passed them on to present and future generations who were living and would live in the countries through which they passed. The *Djanggawul* epic, for example, is sung by the Djanggawul ancestors and details their adventures and how they peopled and sacralised the land. The *Two Men (Wati Kadjara)* epic, which stretches from the Kimberley in north-western Australia to the southern coast of South Australia, is sung by the two Iguana men who marked out this part of the continent. This latter epic is the longest I know and is sung section by section throughout the Western Desert. It has never been collected in its entirety, and when I asked the anthropologists, Ronald and Catherine Berndt, about this songline and if it still could be collected in its entirety they said that it was too late. If this is true, it is sad, for the length of this songline, this epic, is tremendous and the number of verses must be far more than in any other Australian epic.

The recording and translating of such an epic is a heavy task and would necessitate spending years in travelling the songline and exploring the verses of the epic, as well as getting to know the details of the land about which it sings from the custodians of the sections of the songline, for these epics do not belong to a single community or clan, but pass on from clan country to clan country and from custodian to custodian; but the effort would be worth it.

As far as I know, the only two people who once spent considerable time and energy in making the epic oral literature of parts of Indigenous Australia available to be read with some continuity were the two ethnologists or anthropologists, Ronald and Catherine Berndt; but they devoted much of their time to the smaller areas of northeastern and north-central Arnhem Land where the songlines are much shorter. They did marvellous work and it is sad that their two books, *Djanggawul* (1952) and *Kunapipi* (1951), are long out of print. Also, we must remember—and it is an important point—that they were not poets or even linguists, but social anthropologists and more interested in the content and surrounding rituals and ceremonies rather than in the poetry of the languages.

The *Djanggawul* epic is praised by Ronald Berndt as including some of the most beautiful literary efforts of Indigenous Australia. Similar to the *Iliad* and the *Odyssey*, they were poems set to tunes which outlined the adventures of the Djanggawul. Not only this but their divine origin is stressed in that they are said to be the original songs sung by the ancestors in the Dreaming. This is important in that this meant that the epic, owing to its divine origin, has kept to its form and content to a great extent, and thus may be an important source in understanding pre-invasion Indigenous society in Arnhem Land, for although the prose accounts may change over time, the importance of the tradition has been kept in the epics, in that to change a song or verse, in effect, is to render it ineffective and false. Thus, the epics were passed down from generation to generation, being memorised to keep to an exactitude of original form and content.

Ronald Berndt states that the epics of northeastern Arnhem Land have a unique place in Indigenous Australia in that they are longer and expressive of greater detail than those found in other regions. He declares that in structure and approach they differ; but I find this hard to accept in that, as far as I am aware, other songlines remain untranslated in their entirety. Until, if still possible, this is done, it must remain in the realms of speculation, although in his other book, *Kunapipi*, the brevity of some songs indicate a desert origin and source though he seeks to prove otherwise; but then, until a desert songline receives such detailed study as the Berndts have done on Arnhem Land epics, we must reserve our opinion, keeping in mind that brevity is the soul of wit, and that the length and detail of individual portions of an epic do not make for such judgements as to the wonder of the poetry therein.

Ronald Berndt declares that the songlines are poetry in their own right and express the spirit of the culture to which they belong, as perhaps no other medium can do. He writes that they are inseparable from that culture, expressing as they do the Indigenous sense of the beautiful and their feeling of strength, goodness and the vividness of their way of life. But what he does not go into—perhaps it was too early in the acceptance of Indigenous Australia—is that they have a universality for all Australians in that, for a unique Australian nationality to be created, these epics must be accepted as the basis of an Australianness which does not rely on recent European and American cultural imports; that we, as Australians, must hear our land talking and changing us, as the Djanggawul were changed in those Dreaming times when they came and brought a culture and language to the land with less disruption than our recent newcomers.

In describing the epic, Ronald Berndt writes that the songs are not merely traditional, but are sacred in that they stem from the Dreaming ancestors. They are thus divine compositions. They set out, as do most of the songlines, although the ancestors differ, to describe in detail all the incidents that took place after the Djanggawul paddled away from their island of Bralgu, landed on the Australian mainland and explored it until they reached Milingimbi, where the Yirrkala section of the epic ends and where Ronald Berndt promises to extend the epic in a later publication, though I have not been able to find this and which possibly lies unpublished in his papers. He, in his examination, mentions the amount of repetition which he says is beloved of the Indigenous songman, but which may be a signifier of oral poetry in general. In fact, in reading aloud Indigenous epics, the repetition gives that swirling of the senses which the musical language of poetry can create and leads to an understanding of why such epics were labelled, by the Berndts, 'song circles', in that themes and lines occur and recur until they are fixed not in the mind but in the unconscious in a general liberation from the prosaic into the truly poetic.

As in some if not all Indigenous epics, there are inside singing words which are different from those in everyday use. This poses problems for the translator in that we are not given a simple text, but a complexity in which there is not only the open meaning available to all, but other meanings residing in the text. Perhaps this means that a translator of any and all Indigenous epics would have to be an initiated member of the clans which own the particular sections of the epic; though, in the spirit of reconciliation, this would have to be worked through by the translator poet. What would and could not be done would be a literal translation so beloved by linguists, but the work of a poet who would with close collaboration produce a text of a beautiful aesthetics, as has been done by those poets, such as Alexander Pope, who translated the Greek epics.

Ronald Berndt, as a social anthropologist, produced texts which were not poetic. They hint at the aesthetics inherent in the epics, but they suffer from a prosaicness of language that detracts from the poetics, which is what I am concerned with in this book on Indigenous literature. I feel that, first of all, there must be texts of sufficient aesthetic attractiveness that they will be read as poetry, as language in motion, rather than as static texts detailing the dry facts of culture and society. Such texts have their place, but I declare that they are not poetry, that with the interest in Indigenous culture readable texts must be produced as a source of inspiration for the poets of Australia who I feel are slowly, if not quickly, growing tired of a suburban inspiration which ignores the bush and the land. In furtherance of this approach there is a book which when published quickly sank into obscurity. In fact, in seeking to do a detailed study of one area of Indigenous poetics, the author produced a dense text of German thoroughness which might be studied as a biography of a son of a missionary, but then, perhaps, we are all victims of our times and must avoid rendering an account. The volume I am talking about is *Songs of Central Australia*, by T.G.H. Strehlow (1971).

The Council for Aboriginal Reconciliation has produced glossy booklets of absolutely no literary merit and with few readers. The Council stresses the importance of Indigenous culture and history and then hires European scholars to do their work, resolutely ignoring Indigenous writers and even those Europeans who have produced worthy books which now languish out of print. Indigenous culture, especially that termed 'traditional', is ignored while contemporary and urban manifestations, more often than not based on imported cultural models, are sanctioned. Culture in itself is defined as what a person thinks and feels and any formal attributes of Indigenous culture and literary forms are ignored. In fact, in the Berndts' last book, *The Speaking Land: Myth and Story in Aboriginal Australia* (1989), Indigenous form is ignored and they produce a rather ungainly volume which is really another anthropological text, rather than a literary one. It is prosaic rather than poetic and the land writes according to the Berndts rather than being allowed to speak, rather than being allowed to be an inspiration for Australian writers in form as well as content. They stress the sociological aspect of their material, ignoring any universality in Indigenous oral literature while stressing locality. 'However, notwithstanding its common human qualities, such land-based mythology is not necessarily amenable to being removed outside its own socio-topographic context, ...' (p. 426). It might be argued that the Berndts, by publishing a haphazard collection of myths and stories, have done precisely this.

In the last section they turn their attention to contemporary Indigenous literature. They attack those Indigenous writers who use the past in their work and even declare that the oral literature of the past has little relevance for contemporary Indigenous writers and that the land cannot speak through their work. I wonder if the Berndts would say this about the continuing use of the *Iliad* and the *Odyssey* for literary inspiration and why the old Indigenous literature on which they have done so much work is not allowed to have the same status in contemporary Australia. Of course, the songlines are locality-based and not only this but they are owned by local clans; but if a writer wishes to write about a country crossed with songlines and wishes to use either the form or content to give a relevance to his or her work, should he or she be banned from doing this? In fact, the exclusivity of the Berndts' position may be challenged and has been by Galarrwuy Yunupingu who comes from Yirrkala, the place where Ronald Berndt took down and translated the *Djanggawul* epic many years ago. Galarrwuy declares:

> Those people who are Aboriginal and Australian-born have the main rights. Those cultures should be dominant, instead of Australia being multicultural. It's an insult to say multicultural. You're trying to hide behind other cultural groups. This is Australia—it should have a culture of its own.
>
> (Weekend Australian, January 6–7, 1996)

This is my position and where else should Australians go for cultural inspiration than to Indigenous culture? It is about time that we gave away such words as 'appropriation' and 'misappropriation' and set out to build an Australian culture and literature which is based on and in Australia, that is, on the land and on the songlines which make known the land. Universality should be the aim rather than an exclusivity which will not work and which will only allow the songlines to become forgotten. Culture is never static and the past is there to be used and built upon. Thus,

Strehlow in his monumental *Songs of Central Australia* stresses the universality of Arrenthe song-poetry which he sees as poetry in its own right and able to stand with other world poetry. This is different from the Berndts' narrow anthropological approach with its emphasis on content and an ignoring of form.

T.G.H. Strehlow was the son of the German missionary, C. Strehlow, who founded Hermannsburg Mission in Arrenthe country in Central Australia and then proceeded to christianise what both father and son call 'Pagans'. This meant in practice that Arrenthe culture was damaged and the authority of the elders undermined. T.G.H. Strehlow in his introduction does not recognise this, but attacks other ethnologists who worked in the region. This detracts from the value of the book and if it should be republished might be removed, or drastically pruned, as really not being relevant to his subject matter. He also ends his introduction with the assertion: 'In accordance with the Arranda rules of tjurunga inheritance, these traditions would be regarded as becoming my personal property after the deaths of their owners.' This assertion a few years ago was denied by Arrenthe elders who wished for the return of their sacred tjurunga, which they saw as still belonging to their community. I write this paragraph to show that the place of T.G.H. Strehlow in Arrenthe history is not without controversy, though this does not detract from the great value his volume has for all students of Indigenous literature. He, it seems, at the time was the only person in Indigenous studies able to write such a book and I doubt that its value will ever be surpassed. It says a lot that such a volume, the only one of its kind, should be allowed to remain out of print, especially when there is an institute of Indigenous studies with a programme of publishing books on Indigenous studies.

The volume begins, as I feel it should, with the rhythmic measures and music structure of the songs which Strehlow discusses as songs, then chants and finally concludes that they are poems along the lines of *Beowulf*, the old European epic. He points out that the songs are akin to chants, with the words being as important as the music. It is interesting to learn that, in Central Australia as in other regions, the Arrenthe songmen memorised thousands of songlines with intricate rhythmic measures which often are difficult to transcribe onto paper. There are many examples of these rhythmic measures in musical notation and from this important first section we learn about the rhythmic underpinnings of the songwords and also how the words are changed to fit the measure.

Part Two deals with the language and verse structure of the songs. Strehlow writes that Arrenthe couplets or quantains tend to consist of two individual lines which stand in a complementary relation to each other, with the second line either identical in rhythm or construction with the first line, or balancing it antithetically and rounding off the couplet with a contrasting rhythm of its own. This parallelism and antithesis also characterises the song language. To illustrate this, Strehlow translates the first five couplets of the 'Ankota Ancestor Song':

> I am red like a burning fire;
> I am covered with red down.
>
> I am red like a burning fire;
> I am gleaming red, glistening with ochre.
>
> I am red like the heart of the fire;
> Red is the hollow in which I am lying.
>
> A tjurunga is standing on my head;
> Red is the hollow in which I am lying.

Strehlow makes the point that, as in most other regions of Indigenous Australia, such songs—and this is an important point which should be remembered—were the property of the fully initiated males of the local totemic clans and were believed to contain magic virtues which gave power over nature and the environment of the locality where they were first sung.

They were first sung by the ancestors, who insisted that they be passed on from generation to generation unchanged. According to the Arrenthe elders, the magic residing in the couplets came from the ancestor who first called out his name, then the place where he originated, the trees or rocks growing near his home, the animals nearby, any beings who came to visit him and so on. He named all these and by so doing gained the power to control them. In each instance, he not only gave them a name, but also described them in the couplet. In this way a series of couplets, associated by time, space and story, was sung into being and this songline the ancestor left behind for the benefit of those human beings who were to be reincarnated from himself. A songline will contain the name of the ancestor and of his sons, if any. It gives the name of his home and describes the scenery, such as the rocks and trees, hills, creeks, around his birth-place. The songline also relates his journeys and his quests for food, and finally concludes when the time comes for him to pass to his final resting place.

Strehlow gives an example: 'The Bandicoot Ancestor Song of Ilbalintja'. The first six verses give a general description of Ilbalintja in the rainy season when the country is green with yams and purple with everlastings. It was in that season that the ancestor emerged from the sacred soak or waterhole in which dwells the Latjia yam. The soak is what is called an increase site and it is from here that the yams originated to flow over the countryside. The songlines continue on to describe the coloured soils of the soak. Songline fourteen introduces us to the bandicoots who emerged from the bottom of the soak. Songline twenty-two introduces us to the great ancestor Karora himself, and songline thirty introduces us to his sons and also refers to a ceremony. Ilbalintja is also a sun totemic site and in songline thirty-three the sun makes an appearance. Songline thirty-seven introduces us to the *tnatanja*, or sacred pole, which is used in ceremonies. Songlines forty-three to forty-four concern the bandicoot ancestor, Tjenterama, who in an encounter with Karora's sons is lamed. The next two couplets are centred on the arrival of two more bandicoot ancestors, while the remaining songlines bring the series to an end with a flood of dark nectar from the honeysuckle blossoms. The ancestors are swept back into the soak or waterhole where they are at rest until called forth in ceremonies.

The songline series is much more complex than I have

indicated as there is an entire story or stories encoded in the verses. Still, one can glimpse the profound beauty of the poetry and how it encompasses the subject matter of the myth:

> Lo, the dweller in the deep pit;
> Lo, out of the deep pit it is overflowing far and
>   wide.

> Lo, the mate of the ilbalba grass;
> Lo, out of the deep pit it is overflowing far and
>   wide.

> Lo, it ties together a pole;
> Lo, it coils around it ring upon ring.

> Lo, the purple everlastings;
> Lo, out of the deep pit they are overflowing far
>   and wide.

> Lo, the milk bush;
> Lo, the maiden's friends.

> Lo, the ground where he lies stretched out;
> Lo, the down-flecked painted ground.

> The crimson soil is grating under the heel;
> The white creek sand is grating under the heel.

> White creek sand!
> Impenetrable hollow.

> White limestone band!
> Impenetrable hollow.

> Rich yellow soil!
> Impenetrable hollow.

> Red and orange soil!
> Impenetrable hollow.

> Plain studded with whitewoods!
> Impenetrable hollow.

> White saltlake!
> Impenetrable hollow.

They are frisking about at the back of their
    nests.
In the thick arabera grass, in the thick arabera
    grass.

Lo, they are running out of the nest—
They all are running out.

The bandicoots are rushing through the grass;
In and out of their nests they are rushing
    through the grass.

On the cracked swampflat the fur is brushed;
By bandicoots the fur is brushed.

On the cracked swampflat they are brushing
    their fur;
The bandicoots are brushing their fur.

Crooking their little claws they are raking grass
    together;
With balled paws they are raking grass together.

They are snoring now—
Half-asleep they are snoring now.

There are mounds upon mounds of anthills;
There are masses and masses of termites in the
    anthills.

The great ancestor Karora
Is gazing about watchfully.

Lo, the great ancestor, tall and broad-shouldered;
Lo, the great ancestor, in the pride of his
    strength.

Lo, the great ancestor, in the pride of his
    strength;
Lo, the great ancestor, with his rippling muscles.

Lo, the great ancestor, in the pride of his
    strength;
Lo, the great ancestor, proudly keeping to his
    own home.

Lo, his skull, hard as white quartz;
Lo, his skull, firm, hard and strong.

Lo, the bloodwood tree, hard as white quartz;
Lo, its hollow trunk, hard as white quartz.

Lo, his knees, firm, hard and strong;
Lo, his knees, hard as white quartz.

Lo, the great ancestor of the painted ground;
Lo, his limbs, firm, hard and strong.

The whirlwind is encircling his waist;
Stripes from his shoulders, the whirlwind about
    his waist.

The pendent ornaments are reaching to the
    ground;
The hairstring ornaments are reaching to the
    ground.

Set free you may talk loudly;
Teased in sport you may talk loudly.

The sun is exulting in his might;
The sun is hurling his spears of fire.

They are sliding away in a sitting position;
The flaming face is torturing them.

They stumble, sneak away on hands and knees;
Blood in a gushing stream flows from their
    noses.

The sun spears them with his rays;
The sun speeds them on their way.

Lo, the tnatantja pole;
Covered with rings and stripes.

Lo, the kauaua pole,
Covered with rings and stripes.

Let the feather-top gleam in the sun;
Let the feather-top tremble in the breeze.

Like a pillar of sand it is towering upwards;
The tall ceremonial pole is towering upwards.

Like a whirlwind it is towering upwards;
The tall ceremonial pole is towering upwards.

Karora himself is towering upwards;
The tall ceremonial pole is towering upwards.

He is frisking about at the back of his nest;
In the thick arabera grass, in the thick arabera
    grass.

'Are you indeed a bandicoot;
Are you one indeed?'

'I, Tjenterama, have now grown lamed,
Yes, lame, the worawora flowers are clinging to
    me.'

Nodding sleepily, he keeps on listening;
Fast asleep he is resting without stirring.

Raging and irresistible—
Like a whirlwind he attempts to overwhelm me.

The sound of the bullroarers, the sound of the
    bullroarers is drawing nigh;
Covered with bullroarers, covered with bullroar-
    ers, they are drawing nigh.

The sweet dark juice is flowing forth;
From the centre of the chalice it is flowing
    forth.

From the slender pistil it is flowing forth;
The sweet dark juice is flowing forth.

From the wrinkled cup it is flowing forth;
From the centre of the chalice it is flowing
    forth.

'Let our sweet sap sound from afar like a
    torrent;
Let our sweet sap rush along like a torrent.'

'On the fringes of the cracked rolling plain,—
On the fringes let the flood of nectar roll along.'

'Let our sweet sap encircle them with rings;
Let the flood of nectar encircle them with
  rings.'

'Let our sweet sap ooze forth from the ground;
Let our dark honey ooze forth from the ground.'

'Let our sweet sap rush along like a torrent;
Let our sweet sap sound from afar like a
  torrent.'

'Let it break strong intertwined roots in its
  course;
Let the flood of nectar break down the thicket
  in its course.'

'Let our sweet sap cast him out and away;
Let our sweet sap ooze forth from the ground.'

'Let the rararara flood encircle them with rings;
Let our sweet sap encircle them with rings.'

'Let the flood of nectar encircle them with
  rings;
Let our sweet sap encircle them with rings.'

Of course, in such an English translation, often the meaning is unclear as the cultural matrix in which the songlines emerge is not known; but if the poem is read the cadences roll forth and images of Central Australia spring into the mind. Again, most English poetry, especially today, is written in the straightforward language of everyday usage. Poetic language has not only been stripped of its archaisms, but often its rhythm. This is not the case with the songlines of Central Australia. Strehlow in his investigation comments that the language of the songlines is highly artificial and has never been a spoken language. He says that it preserves many archaisms and obsolete words and phrases. This of course means that the songlines were formally learnt over a number of years, as he later observes. It took years of training and hard work for an Arrenthe man to understand and value his own literature; though, once that he did so, he could then gain aesthetic enjoyment not only from his own group's songlines, but those of his neighbours.

Strehlow's *Songs of Central Australia* is a huge and unwieldy volume, but it is the first and the only one which treats so extensively the oral poetry of an Indigenous community. It is a sad fact that, despite the founding of many Indigenous studies courses in Australian universities, it has been left to wallow in obscurity like some beached whale. For those who are interested in the Indigenous oral literature of Australia and Australian culture in general, it should and must be read. In fact, in contrast to the Berndts' reservations about the worth of Indigenous oral literature beyond the locality of its production, Strehlow declares: 'In point of language, rhythms and forms, Central Australian poetry is highly developed; and the themes of which it treats are of universal interest to mankind' (1971, p. 657). In fact, the importance of poetry to the Arrenthe people is stressed by Strehlow who declares that in Arrenthe society it was the poet, the knower of sacred songs, who had prestige. He ends his huge volume with an appeal which echoes my own: that if Australia is to develop a truly national culture, it is to the land and environment that Australians must go:

> *It is therefore to be hoped that a perusal of the ancient material that constitutes the aboriginal sacred songs of Central Australia will not prove entirely unrewarding to our future poets: the imagery found here does harmonize with the outward shape and inward spirit of our continent.*
> (1971, p. 729)

Indigenous Literature in English

2

Aboriginal writers have a responsibility here, a very important responsibility, to take that message not only to white people but to Aboriginal people as well, so that we can foster within our own communities a very important concept. That concept is that if we are going to survive, we are going to have to do it as a community, we are going to have to do it as a nation and not as individuals.
(McGuinness & Walker 1985, pp. 43–54)

INDIGENOUS LITERATURE IN ENGLISH BEGAN AS THE expression of an Indigenous minority living on the fringes of the majority community. It was the writing of an oppressed people that until the last two decades was completely under the heel of the oppressor. Until recently, they did not do things, but had things done to or for them, and any urge towards protest or expression was fiercely attacked as being the work of others, that is, radical whites. The majority accepted as fact that the Indigenous people were unable to decide for themselves. They had been declared wards of the state, a category usually reserved for children; but this was untrue.

The British colonised the island of Tasmania early in the nineteenth century, and then began a desperate war of resistance by the Indigenous inhabitants against the seizure of their island. Eventually, after a military campaign, an Englishman named George Augustus Robinson collected together most of the survivors with the promise of sanctuary. This sanctuary proved to be a windswept island (Flinders Island) in Bass Strait, where Robinson began an ill-conceived attempt at civilising the people. His attempts met with disaster, not to himself but to his charges. In a dusty file in the Mitchell Library in Sydney lie the papers of William Thomas, an early settler of Tasmania. Included among his papers is a handwritten journal produced by Tasmanian Indigenous men under the direction of the superintendent of their station, G.A. Robinson. The writers were Walter George Arthur, Peter Thomas and Davy Bruny. The journal was titled: *The Flinders Island Weekly Chronicle*, and its object was 'to promote Christianity, civilisation and learning amongst the Indigenous inhabitants, be a brief but accurate register of events of the colony, moral and religious'. In 1837 it appeared every Saturday, was priced twopence and profits were distributed among the writers. Robinson intended the paper to be read as much by Europeans as by Aborigines, for most of the latter never learnt to read.

The writers for this journal appear to have been the typi-cal mission boys, those who were christianised enough to enjoy the privilege of living next to the British and sharing in their lifestyle, while the still-pagan majority were left largely to be fringedwellers around the mission, or to be coerced towards Christianity and civilisation. In this coer-cion, the mission boys, as members of their race, had a large part to play. Thus the men who wrote for the paper were also sent around to the other Indigenous people to keep them in line and to guide them towards civilised Christian values. Divide and rule tactics have always been the weapon of the coloniser and the missionary, though they have always had to be on guard, for it was well known that the native was a treacherous animal, ever ready to turn on his master, and to make altruistic acts seem the opposite.

The Flinders Island Weekly Chronicle was the forerunner of later Indigenous periodicals such as *Dawn Magazine* in that it was controlled by a sympathetic member of the majority and written by those closest to assimilation; but, for all that, it makes interesting reading of how the Indigenous people felt during island exile when their numbers were lessening under the impact of homesickness and a settled life in a camp set up on an inhospitable island. We can read of the despair overwhelming the people in the 17 November issue of the journal:

> *The brig Tamar arrived this morning at Green Island. I cannot tell perhaps we might hear it by and by. When the ship boat comes to the Settlement we will hear the news from Hobarton. Let us hope that it will be good news and that something may be done for us poor people they are dying away the bible says some or all shall be saved but I am much afraid none of us will be alive by and by and then as nothing but sick men amongst us why don't the black fellows pray to the King to get us away from this place.*

This Indigenous newspaper is the first written expression of Indigenous people in Australia and, although it must be admitted that G.A. Robinson had a hand in the production, for in the prospectus it is stated: 'Proof sheets are to be submitted to the commandant for correction before publishing ...', it is still too rash to dismiss it as being completely composed by him.

Indigenous people, although being educated by missionaries, were often denied the ability to write coherently in English by the invaders. This even led to a police investigation in the colony of Victoria in the late nineteenth century. The Indigenous station, or mission or settlement, of Coranderrk was a centre of Indigenous resistance in Victoria. As it was close to the main settlement of Melbourne, the Indigenous people could demonstrate there and write letters to sympathetic newspapers. Not only this but they petitioned the Aboriginal Protection Board and the government. The Board, refusing to believe that Indigenous people were capable of using the pen, in 1882 employed a detective to prove that the petitions and letters were forged by whites. Detective Mahony went to the Coranderrk Station incognito and discovered that the letters and petitions were indeed written by an Indigenous person, Thomas Dunolly, and were genuine expressions of the feelings of his people.

Perhaps from this early investigation began the practice

of prefacing Indigenous texts in English to prove their authenticity. These prefaces and introductions are a part of my study. They are invitations to the reader to accept Indigenous literary productions in certain ways and, in effect, are signals often apologising for the Indigenality of the texts or placing them in the area of academic studies labelled postcolonial. What many of these forewords do is to emphasise (albeit unconsciously) the fact that these literary productions are to be judged in ways different from the standards of the metropolitan literary tradition. In fact, recently, an academic writing on Indigenous women's literature has gone so far as to declare that the notion of any aesthetics should be disregarded when reading such texts. Of course, such assertions are patronising, to say the least, and any discussion of literary worth or not must use some sort of aesthetic judgements.

In 'Evaluating protest fiction', Gareth Cornwall (1980) quotes Richard Hoggart. This quotation is important in that it sets out this aesthetics versus no aesthetic value in some detail:

> *I value literature because of the way—the peculiar way—in which it explores, recreates and seeks for the meanings in human experience; because it explores the diversity, complexity and strangeness of that experience (of individual men or groups of men in relation to the natural world); because it re-creates the texture of that experience; and because it pursues its explorations with a dis-interested passion (not wooing nor apologizing nor bullying).*

Gareth Cornwall sees this statement as being non-contentious, but the very fact of emphasising a 'disinterested passion' would make Indigenous writers and others shudder and dismiss the rest of the paper as 'gammon'. Men and women are passionate beings engaged in the world and writers are part of that passionate collective being engaged in the world. The Indigenous writer, Kath Walker, had a different view of the writer, and her life and works bear it out. Here is part of her opening speech to the Second Indigenous Writers Conference held in Melbourne in November 1983:

Dear Fellow Delegates

Today we have come together to work towards implementing a programme of action in the interest of Indigenous writers and Indigenous people. We can be proud of our past efforts. We, as writers, know only too well, how powerful is the pen, how much mightier than the sword. In our short history of progress, since the invasion, (and let us not forget), with little or no thanks to the invaders and their records, our history according to them began on the 27th May, 1967, when we the Indigenous people, forced a referendum upon the peoples of Australia. So it is assumed by white Australians that we stagnated politically and economically throughout our long history in this our own country. What the mainstream of non-Indigenous people in this country refuse to acknowledge, is that we were and are as a race, politically and economically sound, and have been so, since our Dreamtime. It is time we put the record straight. Through research, we, the writers, must find our own historians and as you know Colin Johnson already leads that field together with Kevin Gilbert and others who have done much. Children's literature is very much to the fore, also. Our poets are well-known and much read. Our playwrights are not only seen but are also heard. But in spite of what we have achieved, there is still much to be done.

FIRST: We must at all times be critical of all fields of Indigenous affairs.

SECONDLY: We must also write about black public servants. I feel sure you will agree with me that the Indigenous input in this field leaves much to be desired.

THIRDLY: Our education field is a mess. The reason being of course that the present education scene in Australia does little or nothing to improve the lot of even the non-Indigenous students. If we must be educated, then we need our own Indigenous teachers and our own schools where, if desirable, non-Indigenous students may attend.

FOURTHLY: The legal services: Let us clean up the bulldust that exists in this very important field. Let us ensure that before long we have our own Indigenous lawyers, barristers, yes, and even our own judges.

FIFTHLY: Medical services: This field, in my opinion, is the only field that is truly dedicated to Indigenous political action. I commend what they have done so far. May they continue to agitate in the interests of our people—but when will we see our doctors and nurses emerge in this field?

These are the things that we must write about. Let the writers lead the field in advising, criticising and scrutinising the ideas and ideals in the interest of all our people. ... Before I officially open this Second National Indigenous Writers Conference, I would like to sum up my speech by reading you the BLACK COMMANDMENTS:

1. THOU SHALL GATHER THY SCATTERED PEOPLE TOGETHER.

2. THOU SHALL WORK FOR BLACK LIBERATION.

3. THOU SHALL RESIST ASSIMILATION WITH ALL THY MIGHT.

4. THOU SHALL NOT BECOME A BLACK LIBERAL IN A WHITE SOCIETY.

5. THOU SHALL NOT UPHOLD THE WHITE LIES IN A BLACK SOCIETY.

6. THOU SHALL TAKE BACK THE LAND STOLEN FROM THY FOREFATHERS.

7. THOU SHALL MEET WHITE VIOLENCE WITH BLACK VIOLENCE.

8. THOU SHALL REMOVE THYSELF FROM A SICK, WHITE SOCIETY.

9. THOU SHALL FIND PEACE AND HAPPINESS IN A STABLE, BLACK SOCIETY.

10. THOU SHALL THINK BLACK AND ACT BLACK.

11. THOU SHALL BE BLACK ALL THE REST OF THY DAYS.

The late Kath Walker (Oodgeroo Noonuccal) in her manifesto espouses for the Indigenous writer a far different role than that espoused by conventional Anglo-Celtic writers. If we need search for comparisons, we might look towards African literature which appears to be concerned with people rather than self, though we should always keep well in mind that there are significant differences between African and Australian Indigenous literatures, and what we are seeking is not an identification with, but an elucidation of, those problems we have in common. To a great extent Europeans have not only physically trodden on all black people, but also on their souls, and continue to do so through advocating the universal supremacy of their philosophical and political theories. I must emphasise that I am not writing about a national majority, but an indigenous minority. The Australian Indigenous experience therefore

equates more with such downtrodden minorities impris-
oned within so-called national boundaries throughout the
world, rather than with any type of racial majority, be it
white or black.

Traditional Indigenous societies were highly functional
and, as the contemporary idealistic writer of Indigenality
identifies with this tradition, he or she does not give an
overriding importance to art for art's sake, but places
aesthetic considerations second to the message, which is
not to say that such considerations do not play a part in the
Indigenous literary product. In fact, aesthetics were important in traditional Indigenous culture, although an unsocial
space for an artist was undreamt of. Art was a social act and
as we see in Kath Walker's manifesto this has carried
through to the contemporary writer. Most are socially
committed and have this commitment firmly in mind when
they write. It is part of the tradition of Indigenous culture to
perceive the artist not as an isolated individual, alienated
from his or her society and interested only in extending the
bounds of his or her own private vision, but as a value
creator and integrator. It must not be forgotten that our
ancestors of the Dreaming were artists transforming the
land and using it as a page onto which to inscribe songs and
stories. In fact, even today, scratch many an Indigenous
person and beneath his or her contemporary skin, or the
persona he or she shows to the white world, you will still
find the old hunter or gatherer. This may lead to alienation
and denial, but to the positive writer of Indigenality, it leads
to an appraisal of Indigenous culture and literature different
from the white critic's approach. For example, the political
activist, Bruce McGuinness (1985), on reading Archie
Weller's novel, *The Day of the Dog*, writes:

> *I believe that Archie Weller has been able to give us an insight into
> the very distinct cultural forms that are kept, and which grow from
> one particular insight that I suppose the Indigenous people on the
> reserves have when they move to the cities—they are forced by
> moving into the cities to come into closer proximity with other
> cultures. They are forced to exist there. They become hunters and
> gatherers within that city, within the new urban life, and to be
> hunters and gatherers there they have to change their weapons. The*

spear and the boomerang and the woomera are no longer acceptable
weapons within the city area. They must change their mode of
weaponry that they used to survive with.

The Indigenous writer is a Janus-type symbol, with one
face turned to the past and the other to the future while
existing in a postmodernity. This creates a tension which
on occasion may lead to an outright condemnation of all
European writings on Indigenous people as being gammon,
and not worth the paper they are written on. It is also this
state of tension which creates the passion with which
contemporary Indigenous people view the world and literature. They find that a literature of non-commitment and of
individualism is not worth the trouble of reading, let alone
writing. It does not lead to anything but the sterile examination of states of mind divorced from communal living. To
be worthwhile, a literature must have social value.

Few Indigenous writers are content with dealing only
with the past. The past is there only to explain the present
and is of utmost importance in that it is the basis of all
Indigenality. This may lead, on occasion, to an idyllic
picture of a past Indigenous civilisation before the ghosts
returned to haunt paradise. For example, the first part of
Maris and Borg's video mini-series, *Women of the Sun*,
presents such an idealised picture of natural harmony and
contentment. Other writers, such as the late Kevin Gilbert,
write about the recent past to expose the hidden underside
of Australian history in which Indigenous people were
butchered, buggered and beaten wherever they made a
stand or attempted to retreat. This past is still with us.
Survivors are still living, and I think that the awfulness of
man's inhumanity to man should be dealt with until we are
sick and tired of it, and until the *Watjela*, the *Gadia*, the
Gubba, or whatever name the European is known as, comes
to acknowledge this historic injustice. It is no use declaring, as some Indigenous people do declare, that the past is
over and should be forgotten. But that past is only of 200
years' duration. It is too early for the Indigenous people to
put aside that past and the effects of that past. Kevin
Gilbert, taking part in an Indigenous writers' workshop,
declared that you must learn to hate and this was objected

to by some Europeans present. But it is true, for it is only when Indigenous people come to realise that many of their problems are based on a past of oppression which is still with us in the present, that they will come to grips with them. If this does not happen, then the self-destructive and community-destructive acts will continue only as sporadic present acts resting on bad housing or ill-health, or even racial weaknesses, without any foundation in the past when the Indigenous soul was brutalised.

In Bruce McGuinness' paper, quoted from above, he calls for a community control of literary production and distribution. Anglo-Celtic writers recoil from this. They see in it an overall tyrannical censorship which they had to fight in their own culture. Unfortunately, their fight was led in the interests of explicit sexuality and the use of taboo words. Censorship meant that the individual felt unable to freely express his Freudian desires and was oppressed. It rarely resulted in political suppression, at least in Australia, thus the fight was between the individual and the state. In regard to the Indigenous people, the writer feels that the majority is the oppressor, that he or she must make his or her work amenable in style (and often in content) to the standards of publishers who have their eyes on the market-place. Thus, the mere fact of writing, of deciding on a style, is a political decision. The Indigenous population is too small, with little economic clout, and so books for and by Indigenous writers are goods of little profit. Thus possibly our best poet, Lionel Fogarty, for many years was forced to go outside the established publishers to have his works printed. His voice was a voice fighting to be heard and it was only recently that a small mainstream publishing company published his work. This is not hard to understand, for the Anglo-Celtic readership find it hard to work through the layers of non-compromising Indigenality with the same dedication they bring to European writers such as James Joyce. This is not difficult to understand, for after all white critics have condemned those more accessible Indigenous poets who use somewhat archaic European verse patterns as being trite and derivative.

In Kath Walker's manifesto, the Indigenous writer is commanded to not only function as an Indigenous voice, but also as a critic of the community. She espouses a dual role for the creative person, partially identified with and partially separate from those sources of power and control within the community who have control of Indigenous affairs. Many Indigenous writers see their works as contributing to the task of creating viable Indigenous communities from the chaos and passivity that have resulted from oppression and paternalism. They are involved in the re-creation of the future health of Indigenous communities and must make choices and affirmations of how this should be done. For example, Kevin Gilbert (1977) has Grandfather Koori declare:

> *I don't care how hard it is. You build Aboriginality, boy, or you got nothing. There's no other choice to it. It'll be easier, now, with bits of land handed back to us, here 'n' there. It means there's no white manager for the people to dob each other in to. It means that you collect your own rents to do your own maintenance. You form a committee to collect the rent. If a family won't pay, you throw them out. You get the young blokes to set up youth committees that backs the elders up. You inspect the houses because rules save lives and health and happiness. You give every man, woman and child his due because life is sacred. You treat your own and every life like that. Every person is entitled to be treated with good nature and dignity. You never steal from the poor. If you steal from a black family you get cast out. If you stand over or hoon from the goomees you get bottled or kicked. If a woman neglects her kids, the women belt her. If a black boy rapes a black girl, he gets flogged and cast out. If two or more men take a woman and abuse her they get flogged and cast out, so as to keep the camp clean.*

Kevin Gilbert's words reflect the values of traditional Law. Indigenous society was never the rather wimpish society as portrayed by the apostles of the noble savage. Justice was hard and direct. The decay of traditional Law, under the attack of the intruder justice, has resulted in the decay of Indigenous communities. Though to some this reliance on Indigenous Law and methods of enforcement may seem a backward step, it is only through such measures that Indigenous societies will become self-reliant and strong, but for this to happen, the effects of assimilation must be wiped out.

Indigenous writers stress Indigenality as a means to do this. It has arisen as a direct counter to assimilation as espoused by the various state and federal governments, and which is still the covert aim of the state educational systems which plonk down strange white school buildings in the centre of Indigenous communities, with walls covered by blonde, rosy-cheeked children, European animals and English words. This type of education leads to a fork in the trail, at the end of one there is assimilation or an alienation in which black is not beautiful, and is a matter of self-contempt. Indigenous writing in English has grown from such a system of schooling, but it has seen a hidden trail which leads to a positive rejection of assimilation and to the stressing of Indigenality, though what this Indigenality is and how much is reflected in this writing is a matter of debate. Bruce McGuinness (1985), for example, sets an extreme when he says:

> We maintain that unless Indigenous people control the content, the publishing, the ultimate presentation of the article, then it is not Indigenous; that it ceases to be Indigenous when it is interfered with, when it is tampered with by non-Indigenous people who exist outside the spectrum of Indigenous life, of Indigenous culture within Australia.

Any Indigenous writer who has attempted to publish or has been published knows how difficult it is to defend complete Indigenality of his or her work, and how, if he or she wishes to be published, compromises must be made. The extent of these are seen in some forewords or introductions which reveal the extent of the editing. Even Kevin Gilbert suffered at the hands of his publisher—to such an extent that he rejected his first published volume of poetry.

The late Kevin Gilbert and Lionel Fogarty are the strongest poets of Indigenality yet published in editions which are readily available. Lionel's poetry makes no compromises in Indigenality and is layered and textured into shapes and meanings which are difficult for European readers to understand. On the other hand, Kevin Gilbert's poetry utilises traditional European verse forms to contain his message. Their meaning is as direct as a bullet and a person of the Anglo-Celtic literary tradition might find them most distressing, but they are impossible to reject, as was Lionel Fogarty's first book of verse (*Kargun*) by a writer on Indigenous literature who wrote: 'In fact the most impressive aspect of this book (*Kargun*) (in terms of skill) is the talented graphic illustrations by Indigenous artist Johnny Cummins of Cairns.'

White critics have been extremely harsh on Indigenous poets:

> *If I had my way I would ban all publishers' blurbs. Apart from their inaccuracy, the dustjacket comments on* The Dawn is at Hand *do Kath Walker a disservice. She is no poet, and her verse is not poetry in any true sense. It hasn't that serious commitment to formal rightness, that concern for making speech true under all circumstances, which distinguishes Buckley and Wright at their best.* The Dawn is at Hand *belongs more rightly to that field of social protest in which Miss Walker's statements are most relevant and most moving. I have a sincere respect for her indignation, her sense of pathos, and her forthright candour. For any white Australian with a conscience her book is often moving and shaming. But to invite us in this case to take the easy way out, to avoid its message (for it is a book with a message) by measuring it against standards and preoccupations with which it has really little to do.*
> (Taylor 1967)

Such reviews serve only to leave us in a semantic fog. What does 'serious commitment to formal rightness' mean: the lipservice paid by quasi-liberals to their ideals? What is 'that concern for making speech true under all circumstances'? We must go to Buckley and Wright ('at their best') to find out. In this single paragraph, the barricades of protest poetry are dismissed as not being poetry, and we are left with the weightier concerns of a late capitalist wonderland filled with such poetry, as 'Dreamt My Teeth Fell Out'. We find ourselves again as fringedwellers unable to enter the elitist fairyland of bourgeois poetry.

Indigenous music is one field of Indigenous expression which, owing to the establishment of such associations as the Central Australian Aboriginal Media Association (CAAMA) and outlets on Indigenous radio programmes, may be seen to have the most independence in that they have the most control of their modes of production. Again, this is limited to Indigenous programmes and venues and has not really been part of the so-called music industry until the advent of Yothu Yindi who with great production found themselves acclaimed worldwide. CAAMA began recording Indigenous musicians many years ago, but their output remains limited to an Indigenous and cult music. Indigenality is to the fore in that some Indigenous languages provide the vehicle of communication and in that there is little aping of American or British speech patterns. Many are in the genre termed Country and Western, but a rhythm akin to Jamaican reggae is employed by some bands, such as Coloured Stone. This type of rhythm appears to fit Indigenous English speech patterns. Native instruments such as the didjeridoo and clapsticks have been successfully employed by just about all of the bands at some time or other. No Fixed Address, originally from South Australia, was the most successful and the forerunner of the new generation of bands which have moved away from Country and Western. Constantly on the road (hence the name), they have recorded two albums which are still constantly played on Indigenous radio programmes, though they were released quite a few years ago. The band members have drifted apart, but the drummer Bart Willoughby has formed another band, Mixed Relations, which plays a hard-edged reggae rock.

Apart from a few attempts which were quickly forgotten, drama is akin to other contemporary forms of Indigenous expression in that the message either determines the form or uses a form ready to hand, though there is an Indigenality which often intrudes or is disguised. Most of the dramas so far produced have a strong realist slant, with intrusions of what may be termed Indigenous reality or Indigenality. I mention, in this connection, Jack Davis' *Barungin (Smell the Wind)* (1988) which centres around the Nyungar funeral ceremony and is structured on it. Jack Davis is the most successful of the Indigenous playwrights. His theatre is strongly naturalistic and his dramas have proved popular and enduring. An Indigenous musical, *Bran Nue Dae*, by Jimmy Chi and Kuckles (1991), was greeted with acclaim and has had a number of productions. It is, on the surface, a rather happy-go-lucky product with a somewhat clichéd plot centring around hippies; but it takes irony to the extreme in that, towards the end, all the characters find their Indigenality in a flurry of Sally Morgans.

Jack Davis began as a poet, and his verses are carefully worked rhythmic structures directed at a European readership. His philosophy of writing has been expressed in the late-lamented Indigenous periodical, *Identity*, where his concern for grammar may have bent his commitment to Indigenality in form and content, though he has modified his stand since those times. Indigenous periodicals like *Identity* have always concerned themselves with Indigenous affairs as well as literature and I doubt that it would be possible for any Indigenous periodical to deny commitment to the Indigenous people and concentrate purely on art for art's sake. Many of the first generation of Indigenous writers were published in *Identity* and novelist Archie Weller had his first stories published therein.

The Indigenous novel is a fragile flower which is still in the process of blooming. Its length is a problem in that only extracts may be published in Indigenous periodicals and the cost of having a novel privately published is prohibitive. It is relatively easy to run off a few dozen copies of a slim volume of poems on the photocopier of an Indigenous organisation, but extremely difficult to do several hundred pages this way. The only recourse at the moment is to approach recognised and sympathetic publishing houses, but this still means that the novel is subject to the editing processes of the publisher and even with the establishment of an Indigenous publisher, Magabala Books in Broome, there still remain problems which pass over from mainstream publishing.

The novel in itself is a tool of reflection and until recently the Indigenous novel was in a state of reflection. This period of inactivity was broken with the publication of Sam Watson's masterly *The Kadaitcha Sung* (1990) which took the novel into a new realm of reality. This is akin to magic realism and I have called this realm 'maban reality'. The Indigenous novel also received an impetus with the founding in 1989 of the David Unaipon Award under the auspices of the University of Queensland Press. Since then

more than a half-dozen novels have been published and
the award has introduced new writers to those who read
Indigenous literature. In fact, the award has resulted in an
upsurge of Indigenous literary production, with people
writing who once would never have thought of doing so:
'What, me write a book? You must be kidding!'

There is also an increasing number of Indigenous writers who do not go through mainstream publishing
processes. Their works are being produced in small
editions on equipment in the Indigenous settlements and
are for local consumption. They are usually in Kriol or the
local language and, because of their limited appeal, can
escape somewhat from the trammels of the publishing
world and its conformity, though in some cases they are
changed by well-meaning missionaries and school teachers
into a standard of English which tends towards a banality
of style. This is not to disparage this work or their work. If
a strong literature based on Indigenous forms is to develop,
the place for this development is among people least
affected by assimilation, and once an upsurge of literature
begins it is only a matter of conjecture where it may lead.
In fact, future Indigenous people may look back on this
literature as having a lost simplicity or a complexity only
brought out through a deep reading of the text.

This literature at the moment consists of a reworking of
the traditional oral literature into written forms and the
recording of incidents. It is but a step further to collect
these incidents to form an autobiography, but when this is
done the resulting lifestory is often determined in form and
arrangement of content by a friendly white man or woman
who naturally knows how things should be written. This
has happened to too many lifestories, though some, such as
Bropho's *Fringedweller* (1980) and Shirley Smith's *Mum Shirl*
(1981), have managed to escape this treatment. Dr Bruce
Shaw has edited two volumes from tape recordings he made
with Indigenous men. He outlines his methods in reducing
his material into the written word in forewords to these
books. Such volumes as these reflect the tampering in that
there is an absence of political comment and no feeling of
outrage or understanding as to the historical process. This is
so noticeable that it may be asked whether it has been
deliberate, either on the part of the recorder or recordee. As

literature these products are hopelessly compromised. If we wish to make a comparison with a product under Indigenous control from formulation to publishing, as borne out by a demeaning note by the publisher apologising for the content and style, we may read Bropho's *Fringedweller* which is so different in tone and content as to suggest that, when Indigenous people begin putting together their own lifestories from start to a finished manuscript without white intervention, these will be vastly different from the editorial interventions that we now have.

It is from such books as *Fringedweller* and Labumore's *An Aboriginal Woman Tells of the Old and the New* (1984) that a future prose literature of Indigenality will develop, but in those areas where the Indigenous language is still strong this is the medium of communication and any English version can be but a translation. In other areas where Kriol is spoken, this may be used as the writing medium. Lionel Fogarty uses Indigenous English in his poetry and this has resulted in a new and striking use of the English language, but for all this approach to projecting an Indigenality in thought, word and deed, it must be understood that Indigenous literature has the important job of projecting an Indigenous presence heretofore distorted on Australia and the world and that standard English has a place in doing this, though creative Indigenous expression should not be distorted for this reason. Although Indigenous people may borrow from European literary traditions—after all, Christianity has entered Indigenality to such an extent that the use of Christian symbols has become both deliberate as well as unconscious—the main source of inspiration should come from the well-springs of Indigenality: the Indigenous communities and their oral traditions. Thus, a literature of Indigenality should be based on the Indigenous reality in Australia and should be true to this reality whatever the technique and form utilised. If a literature of Indigenality is to continue, it must be a community literature addressing itself to the various and serious problems facing Indigenous culture and life in contemporary Australia. It should never be an art for the sake of art, but a dynamic movement reflecting in its structure and content the Indigenous people of Australia.

Indigenous and Mainstream Literature

3

the white.
the rock at the lip of the coast.
the white.
with backs turning, eyes to the desert.
(Amanda Stewart, Kitsch Postcards)

ONE OF THE ABIDING CRITICISMS BY INDIGENOUS people of 'white' Australian works of fiction is that of Indigenous cultural and individual representation. How Indigenous people and their cultures are presented is considered by Indigenous people to be of considerable importance, though the subjectivity of the criticism leaves something to be desired, for example urban Indigenous people complain that too often Indigenous people as a whole are depicted as the naked-and-standing-on-one-leg-with-woomera-and-spear noble savage stereotype, as though they existed in a timeless cultural Dreamtime. This complaint, although it has more than some justification and leads to the assumption that there are the 'real Aborigines' who have retained 'their' traditional culture as opposed to those living in the cities, fails to take into account the possibility that some rural groups might wish to see themselves portrayed in this way. It is not so much the stereotype that is upsetting; but the ownership, the appropriation of that stereotype and the political use that is made of it. To put it in another context, it is whether the Japanese might need to choose between the samurai warrior, or the western-suited salaryman, or have the choice made for them. It depends on whether we have the power to select our stereotype, as a source of empowerment, rather than of negativity and division. What we as Indigenous people must be aware of is that any society, or social groupings making up that society, is made up of conflicting centres of power and prestige, and to select one power centre and to portray it as being a 'true' representation of all Indigenous people is misleading, to say the least. What is important is whether the representation fills us with pride, or not. Pride in our cultures, our histories, in our communities and individuality.

The problem is how cultures and peoples are represented and how peoples under constant examination represent themselves, recapture their representations and empower them. Representations are important politically in that often a generalised political representation is needed as well as a specific community one, especially when dealing with government instrumentalities and the media.

Indigenous representations have a foundation in specific and often very different communities and not in any centralised Aboriginal existential being. A national and unified representation may often be stressed; but this rests on different communities and cultures. Even when I use the singular 'Indigenous' as here, it is but an encoded word which may be decoded, or deconstructed, into many component parts: *Koori* (New South Wales and Victoria), *Nunga* (South Australia), *Anangu* (Central Australia), *Yolngu* (Arnhem Land), *Murri* (Queensland), *Nyungar* (south-western Australia), *Yamadji* (mid-Western Australia), *Wonghi* (eastern Western Australia), and other groups, which form a network through which information is exchanged, though not independence. It is only through this network that a common Australia-wide Indigenous representation may be theorised and actualised.

As a vast land, Australia had and has many Indigenous communities and cultures, and their reduction into the Other, the Aborigine, as opposed to the Subject, the European settler, is a simplified construct. All singular, totalistic representations of the Aboriginal (and the European, for that matter) are suspect, if not downright fictional. Indigenous people declare that any representation begins with and stems from the community, and only the community, or members of it, can claim unmediated access to their representations: all else is but misrepresentation. Thus Indigenous literature says that it can represent Indigenous people because it stems from the community or communities, and defines or explains this community or communities to itself, to themselves, and lastly to others.

What we have are continuous streams of similar practices which often are fractured and parts of a serial which resists totalising tendencies. The settler scholar, C.D. Rowley, has pointed out that Indigenous people have hundreds of local histories handed down through families, some of which have been re-encoded into books, and these are monotonously the same, and cumulatively damn the inhumanity and injustice of Australian 'development'. Now, this may be accepted at least from his position, although it does gloss over the very real differences between Indigenous communities to posit a singular line of development so that these texts may be considered the raw materials of a future condensed narrative of a singular 'ideological fiction', one central discourse of empower-ment, one system of thought which will totalise the heterogeneous nature of the source materials found in our peoples' histories, abandoning all contradiction for a linear and consistent narrative; but this tendency to generalise these histories results in a diminishment of whatever 'truth' (truth as contradiction) is residing in them, and may even lead to a disempowerment. From particular local centres of empowerment (reasons for the family, or community, history to be compiled), the ideology will evolve into a general discourse of Aboriginality with other agendas of empowerment, especially if this is not done by Indigenous people. The localising and community empowerment in these texts will be lost and delivered up to a generalised narrative of an 'Indigenous History'. This generalised narrative has already been attempted by James Miller in his *Koori—A Will To Win* (1985), though an examination of this 'history' reveals that it falls short of actively postulating a 'History of All Indigenous People'. In fact, it concludes with a section on how to research family history, and thus re-enters community history, rather than adhering to a general Indigenous history.

An example of a more generalised historical narrative is Mattingley and Hampton's *Survival in Our Own Land: 'Aboriginal' Experiences in 'South Australia' since 1836, told by Nungas and Others* (1988), in which the editors have attempted to bring quite disparate and fragmentary recollections under a continuous narrative imported from invader documents and given a linear time sequence. The reason for this is political in that it sets out to present an oppositional history which will be accepted as correct, or at least provide an alternative history for Nungas (and others) in South Australia, as is evident in the title of the volume in which Aboriginal and South Australia are in inverted commas.

There are problems in constructing a generalised Indigenous historical text. One such is that Indigenous people may be represented as an encapsulated, almost powerless minority, and their history may be constructed as a narrative based on the settler mainstream and subject–object power relationships, a history of government–Indigenous relationships rather than histories of the various communities and occurrences within them. As an encapsulated minority, or minorities, they are constantly being manipulated by a state apparatus which seeks to better their lot, and represents and re-represents them for settler acceptance and consumption. This fate was once the fate of all subject peoples within the British empire. Dominant European powers constructed, on a class and race basis, a well-defined and enforced ideology which reached its peak in the latter part of the nineteenth century with the spread of British imperialism. This ideology utilised the philosophical and the evolutionary concepts of Charles Darwin to formulate what came to be called Social Darwinism and which graded races (and even classes) from the high of European civilisation to the low of the so-called primitive tribes. Well-known scholar Edward Said (1987) has examined the evolution of 'Orientalism' and how the 'oriental' was constructed for European consumption. His central theme is, quoting Karl Marx: 'They cannot represent themselves; they must be represented' (The Eighteenth Brumaire of Louis Bonaparte). In regard to Indigenous people, 'Orientalism' must be replaced by 'Anthropology', at least in regard to academic theories and how these were used to construct 'the Aboriginal'.

Perhaps the founding father of Australian anthropology was A.W. Howitt who, in the late 1880s, collected together data from widely disparate sources which helped to set the agenda and ideology of the British school of anthropology as an imperialist science which provided information which helped the British colonial administrators to govern their subject peoples. Thus, from the first, it placed an emphasis on field work rather than on the construction of theories, although beneath rested the ideology of Social Darwinism. Spencer and Gillen followed in his footsteps. From the first, they claimed a specialised knowledge of the Other, the subject races, and their texts are still used today. The British school of anthropology is descriptive rather than analytical, thus continental scholars are seldom accorded as much respect, often because they consciously use theories of explanation. One such was Geza Roheim (1945) who used psychoanalytical theory in an attempt to penetrate into the mind of the Indigenous, in this case the Aranda of Central Australia. His works are a quite fascinating, erotic reading of the Other, a creative fiction which is perhaps more alarming than the writings of the British anthropologists, for after all Freud was an evolutionist, and sifted through the knowledge of late nineteenth century ethnographical thought to form his own theory of the primal horde as depicted in his book: *Totem and Taboo* (1919). Naturally, and as I am doing here, when one writes about anthropology, one writes about anthropologists and their associates, and the Other, the Indigenous people, retreat to a respectable distance. This separation between Subject and Other may be summed up in the title of one of C.D. Rowley's books: *The Remote Aborigines* (1970).

Actually, what I am seeking to approach is the hegemonic system (still based on a Social Darwinism) which has saturated Australian settler consciousness and unconsciousness to become the discourse of average settlers and part of what I have termed their 'political unconsciousness'. This system of once-conscious thought rationalised the discourses, or ransacked the discourses of anthropology and evolutionary theory to produce the Aboriginal as Other, and it is too often from this position of Other that Indigenous people are placed within Australian settler literature, whereas in Indigenous literature the position sometimes is reversed, though more often done away with, so that instead of a Subject–Other dichotomy, there is simply Subject–Subject, an engagement much more complex in that points of view, or emphasis, shift from subject to subject and, if a Subject–Other opposition is used, it is played with, as in my novel: *Doctor Wooreddy's Prescription for Enduring the Ending of the World* (1983).

Modernism rests on a foundation of an ideology of Western imperialism, with a genealogy of evolutionism extending through Hegel to modern Australian literature which may be represented by Frederick Macartney, a champion of an independent Australian settler literature who, in an essay titled 'Literature and the Aborigine' in his 1957 collection, denies any intellectual breadth or imaginative ability to Indigenous people. Macartney takes issue with a doyen of Australian settler anthropology, A.P. Elkin, who has dared to suggest that Aborigines are 'natural philosophers'. This upsets Macartney so much that he launches into an attack on this assumption with the assertion that philosophy was an intellectual analysis of ideas and phenomena which had nothing to do with 'primitives' who blurred the distinction between self and external objects.

Of course, this was not a new attack on a non-European people, and it was made about Indian peoples in the middle of the nineteenth century by Hegel who, in his *Philosophy of Fine Art* (1835–38), reduced Hindu thought to 'Fantastic Symbolism', a term reflecting the 'absence' of an historical consciousness in the Hindu. In continuing his discourse, Hegel concluded that, as there was a fundamental unity of consciousness and self-consciousness, the distinction between self and object effectively disappeared and therefore there was no 'object either for imagination or art'. This same argument reappears in Macartney's essay in 1957.

Macartney was too ready to dismiss Indigenous people for being unable, as he asserts, to produce 'a race's finest cultural artefact', that is, the literary text, when unknown to him an Indigenous person had already produced literary texts. At the time he was writing, Indigenous people in a number of areas and among a number of communities had had over a hundred years to seek some accommodation with Western cultural genres. Not only this, but they were taught by those termed missionaries who sought to 'civilise' the native. Being ignorant of any response by Aborigines to settler genres and seeing Indigenous culture through the ideology of Social Darwinism, Macartney had no knowledge of David Unaipon, an Indigenous thinker of the 1920s, who was an inventor as well as a writer.

David Unaipon, a Nunga from Point McLeay in South Australia, was born in 1868 and educated by missionaries into Western genres. He wrote 'Legendary Tales of the Australian Aborigines' apparently in 1929, and the manuscript is preserved in the Mitchell Library in Sydney. Some of his stories which appear in Davis, Muecke and others' anthology of black Australian writing, *Paperbark* (1990), show a grasp of a medium which reflects not the so-called timelessness of the Dreamtime, but a keen mind seeking to recast Nunga and other Indigenous legends into a contemporary form which reveals the intellectual ferment happening amongst Indigenous communities, perhaps from the time of the invasion and which was unknown to such settlers as Macartney.

David Unaipon's narrative discourse owes much to the Christian bible; but his subject matter is the ancestral beings of the Nunga and other Indigenous people. The very existence of David Unaipon's creative writings thus renders Macartney's analysis and his conclusions in doubt, to say the least. It is not known what Indigenous literature he was familiar with. I assume that they were examples of oral literature—spoken or recited, rather than written down—although the extent of his knowledge of

Indigenous literature is open to doubt, for he comments in the main on a supposedly short song, rather than on any lengthy extract; but this does not deter him from declaring that Indigenous oral literature was 'tediously discursive and inchoate' (p. 121). At the time he wrote, other settler scholars, such as the anthropologist R.M. Berndt, had different ideas and he had published a version of the *Djanggawul* epic or song cycle, which was not tediously discursive but had the encoded brevity of Sanskrit sutra literature, which necessitated a long commentary. In fact, with settler Australians searching for a convenient mythology to stress their belonging to the country, the *Djanggawul* epic might one day hold the same place in an Australian literature as do the epics of Homer in British literature, with the flashing paddles of the Djanggawul brothers being appropriated to become the shining sails of the ships of the invasion force of Governor Phillip.

It is difficult these days to defend a singular and dominant European narrative based on Social Darwinism and extending through into modernism with the elevating of certain European cultures at the expense of subject cultures. The subject cultures have been writing back for some time now and the grand world narrative, once seen as leading inexorably to European civilisation, has become fragmented or, as the French theorist Roland Barthes has declared, has become a tissue of quotations taken from the various centres of culture. The fragmentation of the grand European narrative has resulted in what has been described as 'postmodernism', and it is because of the fragmented nature of this narrative that Indigenous people find a place for their own quotations and achieve some degree of empowerment. In doing so, they come to contend with other, usually settler, representations of Indigenous people who are often loath to deconstruct their representations and in fact ignore Indigenous protestations of misrepresentation.

In examining how Indigenous people are represented in settler literary texts, perhaps the place to begin is with the kinds of settler discourses or genres available also to many Indigenous writers. Whether we like it or not, if Indigenous people enter into the settler cultural patrix, as writers they must deal with the use of printing and the development of a style marked by closure, graphology, mechanical production, editorial apparatus, commentaries, critical metatexts and intertextuality. Indigenous literature has been and often still is an oral discourse with different devices, such as absence of closure, narrative dominance, epic style, collective authorship and recitation, generic fluidity, repetition, non-verbal and semi-verbal markers and other devices which are often edited out when the literary text becomes an artefact to be read rather than heard.

The written text seeks to condense while the oral text, especially when it is the formal language of ritual, relies on repetition to make a point. This repetition when written down often becomes tedious, or appears so, for example in the sacred Buddhist texts which keep to the fidelity of the original oral text. As in these Buddhist texts, Indigenous texts do not refer to an author, but to the guardian of the information, and the formation and reformation of the information through a succession of storytellers or reciters. Oral texts when written down still bear the marks of their spoken origins: retarding narratives, prolepsis, bricolage, the surfacing of residual material and so on.

When an oral culture enters into a print culture, an example being David Unaipon, certain aspects of the oral text may be carried over. It, for example, may be more inclined to the interpersonal and how things are or were, whereas print culture texts (those completely within the written tradition) tend to be about how things ought to be, rather than how they are. In Indigenous terms we are talking about 'tru stori' as opposed to 'gammon'. As many Indigenous people enter print culture directly from the oral, we might be justified in thinking that they would, at least in form and style, produce the more authentic text and representation when speaking and translating their speech into writing.

This is becoming apparent as more Indigenous people put in print their own stories and histories using appropriate oral formations, or devices which can be easily handled within the genres of written discourse. Thus, Ida West's *Pride against Prejudice* (1984), Hazel McKellar's *Matya-Mundi* (1984),

Labumore's *An Aboriginal Mother Tells of the Old and the New* (1984) and Robert Bropho's *Fringedweller* (1980) are marked by a mode which is fragmented and centred by the subject. These histories are not so much concerned about the objective terrains claimed by settler literature, as by family relationships, survival and ritual. They are texts of community empowerment.

Georg Lukacs, the Marxist theorist, has stated that the central category of all literary discourse is genre. As positive structures of potentially realisable meanings, genres realise, reflect, distil and mediate what he calls 'the historical real'. As such, they designate the presuppositions upon which any generic actualisation is based. Genres are organising principles which channel discourse towards a particular mediated expression, and perhaps an Indigenous example is *My Place* by Sally Morgan (1987) which fits quite neatly into the romance genre. Genres are bonded to history and are to a greater or lesser extent creatures of a particular ideology, and perhaps this is one of the reasons why Sally Morgan's book, though being so well received by the settler community, has been a contentious subject amongst Indigenous people. In contrast to this, oral discourse fits into its own genres and projects its own generic possibilities. An example may be seen in *Gularabulu* by Paddy Roe (1983). In his stories there are interactions within a powerful interpersonal domain where the forms of representation are fluid, endless and not marked by a self-conscious concern with origins as is *My Place*. This is also seen in the stories of David Unaipon where, though the writing down seeks to condense and lessen the fluidity, there is still a marked episodic quality about the stories which is not a marker of written discourse, but of oral discourse.

Following Lukacs, we may say that written settler discourse with its own genres may be considered more bound and historically determined than Indigenous oral texts, and, moreover, through 'settler education' these genres are becoming widely disseminated among Indigenous communities. Thus, urban Indigenous discourse—for example, that of the Sydney Indigenous area of Redfern—may be analysed through written genres even when remnants of previous oral discourse genres enter into, de-establish, and juxtapose that discourse's appropriation of written genre. In fact, in urban Indigenous situations, written and oral discourses exist side by side and fertilise each other. Texts are formed which draw on the different centres of culture and hybrid forms are created, an example being *Real Deadly* by Ruby Langford Ginibi (1992).

The position of Indigenous people in Australia, often constructed as an encapsulated minority, is reflected in their written literature which is often in a mixed genre which settler critics find hard to contend with. An Indigenous text which approaches closest to a settler genre is considered better than a text which does not. The problem with this, and the use of genres such as romance, is that they organise the kinds of meanings to be realised from the text, and under 'kinds' we may place the representation of Indigenous people.

Before the advent of postmodernism, Australian literary texts were what may be called realist texts, seeking to reflect reality through mimesis, and these types of texts have endured to the present. Such novels as Prichard's *Coonardoo* (1929), Herbert's *Capricornia* (1937) and *Poor Fellow My Country* (1975), and Keneally's *Chant of Jimmie Blacksmith* (1972) attempt to negotiate the terrain afforded by mimesis, and thus slip into genres such as the romantic in which history is trivialised. Xavier Herbert's *Capricornia* is a romance in which history is rendered through nostalgic recollections of a supposedly bygone era and relations of power are glossed over rather than negotiated or actualised; but what is interesting in his two modernist texts is that they seek to negotiate the Other, to render him or her visible as to ontology and motives. Conventional novelistic techniques formulate the characters and more or less render them into caricatures or stereotypes, at least from a postmodern perspective.

Capricornia was written during what is called the assimilation period, and essentially beneath the romance there is this political subtext. *Poor Fellow My Country* and Thomas Keneally's *The Chant of Jimmie Blacksmith*, on the other hand, were written during the period of integration and have a different agenda, and negotiate a terrain of overt struggle for Indigenous empowerment. If power and contestation of power is a subtext of these novels and is dealt with as a major theme or sub-theme, there is no attempt by the authors to question their own Indigenous representations, and, at least in *Poor Fellow My Country*, Aboriginalism is structured into what may seem on the surface to be a very sympathetic text.

Poor Fellow My Country is perhaps the highpoint of the modernist text in Australia and it is a massive, irritating, sprawling work with abundant Indigenous representations, often edging towards the caricature. It is over a thousand pages long and stretches mimesis to the limits. Herbert is not afraid to deal with the political implications of the invasion of Australia and sets up myths of his own, fore-shadowing such later developments as landrights and landrights' legislation. Unfortunately, it lacks the sensitiv-ity of Indigenous people writing on the same or similar subjects, such as Herb Wharton in *Unbranded* (1992), as may be seen in contrasting a passage from Herbert with one from Wharton:

> *Her voice rose with strength: 'Vite pipple of Australia have only vun chance left to cure ze Black Pox zat is vages of sin zey have committ' against ze Aboriginal Race. Give back to ze blackman a vorthvile piece of ze stolen land, and let him live zere as he likes. Zat North Coast Country is ze only vorthvile piece left. If ze kuttabah ... ze stranger, vich mean everybody not belonging, and zat mean halfcaste too ... if zey get out, ze truly native people, if left alone, vill go back to old vay, ze only vay zey really know. Change moost come. But let ze blackman change himself. Do not count zese ozzer blackfellows in numbering ze Aboriginal Race. Zey have lost Dreaming vitout vich zey are like cripples ... to be helped vit pity. Do not count halfcastes even vit cripples ... because zey are really kuttabah, only pretending to be Aboriginal ven it suit zem ...'*
> (Herbert 1975, pp. 1461–2)

> *Inevitably, his thoughts turned to his own people, and once again he wondered just where some so-called Murri leaders were taking them. Back to the past was his guess—how many times had he argued that education should come before Land Rights, otherwise in a hundred years' time, even if every Aborigine was given a thousand acres, it*

would not solve his health or housing problems. As Bindi had said,
once there were ancient Aborigines; now there were modern
Aborigines.
(Wharton 1992, p. 184)

Poor Fellow My Country is a bitter book, and there is little hope given in it of a future change in direction and it effects closure through mysticism. It covers similar ground to the Murri realist book, *The Kadaitcha Sung*, by Sam Watson (1990), but Watson by his clever use of Murri reality, or maban reality, realises his subject with more acuity than Herbert. Both books end with a death; but the death of Watson's character is more hopeful than Herbert's rising from the waters of a great sea serpent, after the death of the hard man Pat at the hands of a mob of angry Indigenous people, and all is resolved in a gabble of Aboriginal words from Herbert alone knows where.

> *As Tommy Gubba's mortal body was lowered into the unmarked*
> *grave, every black man, woman and child on the Fingal Mission*
> *stole away from the reserve and walked north—towards their tribal*
> *lands.*
>   *Jelda travelled on horseback, as she was in the early stages of*
> *pregnancy.*
(Herbert 1975, p. 312)

Poor Fellow My Country is, as I have said, the high point of the settler modernist text in which the author is enthroned as God commenting on things below, and there is no questioning of God's right to represent who he pleases and in whatever way he chooses. In fact, the author enthroned as God is what distinguishes modern settler texts from postmodern, in that the latter are aware of the pitfalls of conventional characterisation in regard to Indigenous people, and try to negotiate Indigenous representation by seeking to render them as part of the backdrop of Australia, by ignoring them, or even by paying them homage; but few postmodern writers seek to contain the Indigenous in the old stereotypes formed from the outmoded conventions of nineteenth century characterisation and Aboriginalist anthropologist texts.

Perhaps a signifier of postmodern, self-conscious writing is Drusilla Modjeska's *Poppy* (1990), which in a memorable passage sets up postmodern Australia, although surely not postcolonial Australia, in these words:

> *Right now in Sydney where I live, the jacarandas are in bloom. In Canberra the Hawke Government announces the terms of the Royal Commission into black deaths in custody. In England the Royals are packing their bags for the celebration of the founding of a favoured colony. In January, on the day Prince Charles will take the salute on Sydney Harbour in celebration of a nation, and the Indigenous People will gather in mourning and in memory of another history, it will be four years since Poppy died.*
> (p. 11)

Poppy is postmodern in that it questions the genre of biography and declares the selective and fictional elements inherent in researching, remembering, compiling and writing. It is as if no genre, no language is innocent, and the author, or compiler, Barthes' intertextualist, must acknowledge this. This is what sets postmodern writings apart from the merely modern, which take genres for granted rather than engaging in discourse as a 'truth-evoking process', with the truth coming from the clash of discourses rather than as a thing-in-itself to be uncovered. In contrast to the modern, Indigenous people are written into the Australian story as in the passage above; but only as a backdrop, though this is important in that previously Indigenous people would not have been there. I see this as an act of reconciliation by settler authors, seeking to write Indigenous people into the Australian narrative. This is one way, and often an important way, in which they seek to deal with Indigenous representation, though it is non-political and leaves any questions of postcolonialism open, or even written out, and any power contestation avoided in their surface narrative. Thus, in the passage quoted above, Indigenous history becomes only a 'memory', and thus not part of the real history show being enacted with all the paraphernalia of a British colony.

Indigenous people as a backdrop can even enter into modernist novels, such as the very conventional, realist texts of authors like Thea Astley who has been described, at least on the cover of her novels, as 'Australia's most important contemporary novelist'. She is a Queenslander and comes from a state which has a large Murri (the Queensland equivalent of 'Indigenous') population, and these figure in her books prominently, though mostly as powerless, flat background material, more or less as a tourist would notice the colour of the skins of the waiters, or people around her, but have no knowledge of them as human beings. In her *Vanishing Points* (1992) which has settler characters working in Murri settlements, Murris are prominent, but distant as the rock art of Laura:

> '*I think,*' *Estelle Pellatier said too loudly for the small dining-room, 'that the art of those from whom the country was stolen would matter more than the burial places of those who took it, don't you? Those layers of painting after painting. Generations of paintings. And those paperbark sleeping platforms. The saddest.' She put down her fork and looked away from the group into the dark beyond the pub veranda where the voices of Aboriginal women on their way to the outdoor movie came through and mingled with the roar of drinkers at the bar.*
> (p. 29)

It is the use of Indigenous people merely as backdrops to the settler story which seems to have become a feature of much of the Australian contemporary literature which I have labelled postmodern. It is as if, from seeking to represent the native or the Other in the modernist text, the postmodern has gone the other way and sought to distance him or her. The Other is other and, although acknowledged, cannot be a subjectivity in a settler narrative. Even in David Malouf, regarded as one of Australia's finest novelists, there is this distancing at work. For example, in his short story 'The Only Speaker of His Tongue', published in an anthology, *Antipodes* (1985), the 'only speaker' apparently refers to an old 'Aboriginal' man whose people have been massacred, leaving him the only speaker left; but the Indigenous character is used only for the main settler character to meditate on the loss of language and how it affects him. The Indigenous character is only part of the natural fauna, I am led to read from the text, of Australia or part of its mysteries. Something or someone of a dismal past and now rendered harmless, as in this quotation from the story:

> *All this is mystery. It is a mystery of the deep past, but also of now. We recapture on our tongue, when we first grasp the sound and make it, the same word in the mouths of our long dead fathers, whose blood we move in and whose blood moves in us. Language is in that blood.*
> (p. 69)

It seems that these days, when the media abounds with representations of Indigenous people and debate on these representations, the acknowledged major writers of Australia have retreated from the Indigenous and have settled for the mysteriousness, the lack of knowledgeability of the Other, the Native. The native is unknown, or to be merely described, though other less well known postmodern writers negotiate representation through the conscious use of experimentation in style and genre. One way which is of recent development, and which is paralleled by the appropriation of Indigenous art motifs, is that of seeing the Other as a repository of wisdom, and in effect the writer becomes a Prometheus entering the Other to steal her wisdom and bring it back to her community. English writer Bruce Chatwin's *The Songlines* (1987) is an example of this type of literature, and another is Lynn V. Andrews' *Crystal Woman* (1987) who enters the world of the Other through a new age shamanism, which is appealing to the settler community for her book is achieving good sales in Australia. What is interesting about her text is that she constructs herself as an innocent (much like Voltaire's Candide), searching out secrets from the ancient subjects of indigenous people worldwide. Her approach is through the ideology that all women (especially shamans) are sisters and there is basically no Other. All cultures may be entered through feminism and shamanism. Her approach is different from the conventional novelist and her texts are accounts of her adventures in faraway lands including Nepal and, in *Crystal Woman*, Australia. Her sisterly approach may be seen in this passage:

By the end of the welcoming ceremony we were no longer strangers.
We were laughing together and had a clear feeling for each other. The
elder women chanted and covered our greasy bodies with ash from
the fires, patting our skin with the palms of their hands. (p. 70)

This seeing women as belonging to a sisterhood which
crosses cultural boundaries or, if not crossing them, at least
allowing some sort of mutuality or acceptance, seems to be
a positive aspect of a feminism which seeks to break down
and do away with the outmoded concept of the Other. This
ideology stresses that women are women first and
Indigenous people or settlers second, and it is through
womanhood that the Other may be done away with and a
common sisterhood formed across racial and cultural
boundaries. It may be seen to be a healthy sign and even as
a marker to the beginnings of a postcolonial literature in
Australia.

Academic research and the writing up of that research
brings us back to 'Aboriginalism' and the defining of the
Other. The exposure of 'Aboriginalism' in many of the
early representations of Indigenous people in settler literature has resulted in a questioning among some writers of
literature and academic works of the constructions of character in fiction and non-fictional writings. Deconstruction
often shows such characterisation to be flawed, limiting
and often racist and sexist in regard to Indigenous people
and women. Some Australian writers have tackled this
problem by distancing themselves from the Indigenous. If
no correct representation is possible, then it is best to let
the Other be the Other, while others have used the tools
of their craft, and the opening up of novelistic and academic genres, to tackle the problem. Victor Kelleher in his
novel *Wintering* (1990) writes about guilt, doubt and the
hope that division and trauma may be overcome as
Australia progresses towards a postcolonial state. In his
text, he seeks to make the Other subject by foregrounding
an Indigenous character as subject and then even allowing
her to edit his text. Thus, certain passages are crossed out
by a heavy black diagonal line. The crossings out are by a
Murri (Indigenous) woman, Bridget, a former lover of the
narrator, and a political activist. The narrator is a settler,

Jack Rudd, who is attempting to write an account of white male cruelty from the aspect of a black female victim who intervenes in the text to address his misunderstanding by wielding a heavy black pencil of disapproval. The device is quite interesting and is an indication of the current experimentation with Indigenous representation by white settler writers.

The representation of Indigenous people by non-Indigenous people has become a matter of contention. Under modernism, when Australia, at least to the settler, was monocultural and he was secure in the inheritance of a European narrative and culture, it was accepted that all representation was grist to the writer's mill. That writing was to a great extent an innocent act, and the settler was at liberty to construct characters from wherever he wanted and whoever he wanted. This privilege, a privilege granted by imperialism and dominance, has been challenged by not only Indigenous people but also non-Indigenous people, especially women who have been the Other to many male writers and also suffered misrepresentation. I have mentioned only a few writers, but perhaps a significant marker is that it is extremely difficult to identify who is an Australian settler writer when many have been born over-seas or have returned overseas or live overseas. This is not my problem and I have used writers of what may be called European extraction who have constructed Indigenous characters or criticised the misrepresentation of Indigenous people. It is difficult to negotiate a terrain which has been sullied by totalising fictions, and this difficulty at least is being recognised and addressed by writers such as Lynn V. Andrews in texts like *Crystal Woman*:

> *I heard Ginevee's voice in my head. She said: 'When you see me in the Dreamtime, you see me as a black swan. Swans have great power. They did not mean to but, as it says in the ancient legends, they helped trick woman and the earth lost her balance. When you see Ginevee in the Dreamtime as a white swan, you will know that her work has been completed on earth and that man and woman swim equally in the billabongs, the sacred waters, and balance has been restored among us.'*
> (p. 266)

The Struggle for Recognition: Oodgeroo of the Tribe Noonuccal

4

... I would like to state that a multicultural society can only successfully occur in this country when seventh-generation Australians recognise the Aboriginal culture. No change will or can occur until the theft of Aboriginal land and the attempted enslaving and slaughter are addressed and compensated ... Aborigines will always be the custodians of their traditional lands, regardless of any other enforced law system, for the land is our Mother. We cannot own her, she owns us!
(Oodgeroo 1989)

OODGEROO OF THE TRIBE NOONUCCAL, CUSTODIAN of the Land of Minjerribah, is no longer with us. She left us in September 1993; but the strength of her spirit pervades this book. She was a writer deeply committed to her people and her land, an Indigenous writer deeply aware of her Indigenality. She is the Granny of Indigenous writing in Australia, and her life and struggle for her people and her craft serve as a model for all writers.

But Oodgeroo was more than a writer and during my long friendship with her never once described herself as a poet. She often said when pressed that she was an educationalist and that her job was to educate both white and black. I believe, therefore, that to wrench her verse away from her life and accepted role is to lose the message for the structure, the polemics for comparison with persons who have described themselves as poets and are taken at this face value through the filtering apparatus of a theory of aesthetics which eschews the political, the polemical, for either the individual or universal truth utterance. In effect, this kind of poetry is meant to be beyond the mundane utterance of the everyday, or to engage in a transformation of the everyday into the universal, as in Alfred Lord Tennyson's 'Flower in the Crannied Wall', or to engage in a fetishisation of language—to translate it into 'a thing of beauty is a joy for ever' (Keats, *Endymion*).

I doubt that this last quotation could be used in regard to the verse of Oodgeroo and I have coined the term 'poet-emics' to separate social verses, such as she wrote and recited, from the more 'serious' business of poetics which exists in and for itself, often as a 'thing of beauty', of an aesthetic form which reminds me of those languorous female muses depicted in Victorian paintings. 'Poetemics' is coined from 'poetry' (verse) and 'polemics' in order to stress that what is important in the poems of Oodgeroo is the message, and the aesthetic pleasure we derive from them is of secondary value. In fact, such poetemic verse may have the opposite effect and repel those in search of an aesthetics. In such verse there may be a deliberate repudiation of aesthetical concerns in order to produce an alienation effect, akin to the theories of Bertolt Brecht in his search for a Marxist dramatics:

> *True, profound, active application of alienation effects takes it for granted that society considers its condition to be historic and capable of improvement. True A-effects are of a combative nature.*
> (Willett 1964, p. 277)

Social protest is thus considered not to be the legitimate field of poetry and, though we might query this especially in regard to poetry which stems from other than the European mainstream tradition, Oodgeroo's work from the first was labelled 'social protest' verse and denied to be poetry. If this position is taken to be a negative judgement, then we are forced into attempts to rescue Oodgeroo for poetry, as may be seen in black literary critic Cliff Watego's spirited defence at the Aboriginal Writers Conference in 1983 (*Aboriginal Writing Today* 1985); but if we accept that

Oodgeroo's verse is poetemical, then it needs no such defence and we are forced to heed the message rather than to drag her verse into the mainstream poetic tradition with all its aesthetical values. Again, labelling Oodgeroo's verse as merely 'protest' does have a limiting effect. Oodgeroo's poems have a wide range of subject matter and often the 'final protest' is left for the reader to make. This is not to say that overt protest is not found in Oodgeroo's verse. In *My People*, her constantly reprinted collected volume of verse written up to 1970, there are poems which rightly may be termed 'protest' verse, such as 'United We Shall Win' and 'Intolerance'; but these are balanced by other poems, such as 'Boro' and 'Community Rain Song', which seek to impart nostalgia for the past and show aspects of Indigenous culture, or hope for the future, or even statements about life in general. Her subject matter is wide and to dismiss all of her poems as being simply 'protest' is naive, to say the least.

Poetry is often judged (as any recourse to reviews of poetry will show) on an assumed originality or, if not, then a playful use of traditional forms such as the ballad metre which are often parodied. Oodgeroo's poetry in contrast to these types of poetry is conservative in its experimentation with verse structures. She usually uses such verse structures which are part of the cultural unconsciousness of Australia. Here I include both non-Indigenous and Indigenous people as belonging to this cultural unconsciousness, with the proviso that Indigenous people are included depending on their proximity to mainstream Australian culture and what they had placed within their minds in that socialisation and often assimilationist process termed 'primary or tertiary education'. Oodgeroo is included in this cultural unconsciousness because she did undergo such socialisation and assimilation, as described in her story 'Repeat Exercise' (*Stradbroke Dreamtime* 1972) and by her later involvement with the Realist Writers Group in Brisbane, as pointed out in Cliff Watego's paper. Because of the conservative nature of both of these institutions, when Oodgeroo began writing verse, she favoured the ballad metre with the necessity of rhyme, though later she used free verse, as in such poems as 'Jarra's Love Song'. In regard to the cultural unconsciousness of Australia, there is also the recourse to the structure of nursery rhymes (or children's play verses) in such poems as 'No More Boomerang' which rhythmically appears to be based on 'Here We Go round the Mulberry Bush'. I wish to stress that we might not find a one-to-one correlation between a particular poem and a particular nursery or play rhyme. I doubt that the unconscious operates like this, but more by way of allusion or invocation. The formula here is that simplicity of rhyme and words evokes simplicity of nursery or play rhymes evokes simplicity of childhood state when such rhymes were heard or used. It is the invoking of this receptive state that prepares the mind for the reception of the message.

In poetemics, with the urgency of getting the message across to as many readers as possible, this of necessity includes those who do not usually read poetry and who were taught only a few of its structures in school, thus recourse must be made to what the adult learnt as a child. This using of traditional structures is very important for it invokes unconscious associations which cause a state of emotional rapport which may then be inclined to accept the message. I believe that structure is just as important, at least in this psychological regard, as content and played a large part in the ideology of the leftist (read: communist) Group of using verse structures which were familiar to the workers. It seems that Oodgeroo through her membership of this group learnt and then adopted this strategy. For her, it proved very successful. *My People* has never been out of print and it outsells all other Australian poetry.

But when such a strategy of using supposedly transcended structures of poetry is adopted, there is a price to be paid:

> *It is to be expected that her reviewer in the* Times Literary Supplement *should write: 'At times the metres of her poems are trite, stemming from the worst type of nineteenth century hymns.' This is undoubtedly true.*
> (Doobov 1973)

Thus, Oodgeroo's verse is placed outside the canons of what, for some, constitutes good poetry; and if we expect our poetry to be experimental and 'flash', we will accept these criticisms as well-founded. Rhyming metrical verse, especially when silently read from the page, can seem trite and contrived and even seem to unintentionally parody itself, at least in the eyes of those knowledgeable in poetic aesthetics. Simple rhyming schemes, as we find in much of Oodgeroo's verse, can make us grit our teeth, or smile disparagingly, or sink to condescension when reviewing it; but what we must not forget is that Oodgeroo has never declared herself a poet's poet. She is writing, as she puts it in a 1977 interview with Jim Davidson in *Meanjin* ' ... for her people'; and this must always be borne in mind, especially when we consider that most poetry published in Australia is completely ignored by much of the population. She might be termed 'a poet of the people' and what this means is that her poetry is easy to grasp and the messages come through loud and clear. The role of the educationalist is to use what tools are at hand and this she does.

Not only are the verse structures of Oodgeroo's poetry known to most Australians, but her language also is akin to Australian spoken language, although at times she does use an adaptation of Indigenous English. The Australian English of Queensland is noted for its laconic flatness and lack of ornamentation and so is Indigenous English. There is, therefore, a noticeable absence of metaphor and simile in Oodgeroo's verse and an absence of striking images which are supposed to be a feature of poetry. If this is so, how exactly does Oodgeroo's verse work? It works by the use of analogy and illusion, just as her verse structures seek echoes from the cultural unconsciousness. This is apparent in 'No More Boomerang', one of her most popular poems, which has been put to music on more than one occasion by Aboriginal musicians like Coloured Stone. There are no similes in the short four-line rhyming stanzas, and the poem proceeds by invoking oppositions between the old ways of life of the Aboriginal people and the newly arrived civilised ways. There is no attempt, except in the stanza on abstract art, to condemn outright; it is left to the reader or listener to draw conclusions. In its brevity and wit the poem is an example of Oodgeroo at her best. Her style is proverbial or aphoristic instead of image-based, and this method, laconic in a flat statement, is not what, we are told, good poetry is made from. In fact, her poem simply titled 'Verses' is a collection of aphorisms or proverbs, which again is marked by no striking images, thus—'appearance is the world's test./Brother, you're treated as you're dressed.'

It should be apparent that it is impossible to use mainstream poetic criticism to aid our understanding of much of Oodgeroo's verse. We are in the presence of a different type of poetics, one which I have labelled 'poetemic' in that the message value far outweighs any aesthetic concerns. Thus, to judge her verse by the usual mainstream methods of seeking striking images and the clever use of other poetic devices would lead to her dismissal as a 'poet'. She declared herself an 'educationalist' and what must be taken into account in any discussion of her written work is her success or lack of it in getting her message across. By any means of measurement, she has been most successful, as the sales of her books attest, as the number of her poems which have been put to music attest, and the number of her lines which are quoted. As an educationalist and a poetemist, she has fulfilled her role, and moreover has introduced poetry to those who otherwise would not have read it.

When the bare garret of Euro-Australian poetry happened to glance at the first volume of Indigenous poetry, the result was horror (see, for example, Taylor's review, quoted in Chapter Two). This horror was tempered by the leftist humanist tradition, still strong among members of the Anglo-Celtic literary establishment, which meant that, although the cause of the poor Indigenous people had to be respected, this respect, in the interests of aesthetics, could not be extended to their poetry which was seen as being too simple and direct. In fact, there was no place for such poetry in the nobler traditions of Anglo-Celtic poetry. It is interesting that Taylor's review began with the reviewer wishing that he could assume the role of dictator and ban Oodgeroo's (then Kath Walker) verse as poetry. He even went so far as to offer a solution as to what genre it should be placed in. Seeing that Indigenous people were the objects of study by anthropologists and sociologists, what better place for it than the, to him, non-literary field of social protest? His message is very similar to the racist comment that Indigenous people are alright as long as they stay in their place, but Oodgeroo was refusing to stay in her place. She was extending the Aboriginal struggle for equal rights and justice into the arena of literature, knocking on the doors of the Anglo-Celtic literary establishment with verse often as simple as a fist. They refused to open their doors and dismissed her as a poor Aborigine whose voice should not be heard in their neighbourhood. The place of an Indigenous writer when this review was written was on the fringe.

But the voices of Anglo-Celtic dominance are not the only voices heard in Australia, and from the first there have been people, often foreigners on a visit, who have no wish to conform to a life in Australia and can appreciate what they find and this often is Indigenous culture. Thus, even in the nineteenth century, English ethnologist A.W. Howitt had praise for traditional Indigenous song poetry which, though appearing simple and direct on the surface, is structurally complex and polysemic. As Michael Riffaterre (1980) states: 'To put it simply, a poem says one thing and means another.' And perhaps if this is kept in mind we may get a deeper reading of Kath Walker. An example would be her short poem 'My Love':

> Possess me? No, I cannot give
> The love that others know,
> For I am wedded to a cause:
> The rest I must forgo.

> You claim me as your very own,
> My body, soul and mind;
> My love is my own people first,
> And after that, mankind.

> The social part, the personal
> I have renounced of old;
> Mine is a dedicated life,
> No man's to have and hold.

> Old white intolerance hems me round,
> Insult and scorn assail;
> I must be free, I must be strong
> To fight and not to fail.

For there are ancient wrongs to right,
Men's malice to endure;
A long road and a lonely road,
But oh, the goal is sure.

The title is ambiguous in itself: does it mean 'to my love' or 'what my love is', or 'what man's love is'? The first stanza begins with the question: 'Possess me?' and the rest of it is taken up with the reply which on a second reading is obscure, except if we take the 'Possess me?' to be a refusal to a certain type of possessive love, though in the rest of the stanza it is the poet who is renouncing the possession, with a further implication that being wedded to a cause is cause enough to forgo such love. The second stanza is essentially made up of two oppositions: the possessive partner and the poet's reply, with the implication that the subject is a man, though again we should keep the ambiguity of the title in mind, 'my love', this is how I love and the passive love object is not for me. The fourth stanza follows the rhythmic pattern of two joined couplets, with the opposition between first and last couplet. The surface structure of the poem is a stylised response and answer, the first couplet giving what the poet sees as negative aspects of love or desire, and the second couplet replying to these.

What are these negative traits? 'Possession', claiming the person, 'white intolerance', 'men's malice'. These are opposed to 'wedded love', 'dedicated', 'free' ('strong', 'fight') and the 'final goal'. It is an interesting little poem in that, although published in 1964, it is (among other things) a paean of praise to the independent woman. It ends on a note of affirmation rather than decrying the fact that the poet cannot give herself in a personal relationship. The poem in effect is saying more than we receive from our first superficial reading, which is that the poet is decrying the fact that her commitment has denied her a true love that will last forever, of the 'possess me, I am yours' variety. A deeper reading reveals that she is criticising the subservient place of a woman in a patriarchal love-relationship.

Oodgeroo's poetry, condemned for being simple and often trite, really is a condemnation of all superficial first readings, though perhaps there is more substance in the criticism that, if Indigenous creative writing is to thrive as a separate entity, it must be independent as far as possible from white Australian influence, thus much of Oodgeroo's poetry owing to its reliance on the bush ballad format is betraying its Indigenality. But it must be borne in mind that Oodgeroo was more than a poet; she was a poetemist who sought out a poetry which would be accessible to as many people as possible. Thus, the strong rhythms of the ballad, the iambic metre with its accent on the second syllable, as in Indigenous clapstick playing, has the strength of rhythm and rhyme to ensure that it is publicly heard. Oodgeroo's early poetry was meant to be recited and if poetry is composed to be heard rather than read, then it must be the rhythm of the metre which carries the words. If we listen to other indigenous poetry from around the world, we notice at once the rhythm, how the words lean on it and are carried by it. Such poems are a joy to listen to, though on a silent reading we may feel otherwise.

Often it is assumed by Europeans that there is a single and unified Indigenous strategy behind Indigenous writing and that some writers are seeking an Indigenous and authentic voice in which to be heard; but this is far from true in the works of writers like Oodgeroo, in which the message is foremost and what experimentation there is, is to get the message received, rather than falling into an obscurity of language which might be labelled Indigenous and mystical, but not political. It must not be forgotten that Oodgeroo is a poetemist and thus we find little Indigenous English. The Indigenality of the text is found in the content rather than in the structure. This is in line with what Bruce McGuinness says about Indigenous writers: 'When Aboriginal people write they write in a style. They're able to adopt various styles of writing so what they really want to write about is hidden. It's contained within their writing … They become actors in fact.'

The need has been to be published in order to get the message across, though this results in problems. Europeans view their literature in other ways and they, being in the majority, seek to impose their concepts onto the Indigenous. It is precisely those texts which correspond closely to the European canon of what constitutes good literature that will be accepted. In this regard, it is the Indigenous novel following closely or copying these canons which is accepted much more than the poetry of Oodgeroo. This is because it corresponds to what is expected from a novel, especially in these times when any experimentation is downplayed and a 'truth-effect' is sought. In fact, to go outside the unexpected is simply not to be published.

The Anglo-Celtic majority culture seeks to condition and explain Aboriginal literature through its own expectations and what has now been constructed as postcolonial. This majority dominates the economic and cultural institutions of Australia and it is their voices which are heard. Thus, Indigenous poets like Oodgeroo and her contemporary, Jack Davis, are judged by Western standards and found wanting, or if not are patronised. There is presupposed an absolute artistic standard identical with the Western standard and this serves as an active agent in suppressing any development of Indigenous arts which are outside this standard. Good Indigenous literature, therefore, is taken to be that which approximates Western literature or now postcolonial literature, especially those texts which stand by themselves away from the creator and deal with what are regarded as universal themes—themes which are to be read by using such Western devices as Freudian psychology or, as in the case of 'My Love', in reading the poem as a simple dedication to a cause rather than as a refusal to accept the Anglo-Celtic standards of patriarchal love, and in reaffirming a love-relationship based more on traditional independent sex roles.

What must be kept in mind is that the primary criticism of Indigenous arts and literature must come from those Indigenous persons and others knowledgeable in Indigenous culture. What must be rejected is any white interference (including that from postcolonial critics) which threatens not only the independence of the text, but the producer of the text. This does not mean that Indigenous works must not be criticised harshly, or that Western critical standards must not be used. But, if these standards are used, we must be fully conscious of their development. Western critical standards are developed in the Western tradition and are applied by critics to interpret and criticise

Western literature to the Western audience. Thus, when Cliff Watego in 1983 said that Kath Walker (Oodgeroo) had been heavily influenced by Henry Lawson, he immediately invoked a whole concept of Lawsonism with which the Anglo-Celtic reader is acquainted as part of his or her cultural education. Most Indigenous people, until recently having had only a primary school education, are not part of this tradition or, if knowing it, reject Henry Lawson because of his stated racism. They are repelled by the non-racist Oodgeroo being compared to him. Cliff Watego does not take into account that, when Anglo-Celtic critics write about Kath Walker, they immediately try to find out what white Australian works her poetry best resembles, then use this to establish communication with their audience. They do not, for instance, seek to establish parallels with, say, traditional Aboriginal song-texts such as the *tyabi*. This is usually because they are innocent of any knowledge of pre-invasion Australian poetry and, if they do seek to use Indigenous sources, are content to refer back to the producer of the text and his or her assumed knowledge of traditional Aboriginal culture.

At the first Aboriginal Writers Conference, Cliff Watego presented a paper on 'Aboriginal Poetry and White Criticism', and recoiled from the bitter response it invoked, which is only hinted at in the published report of the proceedings. In Indigenous aesthetics the producer of a literary text is not divorced from the text and held to account. Cliff Watego, by stating that Oodgeroo's models lay within the tradition of Henry Lawson and Banjo Patterson, slipped over into the realm of non-Indigenous criticism. Henry Lawson is noted among Indigenous people more for his racism than for the quality of his poetry and, ipso facto, Cliff was dragging Oodgeroo into the mainstream of Australian literature which, because of its heavily racist bias at the time, was under attack by Indigenous people. Since then this position to some extent has changed, owing to the work of Indigenous writers and activists like Oodgeroo of the Tribe Noonuccal, Custodian of the Land of Minjerribah. She tirelessly fought all through her life for a transformation of Australia as a whole and thus was more than a mere wordsmith. Perhaps others should follow in her footsteps and further this transformation. Even now such prestigious bodies as the Association for the Study of Australian Literature continue to deny the racism inherent in Lawson's works, and indeed such attitudes show that there is still much work to be done in removing racism from the halls of Australian literature.

The Poetry of Lionel Fogarty

5

Every colonised people—in other words, every people in whose soul an inferiority complex has been created by the death and burial of its local cultural originality—finds itself face to face with the language of the civilising nation ...
(Franz Fanon)

WHAT HAPPENED TO THE INDIGENOUS LANGUAGES of Australia? The British invaders sought to destroy them utterly. The Indigenous person had to be forced into the supposedly advanced state of British civilisation. This in practice meant the destruction of many Indigenous languages and cultures. In colonies such as Victoria and New South Wales, there was imposed a deliberate policy of language and cultural genocide. Under this policy, in a few decades, the Indigenous languages became broken collections of words falling towards English structures of grammar. This forced adaptation of the English language resulted in the rise of Indigenous English, creoles and pidgins which then became the domain of academic study. Indigenous writers in English were even criticised by these academics and white critics for their use or non-use of Indigenous structures of English. The political was

eschewed for the culturally correct and poets like Oodgeroo
were dismissed.

Lionel Fogarty did not enter into these academic
debates. He arrived from the outside, from the old mission
or concentration camp of Cherbourg, armed with his own
unique style. Deeply conscious of the language genocide,
he did not pass over into an accepted standard of English
but used the Indigenous English of Cherbourg to forge a
new style. It is impossible to read Lionel without realising
that he is Indigenous; it is impossible to read him and not
consider the crimes committed against the Indigenous
people of Australia; it is impossible to read him and not
realise that not only are we in the realm of Indigenous reality, but that here is a poet using the English language in
new and unique ways in order to give voice to the maban
reality which is the bedrock of Indigenous culture. Standard
English with its grammatical strictures reflects the reality of
nineteenth century imperialism with its ideologies of scientific realism and Social Darwinism. To give voice to an
Indigenous reality not based on these norms, a new
language must be forged and Lionel has done this.

He does not rely on European models for his poetry. It
is his genius and Indigenality which erupt to shape his
verse. Born a victim in a world in which he and his people
had no say, he revolted against this lack of subjectivity and
became a poet and an activist. And where else could he go
but to the Dreaming to connect up with the voices of his
ancestors? His poems speak of the ancestors and those
who fought against the imposition of European modes of
thought and feeling. His poems are exceedingly complex
and far from those nineteenth century models once
favoured by other Indigenous poets. In a sense, to use
these containers of words, these genres of verse, is to
accept the invasion of Australia and the death of the
Indigenous spirit. To go beyond them is to attempt to
change the structure of the English language, the
language of cultural imperialism, towards a reconciliation
of extremes. Lionel Fogarty is aware that the English
language is not his own, but by using and changing it he
seeks to make it his own. He has had five volumes of verse
published and in each there is an increasingly sure grasp

of what once was an alien means of expression. There are few poets, if any, to equal the strength of his verse; but in saying this one must remember that it has been a long struggle for him to achieve his status.

The first generation of Indigenous writers, such as Jack Davis, Kath Walker, Kevin Gilbert and myself, were representatives of a generation scarred by assimilation. This government policy dominated our lives and passed over to our work. Our lives engaged with the politics of the street and the bush, and the need to express ideas had to be in a clear language to get the message across to whites of the predicament we were in and how it should be changed. White Australian writers have always had freedom. It has been their birthright, but for the Indigenous people there had always been the government over them, represented by the police and the welfare officer. For many of us this is still fact. Graeme Dixon in his 1990 volume of verse, *Holocaust Island*, tells us what it is like to be a prisoner of the state. He writes in short abrupt verses which reflect the lives of those who build up the statistics of those of us who die in custody. It should be read by everyone who wishes to know what drives us to despair and death. Freedom is not the birthright of the Australian Indigenous person and too often, if he or she ends up at the receiving end of the white law, he or she is never treated as a common Australian citizen, but as a boong.

The whole of white Australian history has been the denial of freedom to the Indigenous people. They are denied any history or right of expression, and under the gaze of the white Other they wilt or revolt, or seek understanding by using the techniques of the white culture that surrounds them. The older poets and writers sought to give a legitimacy to the Indigenous world by using them. Thus, Aboriginal poets used the verse structures of Europe to get their message across. It was a strategy which left them open to judgement by white literary critics simply as bad or good poets according to the European tradition focused on aesthetics. It is only when we come to the newer generation of poets like Lionel Fogarty that the standard critical assumptions of Europe break down, and critics are either forced to condemn outright, or to at least attempt to arrive at some understanding by utilising their theory, and to modify it to arrive at a new way of seeing and understanding. In effect, to attempt a reconciliation of their own.

To attempt a deep reading of Lionel Fogarty is to penetrate into another world, which is different from the European, and to come to some understanding of an Indigenous reality which is only now penetrating white consciousness. Lionel Fogarty is the forerunner of those Indigenous poets who seek to establish an Indigenality rising from its own innate creativity, stemming from the time of our ancestors. This Indigenous reality finds echoes across the world in other writers and poets, such as Louise Bennett of Jamaica, and at times approaches the surrealism of African writers like Cesaire or Senghor. Early Indigenous poets often have problems in coming to grips with his verse. It is not the product of assimilation and lacks that precision of meaning which they are familiar with and which they used with great effect; but poetry need not be precise. Preciseness of language often destroys the poetry implicit in language. Rhythm and music are implicit in poetry. A true poet wrestles with language and this is what Lionel Fogarty does. He produces Indigenous verse which is difficult for some readers to accept; but this is the fate of such serious poets, an example being Ezra Pound who produced a dense poetry of often conflicting idioms. Such poets are to be dismissed as poets or accepted as major poets to which some effort must be given if their visions are to be realised by the reader. With Lionel we are reading works that sing not only of the rape of the Indigenous soul, but also of the healing of the soul and perhaps the healing of the land of Australia. His voice also sings of the sad wounds inflicted on a whole people, of hundreds of mouths forced into shaping the harsh sounds of an alien speech so unlike the liquid Aboriginal discourse patterns:

> If I don't succeed, bear with me,
> I see words beyond any acceptable meaning
> And this is how I express my dreaming ...

The language of poetry differs from common linguistic usage and it may even have its own special grammar. This

is the case with Lionel Fogarty and thus there is a displacing, and a distorting, in an effort to create a new language
from English which will reflect Indigenous reality, what I
have called maban reality. Displacing is used by Lionel to
shift the sign from one meaning to another, for example 'So
come on down/and freehold us'.

He uses distortion to create ambiguity, contradiction, or
even non-sense. He uses textual space as a principle of
organisation for making signs out of linguistic items which
may not be meaningful otherwise. We might ask what these
devices do in his poetry? There is but one answer—that
they threaten the literary representation of accustomed
reality, of mimesis, and postulate another reality which may
be magic. Too often the reader expects to be presented
with a context consistent with what he or she believes to be
reality. Usually and most often, except for Indigenous song
cycles, this reality reflects what the European sees around
him or her and is based on nineteenth century European
ideologies of thought which have crystallised. It is a simple
reality opposing true to untrue, and grammar (whose rules
were formulated last century) reflects this. Language and
reality support and maintain each other, even to the extent
that they are identical. Thus early Indigenous poetry could
claim to give a correct picture of the Indigenous condition
in Australia. Words and verse reflected this reality without
taking into account any ideology implicit in such a position.
These signs, these words arranged in chaste verse forms on
white paper, I would argue were not signs of reality in
themselves, but ideograms revealing or encoding the effect
of assimilation on Indigenous writers and their occupation
of a rational world. The ambiguity of the words and the
structures of the language used were ignored for a 'truth
effect' and this had the effect, at least in the case of
Oodgeroo's verse, of it being denied a place in the halls of
poetry; instead, it was placed in the gunya of social protest.

The basic characteristic of mimesis is that it must
produce a continuously changing semantic sequence, as we
find in the work of Oodgeroo, Jack Davis and Kevin Gilbert,
to produce a one-to-one relationship of words to things as
they are supposed to be. The text lessens details, but keeps
shifting its focus to achieve an acceptable likeness to reality.

A masterly use of this shifting of image is found in Jack Davis' 'Tribal Man in the City' where each line of the poem begins with the word 'Black', followed by a definition which makes the reality of the tribal man in the city black. The poem is grammatically laid out and does not have the difficulties and shifts in grammar usage that we find in Lionel's work. These are noticed by the reader from the first, and dominate to such an extent that this common trait forms a paradigm which shifts the complex of meanings away from the familiar reality, constructed by us from formalised grammar, and towards Indigenous reality with its own formalisms. The shifting grammaticalities are components of a different network of relationships and also signify a different reality structure. It is here that the approach of the unsophisticated critic and reader breaks down. He or she does not advance beyond the first reading which seeks to decode the poem from the beginning to the end of the text, from top to bottom, following the syntagmatic unfolding of the familiar. It is in this first reading that the reader attempts to apprehend meaning and to do this he or she brings along his or her linguistic competence which includes an assumption that language is referential and that words do indeed relate to familiar things. Incompatibilities are noted between words, recognitions made that a word or phrase does not make sense in his or her experience, that semantic transfers are necessary and the understanding that a bilinear deciphering of the single linear text is necessary for the perception of irony or humour. But this reading of the text occurs only because the reader has the necessary linguistic competence to perceive such techniques, which may be recognised as a writer's 'style'. In the case of Lionel's poetry, to confuse a simple reading act there is often a double or even triple grammar at work which needs to be read. In Lionel's poems there is the grammatical structure of Indigenous English and the use of Murri language which act as signifiers for Indigenous people. There is often a twofold (or threefold) grammar at work which tends to establish signs as ideotones so that what may seem obscure to a white reader will be clear to an Indigenous reader. There is a further complexity in that the descriptive systems, the themes, the mythology employed, may engage in an

Indigenous or maban reality which is beyond the signifiers of the everyday.

This inability, at first or second reading, to fully comprehend the poem necessitates a third or retroactive reading. The wary reader now progresses through the text, remembering what has just been read and modifying understanding in the light of what is now being read again and decoded. Progress is made through the text, reviewing, revising, comparing backwards and forwards towards the vision of a different reality hidden in the bewilderment of language.

Lionel's poetry is best entered through his latest volume, *New and Selected Poems* (1995). The newer poems I feel are more accessible and the understanding gained may then be turned to his earlier and more difficult poems. A circular reading practice may emerge, the later codes of his new poems being used to decipher the thickness of some of his earlier texts. Retroactive reading is necessary to perceive the underlying reality, the single underlying experience of Indigenality or maban reality. To show how this retroactive reading is done, I will take one of his poems, reprinted in his new volume:

FREE OUR DREAMS

Out of a hole we came out of a hole
    filled with poles of unfolded reasons
As it flies past
    songs came off in blood
We find strength to be blue and red
    ride it to expansion
Yet you people miss what they came as
    miss everything living that lives for
Power.

Don't give then the human power
    that makes green frogs cut open for enjoyment
Make it the kind of compassion
    for establishment rules on love
Smelling noises
    of burning finger tips
Water came falling

like digesting loud rushing pains
Eaten a sickly sight of spirituality.

Treat us to a barking laughter
    like running creeks
Speared out for swimming fish
    dead leaves, dead weeds go with our seeds
Roots grown out
    mingled with shining desire

Free our dreams.

Even with a first reading, we are instantly aware that we
are not in the literal world of descriptive signs, or of mimesis. From the first we are forced to transcend any checking
of language with supposed perceived reality. There is not
even any shift towards symbolism, but a symbolism
implicit from the first line and even oppositions which
create the necessity of a second reading. 'Holes' are
opposed to 'poles', reduced to 'a pole', perhaps a penis
expanding, thus referring back to the hole which may be
equated with the vagina, the womb pregnant with life, with
power. Thus, what may seem at first reading to be simple
oppositions of hole to pole renders down on a second reading to a relationship of hole/vagina, pole/penis birthing into
songs, strength, expansion—all forms of positiveness, of
fecundity, of creativity—finally in the chief word in the
first stanza: power. As words are never isolated but exist in
a grammatical relationship, this power may be ascertained
to refer back to us, the Indigenous people who know our
origins, who know our power which in our maban reality is
the earth, thus extending our first hole/vagina symbolism
to include a literal hole in the earth. Again our pole/penis
symbolism in the light of maban reality may now be
extended to the *rangga* poles of initiation, or of power
bestowing, the meaning strengthened by songs and blood,
components of Indigenous ritual, the flying pole referring
to the mabans, the shamans of Indigenous culture who use
it to fly through the air. Power resides in the ceremonial
pole and it is precisely this power which is missed by 'you
people', referring to the white people. Thus, in this first
stanza, the words make sense only if treated by using the

metatext of maban reality. It is then that the reasons unfold as the magician on his wand flies past.

Significance is more than or something other than the total meaning deducible from a comparison between the variants of the given. Significance is transformation achieved through ritual. This poem is similar to a ritual and there is a circuitous sequence, a grammar of language employed which keeps revolving around a key word or marker. This marker is *power*. The first stanza describes this power, then dances off the word to gesture in the second stanza and another kind of perverted power that tortures animals only for enjoyment. Using our metatext of maban reality, we are aware that frogs are sources of water and that survival may necessitate their being cut open, but not for enjoyment. This cruelty is then opposed to the right kind of power: compassionate establishments based on love. The establishment is often equated with the oppressive system of government, and the first four lines of the second stanza are a plea for a transformation of this establishment into one based on love, but this is followed by a reiteration of the sadistic pleasures of the establish-ment based on their own kind of spirituality, or power, though even here in the referents there are oppositions which stress hope rather than gloom. A heat sign is followed by a cooling sign, pain is digested, and the sickly sight of spirituality is eaten which refers back to the digested pain. Many Indigenous rituals and ceremonies are based around such ingesting and egesting, of the burning pain of the initiating firestick and the cooling waters falling, of being eaten by the serpent and of being vomited by the serpent. Thus, by seeing the last lines in an overall structure of Indigenality, we may discern a meaning that, by being ingested and then egested, is being reborn. The ritual of the second stanza moves on to the third stanza.

Poetic discourse is the equivalence established between a word and a text, or between a text and another text, with text being taken in the widest sense of meaning anything and everything which may be read. Thus I have been seeing maban reality or Indigenality as a metatext or matrix beneath Lionel Fogarty's poem by which they may be read, or by which a first or second heuristic reading may be transcended into a truly hermeneutic reading, one which evokes this reality.

Thus, in my reading, the third stanza may be seen as the end result of initiation, of being reborn, which must be positive and natural. The sound signs scattered throughout the poem—'songs', 'noises', 'loud pains'—are transformed into 'a barking laughter like running creeks', the 'falling water' of the second stanza. Any negativity still remaining—'dead weeds', 'dead seeds'—is seen as fecund with life, 'shining desire'. A last line stands alone—'Free our dreams'—and it is the dreams which are important, the source of power, a referent to the Dreaming, to maban reality from whence comes all our power.

By reading one of Lionel's poems in this way, I have tried to show that they are intense structures which necessitate degrees of thought and knowledge of the underlying metatext of maban reality. If his poems are to be properly read, one must leave the safety of standardised language, placewords and conventional reality and accept this poet, this maban, as a guide to another and more magical reality. It is then that Indigenality will reveal itself in a blaze of revelation or a smile of understanding. This revelation or sudden leap towards understanding is magical and is found in Lionel's poetic texts. I feel that Lionel Fogarty's poetry is great poetry because we are forced to reach towards a new but ancient reality, one that is the preserve of the Indigenous people of Australia, especially of songmen and women who are the guides into this reality. It is this that gives a fascination to his work.

Maban Reality and the Indigenous Novel

6

When sitting with my people and talking about our writing, there are two strands which emerge in our yarns, one is the urge to tell our history as it is, not relying on those documents of the past which after all are the records of the colonisers who had other animals to hunt and plants to gather from a place other than Australia and the other is the magic of our Dreaming, of our own genres and ways of speaking. Language after all is a magic construct and to try and gain truth from it is a dubious undertaking, especially when even now the European way is the best and too often they create and seek to impose hard realities existing on nothing but the words and marks of language, and so if we believe in ourselves we must continue the struggle to define our reality and to live it in this land of ours which thousands of years we sang into culture and spread a tapestry of language over its living reality. Having come from the bush, having listened to those songs defining what is the bush, I feel the urge to return and from this, the shadows, survey those angular geometries called cities, another magic formed from another reality. How does one become reconciled to this reality when there is another reality calling me. It is there, softly in the soft brushings of the night, in the hardness of the bright sunlight on the land where I was born. It is a call to Indigenous people to live in their own reality, to avoid the hardness of the measuring rod and to fall back into the magic of our Dreaming.
(Mudrooroo 1995)

WHEN ENTERING AND LIVING IN A SUBTLY ADAPTED scientific reality (whilst holding on to a more mythic reality), magic begins to work and the resulting intertextuality shifts into strange beasts of quotations which do not belong to those who read books like this, and who often have no entrance into any reality pertaining to another people's reality which passes beyond such a European construction which has been created from eighteenth and nineteenth century scientific discourse, which is static rather than dynamic and allows intrusions from within the scientific field, but not from without. If it does so, there are transmogrifications of the beast into startling shapes of such repelling attractiveness that there are cries for an ethnic cleansing that will remove once and for all such non-scientific intrusions. The beast must become tamed, static and able to be petted, examined and made known. It cannot be strange, it must be scientifically acceptable, and indeed all that that strangeness deserves is a bullet between the eyes, or rather a scientific research grant to imprison it within the folds of properly constituted discourse and theories.

I believe that the so-called natural reality which has achieved an unacceptable dominance of world-shaping is a European construct formed from eighteenth, nineteenth and early twentieth century scientific thought, which displaced the shaman or maban from the world and with him or her the magic implicit in the world. It is this scientific natural reality which changed the consciousness of others as it shape-changed the world, flowing along with the colonial expansion program of the eighteenth and nineteenth centuries, which was not only an invasion and stealing of land, but the imposition of a singular European reality—based on the so-called natural sciences—over the various indigenous realities. This reality dominance proved to be just as disastrous to the native as did the weapons which had manifested from it. In effect, and from this viewpoint, native reality was simply superstition. Thus, colonialism positioned the indigenous inhabitants of Australia as primitive, pagan and savage, and its scientific reality positioned the maban reality of Indigenous Australia as a veritable devil's nest of superstitions. 'Truth' was positioned only in natural sciences, and 'untruth' in maban reality. When maban reality was acknowledged at all, it was considered only an impediment to be destroyed by the colonial scientific reality. There was no either/or, or multiplicity of realities, able to be accepted. There was only one reality and aspects of this had to be proved from the natural sciences as formulated in earlier centuries.

Of course, it should be understood that I am talking about only the discourses of the natural sciences of the eighteenth, nineteenth and early twentieth centuries, precisely that period of modernism which, with its singular enthusiasm, stated again and again that all realities could be proved by recourse to this scientific discourse. Thus, if we seek to read the more occult or other realities of this period, we find that scientific discourse is the mode that these authors use in seeking to capture them. The use of scientific discourse extends far into the realm of the weird (here used in the sense of the eerie) and the uncanny, thus proof of the existence of werewolves and vampires is sought in the discourses of natural science.

And so throughout the colonial empire of the nineteenth and early twentieth centuries, natural scientific reality as the only allowable ideology shaping reality had to be used not only by colonial authorities to write about the natives, but later on by those natives who had been silenced and who then, after eventually becoming acclimatised to natural scientific reality, began to answer the coloniser. Unfortunately, maban reality had been disparaged and driven into the deserts and jungles; and those who assumed voices to speak for the native and to set a political agenda had to appropriate the dominant language and with it the dominant reality: natural scientific reality. This had an effect on the majority of early Indigenous written texts, and even in the poetry there is a deliberate attempt to exclude any hint of a world different from that of the European.

And so the majority of early written Indigenous texts, even poetry which does lend itself to maban reality, were essentially social realist works, natural scientific reality works, with scant regard paid to maban reality. But there was one writer who did not give in to this reality. This was David Unaipon, who did utilise a strong maban reality when writing about his people. His maban reality was a fluid shape-shifting mythic reality, vastly different from the natural scientific reality into which he had been inducted as a child; but his reality proved stronger, though his works received little notice during his lifetime. He wrote in the second decade of the twentieth century, but in the reality of the 1920s, there could not be such a thing as a native writer. Such a person and his or her maban reality were placed firmly in the domain of a reality stemming from the natural sciences, and so we had ethnology or anthropology which was a natural science with a readymade set of rules to render maban reality into natural reality. In fact, ethnologists and anthropologists, especially earlier ones, can be seen as translators, and their works should not be seen as examples of scientific objectivity, but as translations (of varying degrees of worth) of maban reality into natural scientific discourse.

More Indigenous literature began to appear in the mid-sixties when Jack Davis, Kath Walker (later, Oodgeroo of the Tribe Noonuccal) and Kevin Gilbert began to write and be published. What we must be aware of when we read Indigenous texts stemming from that period is that they too are essentially translations, essentially natural science reality texts, often about how the Aboriginal people and communities survived in Invader Australia, an ideological field of discourse which used theories of natural science, such as the evolutionary theories of Charles Darwin, to create a humanity which was evolving on an ever-progressive curve towards an earthly paradise, from which the vast majority of Indigenous people were excluded or rather were to be assimilated into this evolutionary stream of common humanity constructed from natural science theories which were seen as 'truth' and not open to doubt. Scientific reality had dispossessed the Indigenous people not only of their lands but also of their reality. In fact, it was firmly believed that they had failed the evolutionary test and were doomed to extinction. Natural scientific theories provided a reality in which it was the natural lot of Indigenous people to be subject to violence, to live in poverty, to suffer disease and to be the continuing subjects of contempt or kindness from the colonisers who segregated them in missions and reserves where they were studied as evolutionary relics of a long-gone age.

In attempting to get the message of their plight across to white readers, texts, especially those written by Kath

Walker and Kevin Gilbert, were at first polemical and confrontational, using the flat prose favoured by the texts of natural scientific reality to make explicit points. It must be remembered that a critic dismissed the early poetry of Kath Walker as simply being sociological texts without the magic of poetry. This criticism has some validity and could be extended to many of the other texts of early Indigenous written literature.

Even then in the early sixties, critics, perhaps emerging out of a reality formed from the natural sciences and into a different, more chaotic reality being formed by thinkers like Werner Hiesenberg, saw a problem in such reality texts especially when they advocated an Aboriginal way of doing things in a prose style and structure which often was anything but Indigenous. This was very noticeable when Indigenous writing was contrasted with Indigenous oral literature, such as between the novel *Karobran* (1978) by Monica Clare and the *Gularabulu* texts (1983) by Paddy Roe. In such fiction writing, in such poetry, there is a reliance on natural scientific reality which is not found in the oral literature of Indigenous communities, especially those less affected by being further from the invader centres of power. Although an exception to this is Sally Morgan's book, *My Place*, which I have elsewhere described as a Gothic novel to highlight the shift which occurs in the text from natural scientific reality to maban reality. It is precisely this shift that has been criticised by such critics as Eric Michaels who, alas, seems to have missed the magic in the text which is perhaps the best Indigenous lifestory to date because of this movement towards a maban reality. In her search for her Indigenality, Sally Morgan in effect enters a different reality as she triumphantly cries at the end of her book: 'Oh, Nan,' I cried with sudden certainty, 'I heard it, too. In my heart, I heard it.'

Close to the invader centres there were and are strong attempts to educate, to shift, to change Indigenous people and communities into what is espoused by the invader culture, which is still extremely conservative, especially in what is said to constitute 'good' literature. This is even seen in the Australian theatre in that there are certain ways of performing plays, of structuring plays and in creating characters, much of which, if not all, rests squarely in natural scientific reality, even though it is stated in some theoretical texts that theatre derives from ritual and thus should be closer to maban reality, or even to the indeterminacies of quantum physics. Thus, Indigenous people to a major extent are forced to create theatre which is essentially mainstream and prosaic. Natural scientific reality to many is still the all-pervading reality and maban reality is rarely attempted or, if attempted, must hide its head in shame under the cloak of natural realism, though there are interesting examples of an attempt at maban reality to fill the text in such works as Kevin Gilbert's *The Cherry Pickers* in the 1988 revised edition, and 'My Spiritual Dreaming' by Eddy Bennell, or a mix of both in my 'Mutjingabba', or Old Woman's Place. In these examples, if a deeper reading or participation is attempted, the reader or viewer might see that there is a contestation between two realities—maban and natural—with the contest not usually being resolved, or a drifting over from maban reality into a natural scientific reality, which appears to be the only reality that many in the audience can accept. This is very apparent in Jimmy Chi's very successful *Bran Nue Dae* (1991), a musical which extends between magic and the prosaic.

Perhaps what is the most magical of the arts—film—in Indigenous Australia remains underdeveloped. Film is the most technical and money-intensive of the arts. There is an assumed need for technical and indeed cinematic expertise which must be learnt, but the question is: what is learnt? Of Indigenous film-makers attempting films which are Indigenous in content and structure, Tracey Moffatt is the only one who has gone outside the parameters of mainstream Australian cinema. Her *beDevil* creates maban reality and has those elements—the supernatural and symbolic —which make it the most interesting Indigenous film made in Australia to date. Other films by Indigenous persons are usually natural science realist and even those devoted to Indigenous Dreaming stories, such as a short film made by Lorraine Mafi-Williams, fail to move us into maban reality. In fact, we are moved into the other reality in which unclothed, though nappy-clad, Aboriginals fail to come to grips with their Indigenality. It is interesting in this regard that it has been non-Aboriginal Australian film-makers, like Peter Weir (*The Last Wave*), Bruce Beresford (*The Fringedwellers*) and Henri Safran (*Stormboy*), who have not been adverse to including elements of maban reality in their films and it has been urban Indigenous people who have criticised this maban reality as not being 'real' enough. In this regard it is also interesting that a recent book by an American woman, who has been given the honorary title of 'Auntie' by a group of Indigenous women, has been criticised as not being 'true'. I believe that when attacks are made on such films and books as M. Morgan's *Mutant Message Down Under* (1994), we are entitled to ask: to what reality are they being false? Much worse films and texts exist, written from the position of nineteenth century scientific reality, which, while seemingly as objective as a scientific text, completely mislead the reader. In this area, it is pertinent to ask: where did the notion that Indigenous people of Australia were stone-age savages stem from?

Indigenous poetry in too many cases can make you shudder. A reliance on a trite rhyme scheme, a lack of startling language and a plodding from verse to verse are often found. There is often little reliance on formal Indigenous oral literature language or an understanding of the maban reality of Indigenality. Poetry is often said to be untranslatable, and perhaps this may be an indicator of the poetic. If this is accepted, then much of Indigenous poetry might be accepted as prose in disguise. If we do accept a poetics of language and an untranslatability of poetic language, then when we are confronted by a poem by the Murri poet Lionel Fogarty, we would find ourselves, not only in the realm of untranslatability, but also in the presence of another reality, a maban reality, which must be entered if we are to arrive at a glimpse of understanding of many of his poems. Natural scientific reality dissolves into a maban reality of signs and intertextualities which are far from what we would expect from an Indigenous poet if we were only familiar with some of the poetry of Jack Davis or Oodgeroo of the Tribe Noonuccal.

It is through works like some of those by Lionel Fogarty that we are led into maban reality and from them there is not much distance to the great oral discourses and spiritual narratives of preliterate Aboriginal Australia. Of course, I am not laying down a literary line which all Indigenous writers should follow or seek to follow if they lack the knowledge or ability or inclination to do so; all that I am saying is that Indigenous or maban reality does not correspond to the natural scientific reality developed in earlier centuries, and that any would-be Indigenous writer must be aware of this construction of reality and how it is neither more nor less 'true' than any other 'reality'. Writings from maban reality are the most exciting literary products of Indigenous Australia and are akin to the originality or traditionalism of the Indigenous visual arts, which often are done by artists who have avoided being educated into the European traditions.

Some Indigenous fiction has moved away from such early novels as Monica Clare's *Karobran* (1978), Archie Weller's *Day of the Dog* (1981), and my *Dr Wooreddy's Prescription for Enduring the Ending of the World* (1983), towards a more free-flowing form based on the oral storytelling of Indigenous communities. For example, Sam Watson's novel, *The Kadaitcha Sung* (1990), to a great extent frees itself from the strictures of natural scientific reality and moves towards maban reality, as found in our great mythic narratives which are after all part of our literary heritage and which are, or once were, spread all across Australia, a network of meaning for all of us and based on our own reality rather than on the structures of the natural sciences. It is to these mythic structures that we should go to achieve any understanding of maban reality and to see how the tradition does continue on in at least some contemporary written Indigenous literature.

Maban reality is akin to magic realism and I will try to explain what I mean by maban reality using some of the work done on Latin-American magic realism. Maban reality has been used by me in *Master of the Ghost Dreaming* (1991) and by Sam Watson in *The Kadaitcha Sung*. Both Sam Watson and I agree that Indigenous texts should intervene politically and socially in the dominant ideology and that texts should not only be political but also enjoyable and entertaining. Maban reality is how this can be done for, unlike many high cultural or message constructs, maban reality can not only pass on a message, but also find a popular audience who will read the work because it is, at least on the surface, enjoyable. An important point is that there is not an attempt to rehabilitate traditional culture as such which, after all, might be an impossible project, but it is the using of our traditional storytelling content and structures in an effort to gain a wider readership. It must be remembered that the Indigenous visual arts have gained a viewing and a wide acceptance through the use of maban reality, and those Aboriginal writers who have done so have also increased the readership for their work and thus passed over deeper knowledge of Indigenous reality in contemporary Australia.

In the first edition of this book (1990, pp. 102–5), I touched on how the structure of the trickster tale was used in telling the story of how and why an Indigenous community was deported from their country and also pointed out supernatural or magical elements in storyteller Paddy Roe's narratives from Broome. I advocated a flight from natural scientific reality into the Dreaming, which is the field of creation for all our creative endeavour. It was after this that Sam Watson's book was published, to some acclaim, and to date perhaps this is the best example of how maban reality can be used to create an original work.

This maban reality may be found in the complex system of mythologies which underpins Indigenality and also in contemporary narratives which are less influenced by European genres. Narratives by Jack Mirritji of Milimgimbi and Dinah Garadji of Ngukurr, both from the Northern Territory, are a case in point. In reading some of their stories we are confronted by a reality which is definitely not what I have been designating as 'natural scientific reality'.

Maban reality might be characterised by a firm grounding in the reality of the earth or country, together with an acceptance of the supernatural as part of everyday reality. It is difficult for many these days to accept a so-called rational worldview, such as the natural reality based on eighteenth and nineteenth century European sciences, when it relegates much everyday experience to the realm of superstition, when it is precisely this supernatural or magic which keeps spilling over the country. It must be

pointed out that maban reality is not only the preserve of
the Indigenous person, but many popular European narratives refuse to accept limitation, especially with the
growth of postmodernism based as it is on a more contemporary scientific discourse and reality which allows for the
presentation of realities beyond the old natural scientific
reality. Fantasy, ghost stories, vampires and a whole range
of other entities, including worlds, are now presented in
European narratives, not from a position of non-belief, or
of superstitious belief, but from an acceptance that there
are many realities and the writer is simply describing one
such.

It is the same or similar with maban reality. An Indigenous
writer simply presents a world which is different from what
natural scientific reality once presented as the only reality. I
should say that this world, this reality, may be familiar as well
as strange and it allows for the opening of the doors of
perception through language and imagination. Thus the
reader is led to question what he or she once accepted as
'true' and 'real'. One of the problems which arose with
natural scientific reality and its acceptance as the dominant
discourse was that Indigenous mythology (along with other
mythologies) was reduced to children's stories. An attempt
at gaining knowledge of a consistent worldview as found in
such mythologies was not made. Instead it was dismantled
or done away with and the natural sciences had ready explanations for such mythology. It was often seen as the product
of the simple childlike mind of the savage seeking to understand his world and thus seen as being a literature suitable
only for children.

But maban reality is not about the natural world as
constructed by the European natural sciences; it is about
describing a world which is as existent and as real as that
constructed by European thought. This is evident from
Sam Watson's *The Kadaitcha Sung*, which begins with a
maban account of the creation of the universe and then of
the creation of the maban:

> So the great one made a veil of mists that hung upon the South Land
> and hid it from all. Then Biamee called an ancient clan of sorcerers
> from the heavens to stand in his place. They were known as the

Kadaitcha and they were powerful. Then came the day that the tribes farewelled Biamee as he ascended from his most sacred altar, in the vast red rock that sat upon the heart of the land.

It is only after this that we enter as readers into the narrative and the initiation of the main character, Tommy Gubba, into this other reality. The reader, through the character and the initiation, participates in the ancient ceremonies which alter reality to that of the maban, so that he/she can enter the more advanced states of the Dreaming reality, as detailed in the oral and dramatic narratives which explain traditional Indigenous reality. But this maban reality in *The Kadaitcha Sung* is somewhat affected by natural scientific reality which posits a separation between spirit and material, though there is some contradiction in that the Spirit Dingo, for example, is as much material as Tommy Gubba. But this contradiction is set up in that alongside maban reality is natural scientific reality, stemming back to Hobbes and Darwin and 'the Survival of the Fittest', where the survival of the fittest may be seen to be the survival of the most brutal, whereas maban reality stems back to what may be seen as an original split in creation, symbolised as Koobara the Good and Booka the Evil One who aligns himself with natural scientific reality and causes the South Land to be invaded by Europeans.

Perhaps it is impossible to have a 'true' maban reality in the sense that natural scientific reality has entered the South Land to establish a counter reality. This counter reality should be destroyed. It is no accident that werewolves and vampires were beyond the technology of natural science and that recourse had to be made to maban reality in order to finish them off. It was and is the stake of quantum theory which stabs through the heart of natural science reality, though it is a long time dying. Until the sun rises and it is reduced to ashes, the effect of parallel fields of realities may be read in some of the stories narrated by Paddy Roe, especially *Djaringalong* in which natural scientific reality is introduced to explain the Giant Bird Being, Djaringalong, and his eventual extinction, though in other versions, such as that by Butcher Joe Nangan, Djaringalong does not die but is transmogrified into the Southern Cross where he may be seen to this day. In *The Kadaitcha Sung*, natural scientific reality, urban scenes of Brisbane and the Gold Coast exist somewhat uneasily along with a maban reality field which every now and again becomes the dominant. Natural scientific reality usually postulates, or should I say counterfeits, a 'real' world which is considered to be the only one; all else is superstition. But from the side of maban reality, this so-called natural reality is but a construction of the aspirations of eighteenth and nineteenth century natural sciences. Essentially, this natural reality corresponds to or underpins a dominant ideology which uses the power implicit in such a dominant position to establish and maintain what else but natural reality. We have only to see the problems another influential reality such as Islam has had in establishing an alternative to observe how power is brought to bear through such dominant controls as television, to see how important politically natural reality is to the dominant class and ethnicities. They cannot allow any counter reality to be established because it would thus challenge their ideological position of dominance.

Thus, maban reality is political in that it seeks to establish an Indigenous reality which is counter to the dominant natural reality of the invaders, a so-called natural reality which permeates just about every genre of endeavour and constructs narratives such as history which serve to establish and maintain nothing but the dominant position of those in power, a natural realist history, or should I say a science of history, though there are other histories which could exist on their own, but are not allowed to. There is that construction called 'History' and it is a European construct and no other history is allowed to challenge its dominance, although the construction of history as a scientific and seemingly objective document stems from the nineteenth century natural science text which supposedly related the true facts of nature. As scientific facts are true, so the argument goes, so is the historical text.

What this means is that any ways of constructing an alternative history are driven from the 'real' and into the fictional or into fantasy or into the dark areas of occultism, which does present an alternative reality but one which is disparaged and given short shrift. Thus those who have a reliance on maban reality, those who do not accept natural scientific reality and its genre of historical and political dominance are driven to what else but fictional narrative to present their reality and their 'history'. This is because an alternative 'authentic' historical text has been denied the native, and what can the native do but turn to fiction to get his or her ideas of maban history across, even at the very real risk of again being denied 'history'? This may seem somewhat arbitrary, but even a cursory knowledge of what history entails for those Indigenous people still to a great extent outside the whole dominant apparatus of natural scientific realism will show that our ideas about writing our history are different from what the mainstream regard as authentic history. Thus we are condemned to inhabit the reality which is regarded as fictional, which is sometimes labelled 'magic realism', and which I have termed 'maban reality'.

The writer of maban reality is often involved in the contradiction that much of his or her readership will be unfamiliar with other realities, and so the question must be asked: how does the writer handle this passing over into maban reality? Sometimes, as in *The Kadaitcha Sung*, it is through a process of straight prose:

> *The tribes had always measured their wealth in the health and abundance of the next generation, who were the guardians and the warriors of tomorrow. Yet children like Poddy had never walked upon their own land and they spoke English too fluently. Their own language was beginning to fade and they knew nothing of their own Dreaming.*
> (p. 261)

'Dreaming' could almost be a synonym for maban reality, though here I am concerned more with the narrative, the way it is encased in language, rather than an actual state or reality such as the Dreaming. Essentially, with the invasion of the Europeans, there ensued a massive displacement of populations and cultural disparagement under the rubric of 'civilising the native' which lessened, in many areas, the ties with the Dreaming and the living within a maban reality based on the Dreaming, so that, into the chaos created, the nineteenth century missionary and educator could enter to paint over whatever beliefs, rituals and ceremonies had been kept in place by the Dreaming. With the weakening and in some places the psychic destruction of maban reality, natural scientific reality could replace it. There was a shape-change of reality and now everything could be explained through the discourses of the natural sciences. It did not matter that some things could not be explained by these natural sciences. In fact, these things did not have a place in natural science and were but the hallucinations of untutored minds. This is made apparent in *The Kadaitcha Sung* in which natural scientific reality refers to a heavenly apparition as 'Halley's Comet' and maban reality refers to it as the 'Eye of Biamee'. The Jesuit priest in the story dismisses the latter as 'rubbish' and observes: 'These poor devils have only come out of the trees a few generations back, and they still hang on to the old devil-devil taboos ... and we must bring these poor ignorants into the modern age' (p. 89).

Of course, it might be easy to enjoin, from our position of postmodernism, that the Jesuit might also have had to be brought away from his reality, based on Thomas Aquinas, into the modern age; but this is only part of the myopia which rests with those observing others from a position of dominance and European reality. For whether a Jesuit priest likes it or not, he too is the owner of a 'maban reality' different from that of natural scientific reality. No matter how the natural sciences were brought to bear on such problems as the virgin birth, walking on water, turning water into wine, healing the sick and the lame and raising the dead, the natural sciences of the nineteenth and early twentieth centuries could not help but find these not only unprovable, but to be dismissed out of hand as superstitions akin to those of the savage. It is when the supernatural, the fantastic, the magic is dismissed from the world that empires crumble and apparatuses of realities are discarded like the serpent's skin. It is perhaps no wonder that, after such a dark night of the soul as bequeathed to the world by natural scientific reality, there has not only been a collapse of those societies based on scientific materialism, but at the same time a corresponding growth in narratives resting on other realities. It may be worth a note that some of these realities are described in books which their authors declare to be non-fictional. One such narrative was Morgan's *Mutant Message Down Under* the publishers of which made the author describe her work as being fictional, though she had self-published it as being 'true'; but then I have met other people who have described to me their experiences of realities which do not fit those of natural scientific reality.

Perhaps I am glossing over the philosophical and scientific problem of what exactly is 'true' or 'real' in favour of advocating the treating of alternative realities through the device of the fictional. One of the things about fiction is that, whether we like it or not, it is a 'real', that is, a psychical means of passing across information. There is a thin line between fiction and non-fiction, just as there is between history and fiction, and perhaps it may depend on our own perceptions of 'reality' or of 'realities' which allow us to sieve out 'the truth'. But perhaps the value of the novel or narrative fiction rests on it being a form which is readily available for anyone including the native to use or adapt. Its forms are such that, for example, it is possible for it to be used to deconstruct the awful invader history of Australia and Indigenalise it through such devices as maban reality. In this way, we present a history of the native, rather than of the colonialist, in a startling way which the native may recognise as his or her own. In fact, reversals and alternatives must be found in a maban reality text coming from the native. If they were not, they would be neither a maban reality text nor an Indigenous one. Thus, in Watson's *The Kadaitcha Sung*, we have this example: 'The legal system administered within these walls was foreign to the land upon which the court had been built. The migloo ways—their language and their violence— were foreign to the land of Uluru … a terrible plague that had come upon them with an evil suddenness' (p. 62).

Maban realism, especially in written narrative fiction, allows for a foreshortening of history so that the novel may contain the long process of colonisation and its aftermath. We see this in the 1985 version of Kevin Gilbert's *Cherry Pickers* and also in *The Kadaitcha Sung* in which, while the main elements of the story take place over a period of just four days, the story ranges over the whole period (200 years) of natural scientific reality in Australia. Sam Watson refers this collapsed time, this maban reality, to the Aboriginal Dreaming where time and space are not laid out according to the dictates of European reality.

Maban reality is the foundation reality of *The Kadaitcha Sung*. Aboriginal characters transform themselves from tricksters to warriors, from birds to animals, and we are in a world where those old fixities of European natural reality, such as conformity to character and to species, do not exist. The problems of characterisation in conventional natural reality texts, which again stem from earlier notions of a certain linearity of character, a Freudian soul as it were which keeps the character straight and united by childhood memories and persecutions, does not obtain in maban reality. In fact, there is a problem in identifying Aboriginal character or personality with those of the European. European characterisation and indeed identity has been fixed by psychology until recently when now there is talk of shifting subjectivities. Shifting subjectivities may be found in the un-natural reality of such writers as Samuel Delaney, but rarely in naturalist texts where, in fact, there appears to be a fixed self which must come to some realisation, as in a therapy session, often of the most trite kind.

'Postmodernism', in any number of books, is the term used to describe the reality in which we are now living. It is said that the world has changed so drastically, at least for the European and his sense of history and well-being, that angst pervades all, with no single verities being found anywhere. In fact, everything is there to be consumed and then discarded. Europeans are simulacra without fixity of purpose and even less fixity of identity. This postmodernism extends across the world, much as the natural scientific reality of the nineteenth century tried to do; but postmodernism, with the development of instantaneous means of communication, akin to the telepathy of maban realism, has the means to reach everywhere on this plane of the universe. Does this mean that maban reality will be destroyed by it? It may be argued that postmodernism aims for a homogeneity of product or reality which will change forever each reality it reaches.

But I would argue that postmodernism is not a mono-lithic structure and that it is quite schizophrenic in nature, so that myriad realities may exist within it. Postmodern reality is much like the Internet, in which various nodes link to form a communications net of such diversity that entering it is a bit like contacting parts of the Universal Oversoul. The various multiculturalisms of different nations, as well as the withdrawal of nations from multi-culturalism, are examples of this plurality of realities which deconstruct the term 'postmodernism'. These may exist side by side as realities, at least as cultural realities as long as they do not attack the monolithic economies and dominant structures which preserve the structure of this postmodern reality. Modernism or natural scientific reality was a field of contending forces, all based on the natural sciences which popularised a singular advancement, through natural selection, of the human race into some singular European utopia. These forces, which might be divided somewhat simplistically into Capitalism and Marxism, sought to change the entire world according to European nineteenth century thought. Each crime, each murder, each genocide of race and culture or reality, could be justified as civilising and raising the world to the peak as theorised by natural science. Fortunately, such a rigid system has collapsed and now we are in a time when many realities may exist side by side. One of these is maban reality, an Australian reality which comes from the land and from one of the oldest, continuous cultures in the world. It has endured long and survived the holocaust of natural scientific reality.

Reconciling Our Songs

7

Power to the people;
Power to the land:
Power for cultural revival;
Power for survival.
(Yothu Yindi)

THE GOVERNMENT IN THEIR WISDOM DECREED A process of reconciliation which with its passive undertones is enough to turn people away; but then government processes and policies are like this. Perhaps instead of reconciliation, we should have had cooperation which is a much more positive word and without the undertones of becoming reconciled to one's fate in Australia. Cooperation does not offend the sensibilities of Indigenous people in their urge for self-determination and self-management. Indigenous music, at least in the popular sphere, shows this cooperation. Popular music is a cooperative enterprise between musicians, producers and record companies. Not only this, but the makeup of a group often necessitates a coming together of Indigenous and non-Indigenous musicians. This has happened since the growing away of Indigenous music from its roots, with the formation of a hybrid music which in a spirit of cooperation may be seen to be Australian as well as Indigenous.

Hybridity in regard to culture is a term coined by post-colonial academics to understand or rather talk about such things as contemporary Indigenous culture. It rests on the belief that there can be such a thing as a pure culture uncontaminated by outside sources. 'Culture' in this context seems to arise spontaneously in an isolated community then exists almost as an artefact until it is contaminated by outside influences and thus it becomes hybridised. This is a dubious proposition. I might argue that there is an Indigenous impulse which gives rise to 'culture' based on the environment; but this is process and keeps changing according to the environment and by environment I include influences from other peoples as may be found in Indigenous culture, especially Arnhem Land, these influences arriving by sea before the invasion.

The very word 'culture' is a dubious term in itself. It may mean ethnographic collections and the idea of 'culture' which has passed over to Indigenous people rests on the ethnologist Tylor's definition of 1871 which set up a vague 'complex whole', including everything that is learned group behaviour, from body techniques to symbolic orders. Defining 'culture' as pure or hybrid seems to be a trap into which postcolonialists have fallen. It postulates a prehistoric time for those once-colonised peoples when there existed 'pure cultures', then along came imperialism and contaminated these cultures. This belief excludes the subjectivity of such peoples, both individual and collective, rendering them into objects to be acted upon by a superior conscious force, rather than conscious subjects reacting to actions, modifying and adjusting their communities and cultures (as they had always done) to new influences. This is how Indigenous music has grown and continues to grow, though I do not discount the effect that the overwhelming force of the coloniser had on the colonised, a force which bore most strongly on those communities of Indigenous people not bound together in a highly structured nation.

The formal government policy of assimilation was a weapon aimed at all aspects of Indigenous culture. The Indigenous people were to be civilised and this did not mean a slow evolution of their cultures to accommodate the new ways, but drastic and enforced change. Religious practices centred on exposed bora circles could be found and forbidden. Then, as Indigenous people were denied native title, the land was parcelled out to settlers who did not want congregations of Indigenous persons on their land. Secular songmaking and singing continued on for a time in the camps of the people; but when missionaries were doing their work of education, these were replaced over time by hymns and the more chaste song forms of England. In the outback areas, where a few settlers held huge tracts of country and reserves had been established for Indigenous people, they could continue the process of their cultures and produce original works in language and dance such as 'Little Eva at Moonlight Creek'. As more and more Indigenous men and women went into the cattle industry and the wireless came into widespread use, new songs began to be heard. These were attractive to many Indigenous people and resulted in secular Indigenous song forms being abandoned. Older people continued the traditional song forms such as the *tyabi* and many songs are still remembered, though as nostalgic remnants rather than as part of a dynamic composition tradition. The younger people, especially those working on the large cattle stations or living as fringedwellers around the towns, listened to new melodies and in a foreign language. These forms at first influenced Indigenous songs. English words replaced Indigenous words, as in this 1880s example from south-eastern Australia collected by the ethnologist A.W. Howitt:

> Galagala binja buninga ngali
> winbelow jena ngarauan udja
> kandubai buninga melinthi buninga
> ngali mulari binja buninga.

The use of the word *winbelow* ('wind blow') shows how English was entering the Indigenous languages there and this is found today in the regions where Indigenous languages are still spoken. A further modification occurred with a second stanza being added to the traditional single song stanza. In those coastal and fertile regions which had become heavily settled by the invaders, the pressures of assimilation were greater and this meant that not only were songs lost, but even language. Eventually, Indigenous songs were replaced by Christian hymns or by simple diatonic tone structures, directly taken from American country songs which were becoming popular throughout rural Australia and replacing the music-hall ballads of Mother England.

A feature of the rural scene in Australia, until very recently, were the nomadic shows travelling from town to town. These were usually headed by a cowboy, western or hillbilly singer of renown, for example Buddy Williams and Tex Morton, who had gained popularity through their radio programmes. These shows featured such acts as buckjumping, stockwhip cracking and rifle shooting—acts which appealed to Indigenous people, many of whom were working in the cattle industry. There was a similarity between their lives and that of the American cowboy— both were itinerant agricultural workers—but through film and song the lifestyle of the American cattle worker had been glamorised, and an Indigenous stockman working often for only rations had little power or glamour. Still, symbolically, they often found personal worth by identifying with these American cultural heroes. There could be little or no identification with the indigenous American people, too often victims as they were. Also, the films and songs were so structured with ideotones of complete white dominance that identity with the masters was almost forced. The dominant structure and ideotones of the discourse glamorised Anglo-Celts completely. Young Indigenous stockmen, especially if they managed to secure a wage, appeared in widebrimmed hats and boots and modelled their lives on nomadic heroes like those portrayed by Gary Cooper and other American actors. There was also the western musical, starring such singers as Gene Autry and Roy Rogers who became song models in the rural districts for white singers like Slim Dusty. These white singers spread the song form, partially Australianised, throughout the country. It was from such travelling singers that the guitar was taken into Aboriginal communities. It had many advantages, being portable, relatively cheap, and easy to play in the simple major four-chord strum used by these popular singers.

Country and western (hillbilly) songs in time replaced most Indigenous secular song structures. This was because the subject matter reflected the new Indigenous lifestyles: horses and cattle, drinking, gambling, the outsider as hero, a nomadic existence, country-orientation, wronged love, fighting and fucking—the whole gamut of an itinerant life romanticised in the stockman/cowboy ideotones. Some Indigenous men creating in this genre used it for social protest. One such song, 'My Brownskinned Baby', by Bob Randall, protesting at the forced removal of children from their parents, has remained popular among Indigenous people to this day, being found in plays and films. Other songs by singers such as Herbie Laughton reflect the sentimentality and artificiality of the ideotones. His 'Alice Springs Waltz' owes much to the long-popular 'Tennessee Waltz'.

After the second world war when many Aborigines began moving into the cities, they began adapting to the urban situation with its tighter music. Country songs remained popular among the immigrants for a time, with bands like Harry Williams and the Outcasts continuing to play and record this music, but young city bands, such as Us Mob, sought their models in American popular song structures, such as rock'n'roll, which were constantly played over the radio and television. By this time Indigenous music structures had been almost forgotten in the city and if heard were heard only from visiting country cousins.

Except for a few singers like Alan Mooriwalla Barker experimenting with the blues, black music from America had little impact on Indigenous singers, except for Jimmy Little (Mr Smoothie) who sang in a similar style to Nat King Cole. Then, in the late seventies, began the growth of alternative music stations and these played reggae from the Caribbean. The sixties with its more social music had vanished and reggae seemed to fill the hiatus, especially when it advocated the smoking of marijuana. This was not as important to Indigenous musicians as the strength of its lyrics which stressed an ideology of blackness and a sense of belonging to a land.

It sang a unity with oppressed people, directing its lyrics

at all black people and condemning European cultural influences. By this time many Indigenous young people had found the city an area of suffering rather than an opportunity to better their lot, and Indigenous people had entered a phase of political activism which had broken through the malaise of the Australian political scene. The most influential Indigenous music of this period, the late seventies and early eighties, came from the band No Fixed Address who stressed in their songs the need for political activism. Heavily influenced by reggae, they declared at one time that it was Indigenous music; the tightness of their music and the strength of their lyrics have never been repeated since. After they broke up, drummer Bart Willoughby switched to guitar and eventually formed the group Mixed Relations, with some success among Indigenous people, their song 'Aboriginal Woman' being very popular. But the hard lyrics and music of the activist days are gone and have been replaced by a reconciliatory message, the name of the group meaning that it is formed of both white and Indigenous persons.

A strength of reggae and also a weakness is that it often presents an ideology based on a back-to-Africa theology, complete with an African God-King, which few Indigenous people are prepared to accept, though an article on the Rastafarians—the religious sect which at one time more or less dominated the music—did appear in one of the last issues of the Indigenous periodical, *Identity* (1982, p. 5). But this religious aspect was countered by a strong political line which stressed the underdog, racial black pride and the adoption of an ideology of struggle. Reggae did not achieve the status of a popular music, but it was heard on alternative music stations and thus could influence Indigenous musicians. Other bands, such as Coloured Stone, Blak Bela Musik and Kuckles, were also influenced by reggae; but the influence has diminished since the disbanding of No Fixed Address and the death of Bob Marley, the major crossover artist of the music.

It was with the growth of alternative radio stations and later Indigenous radio programmes, such as those by the Central Australian Aboriginal Media Association (CAAMA), that there has been an outlet for Indigenous music. Based in Alice Springs, CAAMA runs a radio and television network which uses black musicians and plays their music. Apart from media access they have furthered Indigenous music by setting up their own recording studio, Imparja, which has produced cassette collections of songs in both English and Indigenous languages. These perhaps reveal the precarious state of traditional Indigenous song, in that no collection of traditional songs has been released. Essentially, Euro-Australian forms—from hymnal, through country and rock to the more polished reggae and black American-influenced music—is heard on their cassettes and recordings. Perhaps the best bands they have recorded are Blak Bela Musik and Wedgetail Eagle. They also have released a few compilation CDs of better quality and also the soundtrack of the popular Indigenous musical *Bran Nue Dae*; but to date they have not had a major success with their music, though it is played all through the Northern Territory and on Indigenous radio programmes.

In 1988 occurred the bicentenary of Australia which resulted in much soul-searching and an examining of what exactly an Australian is. Since that year, advances have been made which have seen Indigenous cultural products enter the mainstream now stressing the reconciliation policy of the federal government. A number of singers and groups have achieved national exposure, all with a strong ideotone of reconciliation and a message that we are all Australians. Indigenous music is an important part of contemporary Indigenous culture and with the growth of Indigenous radio programmes, it is being heard widely. Both the lyrics and music are important, and I use the concept of ideotones in my discussion.

Dr Hugh Webb of Murdoch University, studying contemporary popular music, developed the concept of 'ideotones'. These he describes as audio-narrative units which appear to flow from and to suggest certain inevitable conjunctions occurring in the word/music nexus. These ideotones may be seen either to affirm or to challenge the apparent unity of the dominant ideological discourses playing at any one time. This seems to mean taking, for example, those drug songs of the sixties which developed a nexus between words and music which acted as signs to be decoded by the then counterculture. Those in the know, or in the culture, received a different meaning from those in the general population.

Using Webb's theory, I would like to analyse two songs dealing with the same subject: one is by the popular Anglo-Celtic folksinger from Alice Springs, Ted Egan, who became a member of the Council for Aboriginal Reconciliation, while the other was written and produced by Mark Binh Barker, a member at one time of Kuckles. Both are outside the mainstream music industry in that Ted Egan produced his own cassettes and sells them during his tours, while the other was produced and marketed through Abmusic in Perth. It is interesting that Ted Egan's tape has what has come to be identified as traditional Indigenous music (tapsticks and didjeridoo), which is not found on Lucy Cox's tape. The folksinger's cassette contains songs made up of the standard repertoire of such singers, but these are absent from the other tape. There is little of the folksinger in Lucy Cox and her songs are unideological in that there is none of that seeking to define a country by its materialist history made up of working class heroes and other 'folky' types, nor is there any Indigenous traditional music. For Lucy that music is no longer relevant. Her music is contemporary Indigenous and she sings in a light popular style about love, touching on race, religion and history. There is no sweep of history or the seal of man on her Kimberley region as we find on the Egan tape. But the reason why I have selected these tapes is that there is a song on each dealing with the same subject: the Indigenous fighter, Djandamara, and using Webb's theory of ideotones I want to compare and contrast the treatment of this Indigenous hero by these two singers.

In terms of ideotone identification, the songs may be placed in genre blocks. Ted Egan is considered a 'folk' singer and his music may be placed in the genre of folk music (Australian). Lucy Cox sings a type of popular music similar to that of Swedish group Abba, with lots of harmony and soft electric guitar. I shall shorten the genre classification markers to 'Folk' and 'Pop'.

IDEOTONES

FOLK	POP
Authoritative and authentic didjeridoo and clapsticks.	Strong bass guitar, drums sometimes sounding like clapsticks.
Story-sequence narration leading into the song. Voice recorded above instruments, standing individual and alone. White Australian voice, with rural gruffness.	Aboriginal voice, sometimes falling into the distinctive accents of Kriol.
Tone assertive. Confident voice of the insider. The folksinger with liberal views. A white voice calling for fair play. Aboriginal rhythms, very authentic.	Non-assertive. Flat style of delivery. Statement of fact. Acceptance of song-words. The sound of the wind, reggae-influence.
Images of history, sequential narration, call for a reinterpretation of historical facts.	Identification of ancestral male, Pidgin, with present generation. Non-commitment. The past is dead. Pidgin exists in mythical time. Always present, accept this and his deeds and not feel at fault for doing so.
Questions? Was he a murderer, or a Che Guevara?	Answers. A freedom fighter who fought for his land.
Use of dominant discourse, and language selection reinforces the idea that he was a murderer.	Statement of fact. This is what he was.

The basic idea behind both songs is to narrate the story of
Pidgin, the Indigenous resistance fighter in the Kimberley
region of Western Australia. Ted Egan's ideological stance
is to reinterpret history or rather to seek a reinterpretation
from his Kimberley audience at which his song is directed.
He reinforces his song text with an authenticity seeking to
be Indigenous. This is seen in the use made of Indigenous
musical instruments. His approach is non-poetical, a
straight historical narration broken by a chorus or refrain.
Barker, the composer of the Indigenous song, and the
singer Lucy Cox, approach the life of Pidgin from a different perspective. It is poetical; history is discarded in favour
of an identification with the fighter, who is urged to fly
away and be free. In a sense there is an opposition between
white history and mythology or even historical being and
freedom. There is no question of historical reinterpretation
and none of the ambiguity of Egan. For Lucy Cox this has
already been done, and she stresses that this is how it was
and all Indigenous people should cast away any shame at
his methods and be proud of this Indigenous man who by
his actions has passed into legend.

Thus we are presented with a white and a black version
of the story of Pidgin. Ted Egan, as a white man identifying with the pioneers of the Kimberley, feels unable to
alienate his audience by making a definite statement.
Djandamara/Pidgin after all was a black man who fought
not only against the whites in the Kimberley, but in an
ideological sense against the whole tradition of the
pioneers and their heroic opening up of a new country, a
tradition which Australian folklore glorifies at the expense
of the Indigenous people. Thus, although Ted Egan does
not fully comprehend the ideological implications in calling for a historical reinterpretation (or does he?), in effect,
he is calling also for a re-examination of his own role as a
folksinger who in many of his songs glorifies settlers who
brutally decimated the local Indigenous population and
murdered those who stood against them. His questions
therefore receive no worthwhile answers and he even, in
an ideological shift, transfers the eventual murder of Pidgin
to the Indigenous people. He was betrayed by them, and
thus the settlers are free from guilt. Ted Egan also appeals

to history, and for him history is a folk history filled with wild and woolly characters who were taming a wild country. In the end his history becomes a white mythology seeking to evade any acknowledgement of historical injustice. What happened is past, though the legend might live on with any decision being decided in the framework of Che Guevara, Robin Hood or Ned Kelly— all white heroes —and who will decide this but the mythical people unspecified in future, though in these days it might be the Council for Aboriginal Reconciliation of which he is a member. But in his song there is no acknowledgement that the issue has been decided already by the Indigenous people, but then for Ted Egan perhaps Indigenous people were not part of 'the people who will decide'.

FLY AWAY PIDGIN
(Music: synthesiser, bass guitar, guitars, drums)

Fly, fly away Pidgin,
Fly, fly away and be free;
Fly, fly away Pidgin,
Fly, fly and be free.

I dedicate this song to a man of my race
Turn the pages, back to a Kimberley place.
They call him Pidgin, why?—nobody knows,
His real name was Djangamarra, so the story goes.

Fly, fly away Pidgin,
Fly, fly and be free;
Fly, fly away Pidgin,
Fly, fly away and be free.

He fought for his people, he fought for their rights;
He fought for their freedom, and he stood up to
    fight;
He was sent to capture, a man of his own race,
He found fifty, he felt the disgrace.

Fly, fly away Pidgin,
Fly, fly and be free;
Fly, fly away Pidgin,
Fly, fly and be free.

They shot him dead, in a Kimberley cave
His spirit lives on, so I singim my song;
They standard subjects, and we're part of it;
We carry no burden—no burden of shame.

Fly, fly away Pidgin,
Fly, fly and be free;
Fly, fly away Pidgin,
Fly, fly and be free.

TJANDAMARA
(Spoken) *The white settlers called him Pigeon, the outlaw. His proper name was Tjandamara. The former police tracker became convinced that he should take up arms against the whites who were taking over control of the land previously occupied on an unfettered basis by the Aboriginal tribes. During the years 1894 to 1897, Tjandamara and his followers raided, killed and plundered. How will history judge him: callous killer, or freedom fighter?*

(Didjeridoo and clapsticks begin for song verses)

In April 1897, Australia's whites rejoiced,
For the telegram came to say that he was dead.
The famous Kimberley outlaw betrayed and shot
    at last,
And as proof the police paraded his severed head.
The whiteman called him Pigeon, but none quite
    knows why,
Certainly he had a great ability to fly,
But his proper name was Tjandamara,
Honourable man of the Djeriya dreaming,
Born and raised in the Kimberley,
A hunter through and through.

(*Chorus*) So what do you say about Tjandamara?
What do you think of Che Guevara?
Were they justified?
And have they really died?
What's your opinion of Robin Hood?
Can you call Ned Kelly good?
Are you satisfied when you speak with pride?
Were they freedom fighters, or agitators,

Bloody killers, or liberators?—
Jokes aside.

It's the people who make the legends,
So let it be cut and dried,
What's the verdict on Tjandamara?—
The people will decide.

He once was a famous tracker,
For the Kimberley police,
He was sent one time to capture a man,
A member of his own race;
But the old man told the tracker
'It's time to make a stand,
Don't be a whiteman's puppy dog,
Drive the foreigners from your land.'

So he stole the whiteman's weapons,
Shot the police on sight,
Freed their chained up prisoners
In the middle of the night.
He formed a gang of fighters,
And he gave each man a gun,
And Tjandamara the tracker,
Became an outlaw on the run.

The police poured reinforcements,
And trackers by the score,
For three hard years they chased him,
While he taught them tricks galore.
He tricked the trackers, stole their rifles,
Tunnelled his way through stone,
Until at last he was betrayed
And trapped in a cave alone.

There in a place called Tunnel Creek,
He fired his final shot,
And one of his own race killed him,
The ultimate tragic blot.
They took his head in a bag to Derby,
Evidence for the court
The end of Tjandamara,
Or that is what they thought.

(Chorus) So what do you think of Tjandamara?
What do you think of Che Guevara?
Were they justified?
And have they really died?
What's your opinion of Robin Hood?
Can you really call Ned Kelly good?
Are you satisfied when you speak with pride?
Were they freedom fighters, or agitators,
Bloody killers, or liberators?—
Jokes aside.

It's the people who make the legends,
So let it be cut and dried,
What's the verdict on Tjandamara?—
The people will decide.

Ted Egan's song was written before there was a Council of
Aboriginal Reconciliation, but it is reconciliatory in that it
does call for a re-examination of Australian history which is
part of the reconciliation process and which since 1988 has
become the dominant policy in Australia amongst both
Indigenous and non-Indigenous people, with both sides
contributing in songs such as these. But I have said that
music is often a cooperative event and, to finish off this
section, I would like to show how Indigenous music has
progressed since 1988. This is relatively easier now that a
number of Indigenous singers and musicians have crossed
over and their music is readily available.

Indigenous writer Kevin Gilbert called for a healing of
the Indigenous soul and the construction of Indigenous
Israels where Indigenous people could go to repair the
damage done after two hundred years of oppression. Many
Indigenous people might agree with this, for after having
flocked to the cities to escape the blight of the rural areas,
they did not find a better life and sank down into the soft
underbelly of Australian society where crime, drunkenness
and drugtaking are the norms of everyday life. To many
Indigenous people living in the cities, Indigenality exists
as a remnant pride, a clinging to a few symbols which
continue to erode under the thrusts of life and a white
despair. Land and country have receded into the mythic

past and maban reality loses out to the harsh reality, the square geometries of the city streets.

This despair has been captured by the Koori songwriter and singer, Archie Roach (1994), who puts this bleakness into stark lyrics which predominate over stark guitar chords. The rhythm of the land is absent, the ceremonies and the thudding of feet are gone and what is left is the victim and the pain:

> Then we'll all get drunk
> Oh, so drunk,
> And maybe a little insane
> And we'd stagger home, all alone
> And the next day, we'd do it again.

Archie Roach was a victim of the Welfare, taken away from his family as a child, and his songs reflect the aspects of deprivation and tragic loss. There is little of the sense of community, of Indigenous culture, and other urban Indigenous singers and songwriters to various degrees glance off the bleakness of this existence. His partner, Ruby Hunter, also sings of the pain of the streets, but with more optimism, though there is still an urban blight for which there is possibly no solution within the city domain except access to jobs, better housing, health and education.

Then there will be a gradual merging into the main-stream culture as seems to have happened to such singers and performers as the female group Tiddas, who construct their music around an a cappella style which is vastly different from the Doowop of Afro-American culture and bereft of the joyousness found in that music. Tiddas, consisting of three women, two of them Kooris, might not even be an Indigenous band at all, for their main singer is a Scotswoman, Salley Dastey. This perhaps explains the absence of Indigenality in their music which concentrates on women's concerns.

In this book I stress a positive Indigenality, which might not fit the stereotype of the victim which too often is perpetuated as the state of all Indigenous people in Australia. Many cultures and people have been completely destroyed, and this is to the shame of Australia, but not all.

Still, a nation resting on a short history of bloodshed and tyranny must make amends if possible, and at least under the late Keating Labor government there were attempts to come to grips with this bloody past and even with the land itself, seeking to do something about the mass exploitation of both land and people which came with the invasion and continues to be the legacy of Australia. It is this legacy which has created the sadness of many Indigenous people and which literally drives us to drink and drugs.

But there were parts of Australia which to a lesser or greater extent managed to escape many of the debilitating effects of the invasion and one such is Arnhem Land, the country of the Yolngu people. Though the peace and security of Indigenous land is often under threat, there it is secure enough to provide an Indigenous Israel for the people who can enter white Australia and return in safety. In Arnhem Land Indigenality is strong and the cultural processes keep changing and adapting according to the dictates of Indigenality. If there is an area which shows what might have happened to Indigenous culture and people if a more benign invader had come to our shores, it is Arnhem Land. The people are strong in their culture, own their land, have mining royalties from a mine forced on them and which they strongly contested in the first landrights case, and speak and sing their language. Not only this but they have strong leaders who can handle the effects of change.

It is from Arnhem Land that the four main members of the group, Yothu Yindi, have come. The other three members are of European extraction, but they have been adopted into the Yolngu social system which can accommodate itself to such strangers. The group is willing to adapt their music to the trends of a popular music which might have its roots in the European and African traditions, but which has become world music over the last decades. Yothu Yindi sacrifices nothing of their Indigenality in the process of creating an accessible music.

Their greatest success, 'Treaty', a 12" 'house' remix was the idea of the Razor Gang at Razor records in Sydney, and important white Australians Peter Garrett of Midnight Oil and Paul Kelly helped to put the followup album, *Tribal Voice*, together. The song and the album were released to worldwide acclaim and for the first time people all over the world were dancing to Australian Indigenous music, often in the Yolngu language. Not only this, but the whole world learnt of the perfidy of the then Prime Minister of Australia, Robert Hawke, who had promised the Indigenous people a treaty in 1988 but reneged on his promise. Yothu Yindi set out the position of Indigenous Australia in defiant lyrics:

> This land was never given up
> This land was never bought and sold
> The planting of the Union Jack
> Never changed our Law at all.
> Treaty, yeah!

Yothu Yindi is a political group and sings about the concerns of Indigenous Australians in their songs, as had No Fixed Address in the seventies. They are songmen who pass the word on Indigenous culture and its continuing strength across the world. Not only this but they challenge Australia to achieve a solution to their problems of victimising Indigenous people whilst criticising other nations about human rights. Australia is searching for a national identity in the debris of a past consisting of vegemite and Arnott's biscuits; but the true basis of Australian identity is Indigenous culture and Yothu Yindi is stressing this in their songs. Indigenous writers are committed writers, dedicated to getting their message across, and this is also the dedication of singers and musicians such as Yothu Yindi:

> Get it right this time, poor boy
> You got inside information
> Hope for the future now
> And we will sing and dance
> Under the honey sun
> For ever and ever.

Framing Our Indigenality

8

WHEN OODGEROO OF THE TRIBE NOONUCCAL, Custodian of the Land of Minjerribah, passed on in September 1993, it is said that two whales surfaced when she was being buried and then left at the end of the service. *Oodgeroo*, a biography by Kathie Cochrane, appeared a year later in 1994. The cover is overpowering: a stark black-and-white extreme closeup of the elder Oodgeroo, one hand framing her chin and her eyes ever-watchful. It is a strong cover and reveals how far the early Kath Walker had come in her quest for human dignity and rights for herself and her people. This biography had a companion volume, also titled *Oodgeroo*, but with the word 'tribute' attached to it. It was edited by Adam Shoemaker. The cover of this volume is in bright colours, with the title prominent at the top and with a photograph of Oodgeroo clad in a snakeskin-patterned dress and with her arms raised as if in triumph. There is a smile on her face to add to this feeling of triumph. On each side of the long photograph is a reproduction of her drawing of the rainbow serpent—her totem, the carpet snake, represented this deity on earth—but these illustrations are somewhat flawed. The one on the left has been beheaded by the edge of the book and part of the body has been similarly cut on the left. In a sense this lessens the feeling of triumph, for Oodgeroo's work has not been absolutely successful and, while she has moved into the centre and into the canons of Australian literature, too many of the Indigenous people remain on the fringe. Still, individually, her life is a triumph and does show the movement of the Indigenous people of Australia into the national awareness.

Jack Davis is still going strong and has written a tremendous body of work: poetry, prose and his well-known dramas. He too has had biographies and autobiographies published. One is *A Boy's Life* (1991), which is a simple text of his childhood with a cover reflecting this, and the other is *Jack Davis: A Life-Story* (1988), put together from transcriptions by a lifetime friend, Keith Chesson. The cover of this book is in stark white surrounding a colour photograph of Jack Davis in closeup, not as extreme as that of Oodgeroo but there is the same look of wary acceptance in his gaze. It was first published in 1988 when the Indigenous struggle had peaked with the bicentenary of Australia and there was a struggle with that encompassing whiteness which both writers had fought against for many years.

This struggle had achieved a literary dimension with the publication of their first volumes of verse: *We Are Going* (1964) by Kath Walker, and *The First-Born* (1970) by Jack Davis. Both books, although from different publishers, have similar covers, with photographs of the poets. Kath Walker laughs sideways, her white teeth challenging the whiteness of her beads. Her hair is neatly arranged and we may be sure that, if we could see the rest of her, it also would be as neat as a pin—the proponents of assimilation loved to use platitudes when dealing with Indigenous people. Jack Davis, on the other hand, gazes into the distance. His hair is short and his clothing is casual. Assimilation did not create middle-class blacks; worker, stockman, perhaps an odd-looking missionary boy, this was all a black man could hope to be in Western Australia, and in Queensland a black woman might become a domestic, as did Kath Walker. From this she escaped into the army during the second world war to become a switchboard operator.

Both volumes have prefaces. In Jack Davis' book, this is titled: 'Introducing the Author'—though, as this is a book of verse, perhaps it should read 'introducing the poet'. It has endured unchanged through two reprints (1983 and 1986), however, so this must be what the poet wishes to be and for that matter is. It has been taken from a tape-recording made by Jack Davis in an interview with Richard Beiby, who, we learn from the flyleaf, is a novelist. At first glance it is apparent that the transcript has been cleaned up to remove any signs of true orality, such as false starts, sudden switches in subjects, use of pause markers and so on. Instead we have what may be described as a narrative discourse in the first person, and though there may be occasional deviations hinting towards the tape, scraps thrown to verisimilitude, such as the use of contractions, there is little feeling of the spontaneity of the spoken word. But there are many problems inherent in transcribing an oral text, including the very fact of it being written down, and thus it may be better to have a clear narrative text. It after all is a matter of strategies of communication rather than a mere matter of being 'true' to the spoken word.

The foreword to Kath Walker's book is written by James Devaney. Who he is appears in her next book, *The Dawn is at Hand* (1966), where she writes the foreword herself. He is her good friend and critic who taught her much. This foreword, in comparison to that of Jack Davis, is quite short and may form the basis of a comparison between the textual reconstruction of two lives, before they blossomed into full-fledged biographies.

James Devaney begins with the obligatory 'first': the first book of poems published by an Australian Aboriginal. Then her credentials are given, and these are not those of a poet. Does this refer to the coming claims of 'this is not poetry but social protest'? Kath Walker at the time was: Queensland State Secretary, Federal Council, Aboriginal

Advancement League; Executive Member, Queensland Aboriginal Advancement League; Member, Union of Australian Women; Member, Realist Writers Group, and so on. This is followed by a quotation from the poet herself:

> *I am of the Noonuccal tribe of Stradbroke Island, near Brisbane, my totem the carpet snake. I was born in 1920 and arrived a week before expected, at the home of white friends where there was a wedding in progress; and the little black baby stole the show from the star performer, the bride. They named me Kathleen Jean Mary Ruska.*

Kath here is stating her Indigenality, giving her tribe, her country and totem. There is only one incongruous note: she is named by an anonymous 'they'. Who 'they' are is not stated, but it is significant that her names are strong Christian names, indicating that the little black baby is to be assimilated into the naming clan. Grammatically, 'they' can refer only to 'the white friends'. This is borne out by the rest of the foreword.

The opening paragraph of 'Introducing the Author' is in opposition to this. It begins with Jack Davis' father: 'William Davis, tribe not stated, reared by a white family until fifteen, itinerant station hand, but a good athlete'. There is nothing of Indigenality in this account, only the government policy of assimilation which took by legal right Indigenous children from their natural parents and placed them with white people. In this context family can only refer to white family. The second paragraph is the female aspect of the male first. Jack's mother suffered the same fate as the father. The text then informs us that Jack Davis is 'part aboriginal' and his described life follows along the same lines as that of the father. He is constructed in the text as being assimilated and this is stressed when we are told that he was treated as white, though his creativity, his poetry, is coupled with his working with full-blood people. Does this mean that his creativity belongs to his darker side? This is only hinted at in this text; but if we know his literary work, we know that his Indigenality has been a source of inspiration and that he has been a pioneer in the resurgence and continuance of Nyungar culture.

Perhaps Western Australia has other tropes of
Indigenality and racism working within, different from that
of Queensland. Oodgeroo, the then Kath Walker, had the
same upbringing; but in her foreword, though written by a
white friend, there is no separation between part and full.
The subject fills only two short paragraphs and is nowhere
as important as it appears to be in our comparison text. Her
mixed racial origins are mentioned in a few short words
('Kath Walker is not a full-blood'), then dismissed in the
remainder of the sentence, as a full identification is
assumed. She speaks on behalf of her people, puts her race
first, is a dedicated worker for them, but nevertheless
believes in the common brotherhood of man. On the other
hand, with Jack Davis, there is a separation and he feels
sorry for the full-blood Aboriginal people and the conditions under which they work, and even when the word
'our' is used to modify Aboriginal people, it has the tone of
the white philanthropist, who sees an injustice and sets out
to remove it. There appears to be much left out of our text,
but identification with his people appears to come about
through political action. He protests at the curfew imposed
on Indigenous people and is jailed for being the ringleader.
It is then that Jack Davis as constructed in the text makes a
personal decision to become involved in Indigenous affairs,
but there is still that feeling of separation from the
Indigenous people which is lacking in our text on Kath
Walker. A reader must wonder why this is so, especially
when there is not that separation from community in Jack
Davis' life and literary work. But, as I wrote a few lines ago,
there may be some trope in Western Australian racism
which, resting on an assimilationist policy, caused separation rather than solidarity.

The Jack Davis text, refurbished from a tape-recording,
reveals what it was like to be an Indigenous person in
Western Australia and how the policy of assimilation
worked to such an extent that there was a definite problem
of identification and an estrangement from the general
Indigenous community. Placed in an inbetween situation
of neither being white enough to be European nor black-
thinking enough to be Indigenous produced a trauma in
many Indigenous persons which remains to this day.

Western Australia has the most Indigenous people incarcerated in its jails, and too often there occur racist attacks,
which keeps up the pressure on Indigenous people. Jack
Davis comes from such a state and this state of affairs
produced nightmares in the subject as a boy. These were,
at least the text informs us, the result of the sensitivity of
Jack Davis, though this is brought into doubt with the
assertion that he had his share of fights at school, the reason
for these fights being his non-acceptance by white
students. He was called a nigger, for example, and after the
text relates incidences of this sort, still it goes on to declare:
'... so you see all in all, we had quite a happy childhood.
Race relations never worried us.' It would be easy to accept
a facile reading of this as being an ironical statement,
except that the happiness of his childhood is reinforced
constantly and it is this childhood that provides an opposition between the freedom of the bush and the enslavement
of the city. Childhood happiness as opposed to adult
sadness is an opposition in Jack Davis' work to which he
returns again and again, especially in his poems.

Jack Davis' poems usually are well-worked rhymed verses,
often in quatrains, revolving around a simple opposition, as
in 'The First-Born' which laments the position of his sad
neglected race in opposition to a laughter and joy now lost.
But although the poem is framed in a series of questions
asked by the land, they are unanswered and the reader is left
to supply an answer.

Both Jack Davis and Kath Walker have poems about the
future of the Aboriginal people in what was once called
'integration'. But the poem of Davis called 'Integration' is
closer to Walker's 'Assimilation—No!' Davis calls for the
worlds to combine, the door to be opened, the walls to be
broken, separation to end, the peoples to stand together as
one under the smile of God. It is precisely this that Walker
is against. Wine poured into a flowing river is lost, oneness
implies surrender and death, and so such assimilation into
oneness is to be resisted. The Indigenous people must
keep their own identity or else they are nothing. Her
message is reinforced by oppositions and the image of the
river is compared to the gum which cannot be trained into
an oak. There is a consciousness of keeping the past things

which matter and not joining into a oneness with a stronger other in which the Indigenous people will be the losers.

Oodgeroo's early poetry was more political; later on, with her poems stemming from her visit to China, they became less so. In contrast, Jack Davis' later poems in his last two volumes, *John Pat and Other Poems* (1988) and *Black Life Poems* (1992), are more conscious expressions of what is happening to Indigenous people within Australia. These protest poems are mixed with gentle reflections on nature and life which are pleasant to read, much like enjoying a pleasant spring or autumn's day in the west. Kath Walker's early poems, on the other hand, are less well constructed and are sometimes strident protests which ring out problems and demand solutions. She names the enemy and by so doing achieves a catharsis which enables her to sing of other things, such as her son or her country. Jack Davis, on the other hand, rarely offers solutions to political problems and any catharsis is achieved by taking refuge in the bush of his childhood.

Jack Davis' first volume of verse, *The First-Born* (1970), was a plea for understanding and help. His second volume, *Jagardoo* (1978), is much stronger. His verse has become 'poems from Aboriginal Australia' and there is a sweet blackness in some of them which is not found in his earlier volume. The softness of 'The First-Born' has given way to the stronger verse of 'Urban Aboriginal':

> With murder, with rape, you marred their skin,
> But you cannot whiten their mind;
> They will remain my children for ever,
> The black and the beautiful kind.

Even the metered and rhymed verse has taken on a new strength of blackness in which the disciplined verse structure begins to echo the chant of Aboriginal song cycles in which no word is superfluous. 'Tribal Man in the City' is a fine example of how rhyme and metre may be used:

> Black the night my mother bore me
> Black her pain to give me breath
> Black the wailing ever o'er me
> Black my tribal death.

This volume is illustrated by Harold Thomas, an Aboriginal artist from South Australia, and one of his drawings, illustrating the poem 'Tribal Girl', is featured on the cover. In traditional times, women were the peace offerings and often they were sent ahead of the men as negotiators. Women and children often appear on the covers of Indigenous books. They are there to allay suspicion, to open a dialogue into Aboriginal culture. When we come to the illustration in the text, we notice that it illustrates a love poem, a poem of forbidden love in that the 'I' of the poem is in love with a woman who is forbidden him by tribal law, and the poem, which opens on a promising note of acceptance, ends with a scream of rejection:

> Gin, barefoot black gin,
> Keep your red earth and your wurley,
> I can walk my own path,
> In the sun or in the dark,
> And find my own affinity.

This tension of rejection and acceptance, of Indigenality and assimilation, is featured in many of the poems in the volume. It begins with ten poems depicting the joys of contemplating nature, and in most of the imagery we find not an Indigenality of image but a Europeanisation of the Australian landscape, as found in the work of white poets. There are 'gossamer curtains', 'a coat of green', 'scarves and bonnets', 'weavers and dresses' and so on, all harking back to an industrialised age, with none of the imagery being found in Indigenous culture. It is when we come to the next set of poems, which are concerned with social protest, that the images become crisp and Indigenous: 'freckled mind', 'akin to the colour of the belly of a dugite', and the beautiful line, 'she was born with sand in her mouth'. But then, again, the images waver away and ogres appear and other images which a poet of Indigenality should leave to European poets. This is what he does in his latest volumes, written and published in 1988 and 1993. These show a maturity of image and an awareness of what is happening to Indigenous people which lifts them beyond his first two volumes. *John Pat and Other Poems*

(1988) marks his concerns and subject matter: injustice towards Indigenous people and an awareness of nature, which continue to be the themes in *Black Life Poems* (1992). Interspersed among these are interesting vignettes of life which perhaps show that, for Jack Davis, his poetry is second to his drama for which he is better known.

The foreword to Kath Walker's second volume of poetry is by the poet. She informs us that *We Are Going* (1964), her first volume, had quickly passed through seven editions, and that this was because it was the work of an Indigenous person, together with the fact that its publication had coincided with a rise in white awareness of their plight. She mentions that the chief criticism had been that some of her poems had been angry and bitter, that she had been labelled a communist, that James Devaney had suggested that propaganda might not be good poetry, and so she, as a good little Mary, has deleted these facets from her latest volume; then she ends with the statement that the old tribal tales are not her invention, but heard from the old people when a child. Of course Kath is not a good little Mary and so many of her poems are similar in protest as in her first volume. She has thus subverted the volume, though the continued use of metered rhyming verse is sometimes an annoyance. She seeks to pass beyond this in a number of poems, such as 'Community Rain Song', which attempt an Indigenality not only of subject, but of form, in that the free verse of the storyline breaks up into the staccato song chants of traditional verse. In this poem there appears to be a traditional form of storytelling at work, and this comes through on occasion to break up the straight prose lines of sentences, thus:

> This was nardoo-gathering season
> But now little nardoo. Too long dry,
> Grass all brown, birds not breeding,
> Creeks not running, clouds gone long time.

But too often there sounds another voice speaking in straight English and destroying the orality of the piece, thus:

> Throughout all the laughter muttered strange words
> Of magic-making as old as the race.

A poet like Lionel Fogarty would have handled it differently, but then it must always be remembered that the
heavy ideology of assimilation sits heavily on these verses.
Indigenous people were not allowed to do their own thing,
but had to obey the white man's dictates. This was beaten
and voiced into them. Indigenous modes of expression
and language were to be replaced by a voice speaking
standard English in chaste tones as close to the accents of
the colonial motherland as possible.

Jack Davis' *Jagardoo*, dedicated 'To all who fight for
freedom's sake', has a foreword by the Anglo-Celtic poet,
Judith Wright. Thus, in the first pages, a white person is
speaking for an Indigenous person, but she is an eminent
person and is introducing an unknown poet, though Jack
Davis was not entirely unknown in that his first volume,
published in 1970, had been reprinted in 1971—a rare
event in the poetry world—but then Indigenous people at
the time were only a fringe people and this is reflected in
their literary works. They must be more or less stamped
with the seal of approval by a white person: a missionary or
anthropologist or, failing this, a philanthropic person from
the field of endeavour into which Jacky seeks to enter.

The first paragraph establishes the place of the
Indigenous people in Australia and also establishes Judith
Wright's views on the subject, as well as enabling her to
distance herself from any guilt arising from their treatment. Thus, a government on the other side of the world
gives them the status of British subjects, and this allows
the British and later Australian governments to take their
land and then children away from their parents. And so it
is the government who takes Jack Davis' parents away
from their community. The objectivity of the style, a style
aimed for by Anglo-Celtic writers, is almost transparent in
its ideology which places the blame on an unfeeling
government. And it is this objectivity which is praised in
the verse of Jack Davis. Any emotion, any resentment, any
anger, any hatred, is to be seen objectively. It should never
be seen as propaganda, as protest, but as springing directly
from life's experience, and thus we may read the poems
thoughtfully—in fact we should read them, not because
they are good poems, but because we owe a debt to the

Indigenous people which cannot be redeemed by any
Budget allocations. She declares that it is only recently
that the Indigenous people have found a voice, and this at
a time when the last remnants of Indigenous culture are
being threatened by the incursion of mining companies
onto Indigenous land with the result that the dispossessed
people are becoming fringedwellers of towns and cities,
which is reflected in the poem, 'Tribal Man in the City'.
She goes on to write that perhaps the strongest feeling
about Jack Davis' poems is that of sadness, a sadness
which manages to swamp any feelings of bitterness and
violence. Judith Wright commends Davis for his wisdom
in eschewing these feelings in his poetry and gives as an
example, 'Self', which is an interesting poem and I find it
amongst the strongest verse Davis wrote up to that time:

> Today,
> I will turn down
> The corners of my mouth,
> Erase my smile,
> Replace it with a frown
> Then see if it will own me.

Here Davis' taut mastery of the English language is evident,
but in the second verse the lines become longer and flab-
bier as the promise of the first stanza is left, and there is a
retreat into childhood, safe and secure, as in the succeeding
two poems, 'Balloons' and 'The Adventurer'. It is the
second verse that Wright quotes as an example of Davis'
wisdom, but I would say that this refusal to accept the latent
violence within has altered and transformed his poetry so
that Judith Wright may describe many of his verses as
simple appreciations of natural beauty too naive for a sophis-
ticated audience and that they should not be taken on merit,
but in the light of the poet's own gentle personality and
background. I doubt if Jack Davis would agree with this
summing up of his work or even with the summing up of his
personality. This text of Jack Davis as presented leaves not
much to the imagination, and results in the downplaying of
a man's work, though his poetry continues to impress me
with its sense of dignity and appreciation of nature.

How Indigenous texts are presented to their readers is a
subject which is quite interesting, from covers to forewords
to publishers' blurbs. Indigenous books these days are
presented in a different way, with the forewords, if needed,
being written by other Indigenous persons. This does give
a certain degree of autonomy to the work. We must beware
in approaching Indigenous works not to approach them
with the attitudes of ingrained paternalism, as a recent
reviewer noted:

> *In a culture that ignores or undervalues almost everything the herd
> does not endorse and that harbours a distrust of ideas, originality
> and inspiration, it seems only natural to avoid confrontation, to
> accept what the so-called authorities tell us, despite those inner
> urgings that quietly challenge one to look beyond what is fashionable.
> This is particularly so with Aboriginal writing, where, instead of
> criticism, there is more often than not merely a patronising accep-
> tance—engagement avoided in favour of a pat on the head.*

(Billy Marshall-Stoneking)

Talking and Writing
Our Indigenality

9

PADDY ROE IS A STORYTELLER IN BROOME, WESTERN
Australia. His stories were taped, transcribed and
edited by Stephen Muecke, a critic and academic
from Sydney. The stories are in Indigenous English,
together with an added synopsis of each story in standard
English, and were published under the title of *Gularabulu*
by the Fremantle Arts Centre Press in 1983. In putting
them onto paper, Stephen Muecke used a method of tran-
scription that he claimed gave a more authentic written
version of the spoken word and presented in a more correct
form the cadences of Indigenous speech patterns.

> That's Djaringalong, Djaringalong,
> You know he used to travel from there
> [unspecified].
> He come up here to pick up lil-lil fellas,

You know that's for his nest—to feed his young ones.
He gotta get something for them to eat,
But he pick up babies from there,
Boy, girl—anyone babies—
When he pick up these fellas,
Then he go back all time—back to his nest—
Feed all his young ones too.
(Paddy Roe)

Long, long ago in the Dreaming days, in the far North, there lived a giant eagle named Djaringalong. She had a nest in the top of a Largardi, a Boab tree, near the sea, and the bottom of the tree was strewn with skulls and human bones—for the she-eagle lived on babies and small children that she snatched up in her long, hooked talons.

Djaringalong was a fierce hunter and she would swoop down from so high in the sky that at first she was only a tiny speck. Then, with a sound like a rushing wind, she would hurtle across the tree-tops, while mothers ran in panic to hide their children. But the eagle was too quick and too cruel, and she seldom missed her prey. In time, Djaringalong ate all the children of the Nygina and Wilangu tribes, and also the babies of the Worrora, Unambal and Ungarinjen. All the camps were in mourning, and the death wails filled the air—and still the eagle flew, her cruel shadow a black cross and a curse over the land below her soaring pinions.
(Butcher Joe Nangan)

In these two extracts of the oral narrative of Djaringalong, we are immediately aware of the vast difference in discourse texts. The series of events are more or less similar in that they add up to essentially the same story, as long as we know that, in oral forms of narration, there is never the same story told twice even by the same storyteller, and that it varies according to such things as audience, place, time and so on. In written discourse, however, the text implies a fictional narrator transmitting a narrative to a fictional listener or reader, with a single written text, usually the only one directly available to the reader and it is through this that the reader acquires knowledge of the story (its object) and of the narration (the process of production). The oral process is different in that the storytelling is immediate and the communication is directly from narrator to listener. There is a problem with the oral text in that it is not an icon, a book or part of a book, but a script liable and open to change. Without the intervention of the recording apparatus, it is a once-off textual event, and perhaps for this reason is very precious in that, once spoken, it is gone forever, though it is highly probable that the storyteller will continue to recreate variants of the basic storyline.

In the discourse of Paddy Roe, we are aware of the fact that he is addressing a particular audience, and is even stopping the narrative flow to emphasise and even elaborate on certain points to this audience which might not be familiar with certain aspects of the narration. This is not so in our second narrative discourse where the orality has been edited out and the story changed to permit the imposition of a fictional narrator transmitting the narration to a fictional reader. I have given both these versions in order to show the extremes of rendering an Indigenous oral narrative structure into a written discourse form. Strategies used shudder on the brink of two extremes, mediate them in the particular frames we are used to in our dealing with Indigenous literature, then boldly cross over into Indigenous territory. One of these intrepid explorers seeks to be as objective as possible and becomes merely a recorder (or does he?), giving a transcript of the oral discourse and not compromising its Indigenality. The other explorer knows how to deal with natives and ruthlessly edits all Indigenality out. After all, one native discourse is much like another native discourse, anywhere—and, in this second version, it is relatively simple by erasing any trace of place to have a story which might have come from any folk culture in the world.

In the past, Anglo-Celtic recorders of Indigenous oral narratives rarely sought a way to handle Indigenous discourse patterns and preserve them in a written text. Usually there was a complete abdication of any responsibility in seeking to be true to what was heard, in the sense of how it was heard, but then, these Anglo-Celtic writers were not interested in creating Indigenous discourse patterns on the page. Apart from self-interest, there was an underlying ideology at work which accepted that there was only one way in which English could be written and they knew this right way. There might be excuses in the frame about straying from the spoken word, but all in all there was the definite belief that the centre knew more than the fringe about everything, including how Indigenous oral narrative discourses should be written. This attitude was so fixed that it passed over to the assimilated Indigenous persons, so that in the legends appearing in the periodical *Identity*, for example, there was an editing towards the fixed discourse of the European fairy tale rather than towards the fluidity of Indigenous English. This is not to be wondered at, for those Indigenous persons shaped by assimilation had been led to believe that there was only one way in which to write and that was standard English. Our Indigenous English was encased in a straitjacket; there was an abnegation of natural style, and an expunging of all orality from our written texts. It was accepted for some years that this was how it should be and it was only younger Indigenous writers who challenged this view.

The Indigenous people are under constant pressure from the mainstream to conform to its dictates and these dictates are pushed by white researchers onto us so that we acquiesce in producing texts which in effect support the ideologies and mechanisms of oppression characteristic of conquest and colonisation.

Of course, this may not be accepted and it may be stated that there is a discrepancy between orality and literacy, that oral communication works through immediacy or spontaneity, whereas writing is planned, is organised and thought out. This is seen in our two stories. Joe Nangan's story is not the result of spontaneous thought or even of any attempt at utilising any discourse elements of orality, such as repetitions, and a direct addressing of the reader. In fact, it appears that Joe gave a version of the story to Edwards who then questioned him on the salient points, removed any discrepancies in the succession of events making up the narrative, then produced a completely new text based on the sequences of the storyline. This is much like the reader appropriating the text and then reproducing it in his own words. There is little of the role of an editor in such an act and there is very little left of Joe Nangan after this misappropriation, though it must be admitted that there was some remorse at the wholesale destruction of Joe's narrative discourse. In the foreword, which accompanies this collection of stories, Hugh Edwards acknowledges his crime: 'Most of all I regret that Joe could not tell the stories himself in his own way'.

This means that there is little Indigenality in the discourse. Any sense of Indigenality is found only in the place names, the illustrations and the few Indigenous language words allowed to remain in the text. What is assumed by writers like Edwards is that the devices utilised by spoken and written discourse are diametrically opposed, and that a direct transposition of the devices from one medium to another will not work or even result in intelligible communication. Of course, with the oral account of Djaringalong before us, we find that this is not so, and that a more honest editing of the Indigenous text is possible, but then in the argument is an attitude coloured by ideology. The bias is towards literacy and many people would prefer the blandness of the Edwards version of Djaringalong simply because it is literate.

The opposing of orality and literacy is to the fore when some people judge the qualities of written and spoken texts. Editor Stephen Muecke in Paddy Roe's *Gularabulu* confronts this problem, though the contradiction is never resolved on the discourse level, as he acknowledges in his foreword: 'The simple act of writing down stories (as well as phrasing them in good English) inevitably involves departures from Aboriginal narrative style.' The oral texts must be written down, rather than supplied on a tape, then explained in standard English. There is never an attempt to fuse or amalgamate the two styles and perhaps this is not the job for the academic, but for the creative writer, especially the creative writer of Indigenality if he or she is to escape the dominance of standard English and produce a style more in keeping with the spoken word.

Except for Pidgin in New Guinea, the hegemony of standard English in the different ex-British colonies has often been challenged, but rarely overthrown. There has always been an opposition involved between the 'broken English' of the various Kriols which have developed and standard English. Often too this has resolved itself into a direct opposition in that standard English remains the language of the ruling class or elites, while the mass of the people speak Kriol. This is precisely the case in Australia in that those Indigenous people now in charge of Indigenous affairs have, as their first language of communication, standard English, and thus have no desire or see no reason to challenge the hegemony of language which exists in Australia. It is only in outlying regions where Kriol is spoken that some small books have been produced in this language, though the writer Edward Warrigal Anderson has produced a volume of poetry in Kriol which is yet to find a publisher.

Most of the readily available, conventional (in the sense of European-style) Indigenous short stories were published in *Identity*, under the editorship of Jack Davis, and although these were in standard English, there are a number which show a strong degree of Indigenality and attempts at recreating a sense of the Indigenous past, though this is at times heavily idealised. Reg Saunders was an author who contributed several short stories to *Identity*, one of them being called 'Parabar, the Shark', a story about the Tasmanian Indigenous people. This is interesting in that it uses the form of the European folk tale to tell an Indigenous story with a strong maban reality. The narrative is about a girl called Rowra who goes to live with the sea people. The time is during the invasion, the place Tasmania, Cape Portland (Luemerrernanner). Life is idyllic—then the sealers arrive and chase after a girl-friend of Rowra's. She escapes. But the sealers follow after, massacre the men and kidnap the women. They are taken away to other strange islands, but are comforted by seeing the shark, Parabar, swimming by. In the story Parabar links the Tasmanian Indigenous people, especially the women, to nature and to the sea. He does not hurt the women, but when a sealer falls into the water, he is instantly attacked. The story is interesting in that it operates on the level of maban reality and lacks the attributes of the European short story with its use of rounded characters and psychologism. We are in the presence of myth or a tale, hinging on an implied moral, and we are aware that the central preoccupation is Indigenous-white relations. The characters are flat, of cardboard thinness, and

are there only to serve the tale. The story revolves around
Parabar the shark and his presence relies on the menace felt
by Europeans in Australia at the thought of such a fish. In
our story, shark as menace is replaced by white man as
menace and shark is at first protector, then a symbol of the
alliance Indigenous people have with the forces of nature.
Thus the story ends with the two women looking at
Parabar's dorsal fin playing in and out of the water. They
find this sight comforting, a complete reversal of the feeling
a white person would have at the sight of the fin cutting the
water. In effect, Saunders has reconstructed an Indigenous
world in his narrative discourse in which white people have
been excluded, since the last image would cause a shudder
rather than a feeling of comfort to come over them.

Such stories based on the structure of tales, myths or
legends work well, and allow for a reading on different
levels, whereas the so-called modern short story, or piece
of narrative discourse, has lost this capacity to charm, or
even to point a moral. It usually relies on some sort of
mimesis to contrive at a naive masquerade of realism in
which we may feel for a character or a situation vicariously,
then put it aside with the exclamation, 'That was a good
story'. This is what happens with the 'good' stories in
Identity. They can be readily identified as short stories from
their narrative discourse mode and, if we need to be more
specific, we may slot them into a realist frame rather than
that of maban reality. One such story is 'Stolen Car', by R.
Chee, in which the first paragraph sets the style of these
narratives:

> *He was eighteen years old, thin and dark as an ancient snag, hidden
> in a river. Golden laughter of the sun shone from his yellow eyes and
> melted into his blond curly hair.*

We might contrast this with the Indigenous oral style of a
narrative discourse put down on cassette by Robert Bropho,
and later transcribed and published in the anthology of
Indigenous writing, *Paperbark* (1990):

> *The days of old, back there in the yesterdays, in the past ... for us,
> Aboriginal teenagers then, in the fifties, in the late forties, up into the
> early sixties ... back there in the past.*

In these two beginnings, we have in the former what might be described as a typical beginning of realist fiction, and there is an inclination towards simile and metaphor which, as I have pointed out before, are rare in Indigenous styles of discourse, while in the latter we have a beginning reflecting Indigenous oral discourse in that it is purporting to tell it how it is, though the personal has been deleted even on a group level so that Robert can extend a group of Indigenous teenagers as representatives of that whole class. This is extending the realist mode beyond realism and into the realms of Indigenality. His extending a group into representatives of a whole generation may be contrasted with the approach of Chee, with his reliance on metaphor and simile, and may even be extended to encompass the notion or the assertion that the use of symbolism is an aspect of Indigenous discourse and an aspect most likely to be lost with the stumbling steps of the editors wandering into Indigenous territory.

Robert Bropho's and Chee's narratives both stress certain aspects of the Indigenous condition in Western Australia, but there is a bravado in Bropho's work that is missing from Chee's. Chee's work is essentially tragic (is this another Europeanisation?); Bropho's work is not, it is symbolic of maban reality with the central action of the journey reaching beyond fact into mythology. Bropho has used the symbol of journey in an earlier work as a spiritual quest, spiritual in the sense that the material result did not matter. And he uses journey in this short sketch exactly in the same way. The teenagers of his story by undertaking the journey together undertake a form of initiation, hence the maban reality, in the sense that this 'great' journey will establish a bond between their age group, exactly as in earlier times the initiation process did. It is more than coincidental that the band of teenagers do a tour of Western Australia. This, as in the traditional initiation, will enable them to locate themselves in their land. They form a psychic map of their country, but this is not enough, for the old ways are broken and essentially there is no strengthening of community ties through the process. The boys do not return in triumph to their camp, but pass on to Fremantle prison. And Bropho, eschewing the white tragic for the Indigenous matter-of-factness, ends his account with:

*And that's where the journey of the teenage Aboriginals—that's us—
in the late 40's through the 50's and early 60's ended up ... and
that's what us the teenagers in them days went through.*

'Stolen Car' is different. Incident is piled on incident, all of
which lead on to the tragic ending. There is none of the
sense of initiation in the central act, the stealing of a car, no
group solidarity or anything like that, only the triumph of
the individual as found in most modern European narrative:

> *Slender hands grip the wheel and he pushes the beautiful blue being
> to its limit. ... For the first time in a long while Johnny Moydan
> isn't being pushed around. He is in control, he is free, he is
> supreme—he is someone.*

But the car gets out of control, and he crashes. Chee ends
his story with:

> *Pathetic Johnny. The shadowy, formless people watch from the foot-
> path. Watched you and the banshee-wailing police car rush past,
> leaving just a wind in your wake. And who remembers a wind?*

R. Chee is or was the pseudonym of Archie Weller, the
author of *Day of the Dog* (1981), and his work has been criticised for lacking a certain degree of Indigenality, of having a
certain degree of accepting of things which is not found in
other Indigenous prose works. In *Going Home* (1986), his
collection of short stories, there is again an emphasis on a
gritty realism which is gloomy, and the Indigenous characters approximate more to rootless Lumpenproletariat than
to Indigenous people.

Naturally, this may be the situation of modern-day
Nyungar youth in Western Australia, but most writers of
Indigenality emphasise the positive rather than playing up
the negative. His characters are rootless and shiftless, with
little to hope for in the future. They are losers with no hope
of winning, and though the dialogue is straight from the
fringe camps, there is little that any community would wish
to identify with or accept. But, I think, the late Kevin
Gilbert might have accepted these stories, as they do
depict an Indigenous lifestyle which is familiar to other
Indigenous people and one which Archie Roach sings

about. The message is that 'Charcoal Lane' is not a nice place to live in.

In *Living Black* (1977), Kevin Gilbert writes that the original aims of the book were to show the conditions of the Indigenous people through their own testimony, but that this he found difficult to accomplish as he travelled across the country meeting and interviewing people. He found that an automatic self-censorship cut in as they were, he writes, deeply ashamed of 'what they know is the truth about their people today'. He then outlines a number of what he calls 'myths' which Aborigines propagate about themselves: a strong feeling of community, a lack of materialism, an ability to share, a deep caring for their children. He then sums up what he believes is the true position:

> *Aborigines try to believe these fallacies about themselves because they won't face the truth. But you only have to go to any Aboriginal mission or reserve to see the truth; the lack of community spirit, the neglect and abuse of tiny children, and all the rest of it.*

Archie Weller in his stories does show this state of affairs which reveals a lumpenproletarianism of Indigenous communities dominated by woman bashing, petty crime, gambling, drugs and alcohol. This condition creates a tension and duplicity in life which is nasty, to say the least, but the writer of Indigenality while knowing these things prefers to write about or postulate a hope in the future. He or she sees these things as only temporary aberrations, which will be done away with in the future, and not as aspects of Indigenous culture. They will automatically disappear if there is a return to pristine Indigenous values or in Kevin Gilbert's case in the creation of a new Indigenous society. Writers of Indigenality are ideological writers and thus are not content to be describers of naive realistic situations. They believe in a future hope and this often, as in the case of Robert Bropho, leads to political action. Archie Weller's writing is strongly realist. He has been content to describe the present situations as they occur. He describes the individual, and the community as a whole provides a backdrop to his characters. His writings are closely related to those of white writers like Thomas

Keneally and his *Chant of Jimmie Blacksmith* (1972), in which Aboriginal society is pictured as completely decayed. For the writers of Indigenality this is not so. They prefer to see hope in the future. This is seen in most of the short stories in *Identity* which, although they may depict nasty situations, always end on a positive note, reflecting oral traditions in which everything can be resolved or reflecting that simply because the story is being related means that the narrator, who is usually part of the action or at least a relative, has won through and survived. The Indigenous people of Australia, as has been pointed out again and again by the writers of Indigenality, are a great race of survivors and this comes across in our literature.

Our World a Stage

10

One day I realised I was earning my living off misery row.
(Bobby Merritt)

'LITERATURE' ESSENTIALLY IS LANGUAGE REDUCED to an artefact of a book or a recording, or some such permanent record. It is with this limitation in mind that I keep my examination to those plays which have been reduced to some such permanency, with the emphasis on two volumes of drama: *Kullark* and *The Dreamers* (1982) by Jack Davis, and *The Cake Man* (1978 & 1983) by Robert J. Merritt. The covers of these two volumes are similar in that the titles are displayed at the top in uppercase letters. In Davis' volume this is followed by: 'Introduced by H.C. Coombs, with an account of the Nyoongah people of South-Western Australia by Ronald M. Berndt'. Merritt's volume is treated in the same way: 'Introduced by Mervyn Rutherford, with a preface on the stage history by the Author and historical notes on the Wiradjuri tribe of NSW'. After this come the names of the playwrights.

This packaging of early Indigenous plays may be contrasted with the packaging of a collection of later ones, published by the same publisher in 1989, and may show the shift which occurred in Australia in 1988. The Indigenality of the plays is shown in the cover which is an Indigenous painting. The first part of the title, 'PLAYS FROM' is in small uppercase letters in the centre of the top of the cover and below, in large black uppercase letters, is 'BLACK AUSTRALIA'. This is separated from the painting by a thick line the rouge colour of lipstick. The four names of the playwrights are in black lowercase letters on the right side of the cover towards the bottom. There are no other names and, when we open the volume, the only introduction is from the Indigenous actor, Justine Saunders, who introduces the plays rather than the entire Indigenous people. On the whole, the cover illustration is similar to the other Indigenous play volumes. The Davis edition has the face of an Aboriginal adolescent painted with white streaks and the Merritt edition has the smiling open face of an Aboriginal boy. The paint streaks would lead us to believe that there will be traditional elements in the former play and perhaps none in the latter. This is borne out when we read the texts and, if we compare two other published dramas with Indigenous characters with urban settings and an absence of traditional Indigenality— *Crow* by Louis Nowra (1994) and *Close to the Bone* by Ned Manning (1994)—the covers are photographs from a particular scene of the play and have no Indigenous motifs at all.

The shift from the wings to centre stage since 1988, with its emphasis on reconciliation and cooperation and the desire to bring Indigenous people into the mainstream, has resulted in most cases in the abandoning of general introductions. There is, however, an introduction in *Close to the Bone* by the Indigenous person, Mark (Peacock) Leon, who intervenes to sway our reading of the text, and at the end there is a suggested reading list. This gives the drama the appearance of an educational text and detracts from the subject matter of the play which, it seems, is not enough alone to present the message. I feel that the text of the play is introduction enough, but this was not so for the early and some later Indigenous plays which often have introductions that have nothing to do with the drama presented. It is legitimate for us to ask why this has been done. Is there a lack in the texts or, if not, what precisely is the function of these introductions?

H.C. Coombs in his introduction, 'An Invitation To Debate', invites the reader to read the texts in certain ways, though his words are not about the dramas, and it is as if he has not read or seen the plays. He invites us to join in an Aboriginal–settler dialogue. The Indigenous people have reached the stage of being able to open such a dialogue, but this has not been met by Europeans. He says that an Indigenous intelligentsia has arisen and describes them thus:

> Men and women who have seized upon what our society can offer them in education and access to the ideas of our civilisation. ... It is remarkable the degree to which these men and women have chosen to seek their careers and the measure of their achievement in the service of their own people and in the institutions they are creating.

He makes no mention of those Indigenous people who have rejected these ideas and seek to find their sources of inspiration in Indigenous culture. He seeks instead to pull Indigenous artists and writers into his 'intelligentsia', and writes of the emergence of new Aboriginal art forms:

> Naturally, these forms take over much of the structure of those of our own society. But in purpose, in content and in style, Aboriginal artists make them distinctively their own.

He does not write about how it may be possible that Indigenous artists then on the fringe of white 'civilisation' may make a contribution by returning to their cultural roots as has happened in the visual arts and the dance to create new forms of Indigenality. This is not important to him, for H.C. Coombs sees Indigenous artistic productions as being 'consciously and unconsciously directed at us'. He sees them as an invitation towards a debate, 'a search from which some sense of shared identity may one day come'. This is a forerunner of the policy of the Council for Aboriginal Reconciliation and this cooperation is all for the better and is well underway, especially in the cooperative enterprises of music and theatre. Still, dramatists such as Jack Davis also write for their own people and provide an opportunity for Indigenous people to see themselves for the first time holding centre stage and talking back to the white man. This is an important aspect of such plays and a part of writing and acting Indigenous people back into Australian history. They see themselves and their history portrayed in positive terms, though in an environment, the theatre, which is often alien to them.

As if to emphasise this, anthropologist Ronald Berndt's introductory piece is titled 'The Aboriginal History'. This is of importance in that, while eschewing any discussion of Indigenous dramatic structure, he writes about language, and how Jack Davis uses in his play Indigenous discourse in the shape of 'Neo-Nyoongah', as spoken in south-western Australia. He goes on to separate this 'Neo-Nyoongah', which he calls Aboriginal-English, from standard Australian English. He also, perhaps because he is an anthropologist, attempts to see the play from an Indigenous perspective, that is, from a viewpoint of Indigenality:

Pride in being Aboriginal is indelibly inscribed in his writing, indicating firm roots which go deeply within the total Australian scene, far beyond the recent past, into its very beginnings.
(p. xxi)

From both these texts we, as readers, are invited to accept the two plays in the volume as the products of an Indigenous writer who is committed to his people and who writes with a purpose. He is a writer of Indigenality using Indigenous speech forms, though using what appears to be on the surface conventional theatrical forms. It is noteworthy in the introductions that there is little discussion of the plays as theatre which are in the naturalist mode that audiences can follow without difficulty.

Robert Merritt, by writing a foreword to the second edition of his drama, captures the textual space once reserved for a white person and this is a 'historical' first. He invites the reader to see his drama in certain ways. This begins idealistically in that he states that theatre was part of

the natural way of Aboriginal culture before it was shat-
tered, but he does not define what this theatre was or is, and
ignores any discussion of the form or structure of *The Cake
Man*. It is noteworthy that, in the first edition, there was an
afterword from the white director of the first production
who was aware of the difficulties involved in producing a
play which did not fit into the accepted genres of European
drama. He discussed the first scenes of Indigenality, of an
edging towards maban reality which then flowed into the
straightforward reality that audiences accept. The director
saw this, not as maban reality, but as a weakness in the
drama, which actors and audiences accustomed to
European theatre found difficult to accept. It is of interest
that in the second edition this afterword has been dropped,
but the first scenes remain as an integral part of the play.

After the foreword by the playwright, there is a second
introductory text which is a reminiscence by a European
who knew the mission, Erambie, in which Robert Merritt
grew up. By recounting his memories, this person in effect
asks the reader to see the play in a certain way, as a slice of
life:

> *Robert Merritt's play* The Cake Man *depicts with accuracy in
> dramatic form a past way of life as we both remember it from when
> he was growing up in the 60's. It is still the present for too many
> people in Australia.*

Thus, the Indigenality of the beginning with the symbolic
elements which continue throughout the play is ignored.
We are in this reading asked to accept the play as an autobiographical piece. The last introductory text reinforces this
way of reading the play. It describes the real setting of *The
Cake Man* and then details the history of the people and the
settlement. Strangely, this piece ends with a long quotation
from Dr H.C. Coombs, describing a traditional Aboriginal
ceremony, the recitation of a song cycle. This in effect is
contradictory and sets up a traditional dramatic scene which
may be contrasted to the contemporary theatre of Robert
Merritt.

These framing texts invite us to read the dramas as essentially realistic pieces of theatre in the European tradition.

They have a message to impart and they are for both Indigenous and non-Indigenous people. This to a certain extent is what we do get and, taking our cue from the introductory pieces, it is possible that this is all that we shall get.

Robert Merritt, in 1986 on the ABC's 'Impact' television programme, established his view of the social importance of theatre. In his then newly established group, the Eora Centre, he sought to build up the self-esteem of Indigenous young people in the Sydney suburb of Redfern, where little of traditional culture remains. He hoped that such groups would lead to a renaissance or revival of Indigenous culture, but there is a revealing sequence in the programme in which a group sit and watch a film of a traditional performance, thus showing the gap between urban and country culture. In the urban environment of Sydney, the roots of Indigenality have withered and traditional culture has little relevance to city youth. Time, distance and place have given this culture an air of unreality, and in its place the city Indigenous people are trying to re-establish or re-form a culture containing elements of the old and the new, though city experiences are more immediate than the old culture. In the case of Jack Davis, things are different in that, in Western Australia, traditional culture continues strong in country places and migrates down to Perth with the seasonal movement of the people. There is contact and connection between old and new, between country and urban, and from the still-performed Indigenous ceremonies, it is possible to reconstitute Indigenous structures in a contemporary city environment. Of course, this can happen in Sydney where Indigenous dancers are brought down to invigorate and Indigenalise dance companies such as Bangara, who also leave the city to travel into the Indigenous hinterland.

In seeking a renaissance of Indigenous culture in an urban sprawl like Sydney, Robert Merritt must first nurture his artists before achieving any sort of revival incorporating important elements of traditional Indigenous culture. He must first create again the artists which in traditional Indigenous society made that culture creative and a source of strength. He sees the Eora Centre as being the spiritual birthing womb for the creation of such artists:

Through the Eora Centre … I see the emergence of the artist—artists are going to keep our culture alive. I want to nurture those artists just like powerful societies do with their generals, because they're the people with a vision.

Robert Merritt's call for his students to become naked when acting recalls the approach to theatre by the so-called 'poor theatre' of modern Western drama. Jerzy Grotowski, in an interview published in his *Towards a Poor Theatre* (1975), accents a certain holiness, a certain development of the individual, in much the same way as Merritt does in the television programme on his centre. This approach is very similar to the various group encounter sessions of personal advancement and even the acting out of problems as advocated by certain psychologists, though there is a difference in that the confrontation of the individual as actor with the audience—again as individuals—is de-emphasised in Merritt's approach, with the group-as-audience assuming a supportive role which may reflect remnant traditional Indigenous culture in that dramatic performances were essentially communal. They were group performances which were enacted, not for any individual advancement, but for community health and well-being. This accent on community rather than on individual is found in many rural and traditionally oriented communities where theatre is put at the service of the community as a source of spiritual and physical healing, with the emphasis being on leading an alienated or sick individual back into the community. Usually they are held by the community for this purpose and if not symbolic, mimetic when certain areas of concern are identified.

The Eora Centre, but without Robert Merritt, produced a play in 1991—*Close to the Bone* by Gubba playwright Ned Manning—which was a musical dealing with urban Indigenous concerns such as the forced adoptions of Indigenous children taken away from their families and put out with white families. It is one of the reasons the play was written, to show what happened to Indigenous people, and the historicity of the play and its message is stressed in the introduction, 'Discovering Our Own Culture' by Mark (Peacock) Leon, though what 'culture' is being discovered we do not find out in the play. He writes: 'It is this anger and the emotions we feel, that will give the words in this book the power to bring to light the untold history of Australia. A history that needs to be known by all Australians.' It is this history we learn about and the plight of urban Indigenous people. 'Urban' is necessary in this context because it is a very urban piece of work, with no intrusions of Indigenality, and with none of the joy of another musical, *Bran Nue Dae* by Jimmy Chi, which transcended such history in a magic of irony and great songs which presented to audiences all over Australia the fun and humour that is in our life. *Bran Nue Dae* was set in Western Australia: in Perth and on the road north to Broome. It was 'Country' as well as 'Urban' and poked good fun at the white man and his ways, as well as establishing a wonderful character in Uncle Tadpole. *Close to the Bone* lacks a traditional Indigenality of spirit and reminds me of that group sitting in the Eora Centre watching traditional people dancing on film. To a certain extent, this sadness at the lack of culture permeates this play and reminds me of the urban drama of the streets which we constantly hear and look at on those television programmes exposing such conditions.

Contemporary Indigenous drama on first viewing or reading can be accepted as realistic or naturalistic in the European sense, though in certain plays aspects of maban reality keep intruding to bring the genre identification into doubt. Supernatural or surrealistic elements have a place in maban reality and these are seen in Jack Davis' *Dreamers* where they are an integral part of the plot. In Merritt's *Cake Man* these are part of the dialogue and, through never intruding into the action, are so much a part of the drama that they tend to subvert the realist aspects. In fact, it is the Indigenality of *The Cake Man* which lifts it above such social plays as *Close to the Bone*.

In Indigenous life, theatre of the conventional European type did not exist, though contemporary dramatic theories speak of the ritual implicit in theatre and this ritual aspect is seen in some of the plays of Heiner Muller which are far beyond the conventional storytelling of most of Australian theatre. Indigenous theatre was

closer to such 'postmodern' productions and events were
staged using dance, song and narratives. In the sacred
ceremonies, which utilised ritual to project a strong maban
reality upon the world stage, traditional wisdom and
contact with the ancestors were maintained. In fact, during
such performances a magical transformation occurred,
with the participants becoming the very ancestors who had
performed the songs and ceremonies long ago in the
Dreaming when everything was magic and becoming
fixed in static reality. Through ritual and ceremony, the
participants could contact this magic and bring it over into
their own lives. Such ceremonies were essentially rituals
of healing and were seen as being necessary to the well-
being of the land, the community and the natural species.
Dramatic elements were important in the performances in
which transformations were re-enacted or rather danced
out; but these were truly social manifestations, with close
communion between actors and spectators, and often the
whole community took part in them. They were staged in
a special arena with little scenery, though in some communities large barkpaintings were used as backdrops.
Costume, particularly body painting, and props (sacred
symbols) were important to help to effect the connection
with the Dreaming past through symbolisation. The songman (often a maban or shaman) was the stage manager or
producer who supplied the ancestral songs and carefully
rehearsed the theatrical event, ensuring that everything
was done as exactly as had been passed down by the
ancestors.

Storytelling was another dramatic event, with the
narrator using such props as leaves and sand drawings to
dramatise the story. The anthropologist Catherine Berndt
even rendered one of these stories into English within a
dramatic framework, though with the admission that she
left out elements which did not fit in with her ideas of a
theatrical format.

Traditional dramatic elements from maban reality enter
such Indigenous plays as *The Dreamers*. In this drama it is
the dancer who shifts the play out of an essentially realistic
mode and into Indigenality, with different concerns than
a surface understanding of the play would suggest.

Indigenous elements are also found in *The Cake Man*, especially in the stylised opening scene where stereotypical figures mime a primal scene, much as in traditional secular performances. It is notable though that the important element of dance is missing and that this has been taken by dialogue, a dialogue which has been influenced by the art of the storyteller. This is evident in the early narration of a myth and again in the epilogue. The beginning and ending of the play are precisely those parts which have been criticised as weakening it, a criticism that is based on expectation of genre. The intrusion of non-European conventions, of maban reality, and old modes of dramatic performance which are paralleled in the dialogue where there is a constant intrusion of non-English words and mythic elements, again threaten any genre recognition. It is the Indigenality of the discourse and dramatic structures which weaken it as a European theatrical piece. Conversely, it may be said that the reliance on European theatrical conventions weaken it as an Aboriginal theatrical piece.

Indigenous dramatists are schizophrenic in that they must seek to please both non-Indigenous and Indigenous audiences. It is impossible for them to avoid this if they seek to have their works performed in the conventional theatre with its white middleclass audience. Also, as theatre is a cooperation between any number of people, both Indigenous and non-Indigenous, the Indigenous plays under consideration make important concessions to European theatrical conventions and tastes which are quite conservative in Australia. One of these concessions is to edit out that which European ears might find tiresome. We must keep in mind that as most Indigenous people rarely venture into the theatre, their ideas on what constitutes theatre will be different from that of an educated European theatregoer. In fact, until recently, it is likely that the only European dramas that Indigenous people might have seen would have been conservative plays staged in mission halls or town halls and their reading of plays would have been those found in school reading lists. Then there is the influence of television with its emphasis on natural conventions. These may be seen as limiting would-be Indigenous playwrights, but then it can lead to an escape from genre entrapment in that genre is a learnt, rather than a natural, classification. Thus, what we might expect from playwrights with such backgrounds is a mixture of genre, a lack of conforming to the dictates of theatrical convention, unless in the workshop situation the script is worked and reworked towards a genre. If somehow the flavour of an Indigenous drama is brought to the stage, we might find a mixture of genre, though with an increased familiarity with European theatre, unless there is a strong infusion of Indigenality, Indigenous playwrights might be expected to produce more genre-typified plays.

This appears to be the case with Jack Davis whose *Kullark* and *The Dreamers* were quite complex in time and structure, but whose third play, *No Sugar*, has become restricted to a naturalist genre, though it has been staged in the round with the audience being forced to move around the theatre to follow the unfolding of the action and to actively participate in it. This is a way of presentation much closer to traditional Indigenous theatre in that Indigenous audiences are never passive spectators, but then again the restricting of time and reality to a historical period (the 1930s) is a lessening in the Aboriginal structure and a stricter adherence to genre. *No Sugar* (1986) has become Jack Davis' most successful play, perhaps because he stayed within the naturalist genre.

His play *Barungin (Smell the Wind)*, first performed in the fateful year of 1988, was a much more political drama. Its action circled around the effects that the increasing deaths in custody were having on his community and Jack Davis, to strengthen the meaning of 'smell the wind' on which the stench of death was all persuasive, based his drama on the Nyungar funeral service. It was as if the deaths of individuals were resulting in the death of the community, and life in white Australia was in effect like being at a funeral. This was a hard message for Europeans to stomach and his drama has not been performed since 1988 and the 'celebration of a nation'. The drama ends with one of the characters reading the list of those who have died in custody and the ending is utterly pessimistic.

A feeling of pessimism is one of the signifiers of Indigenous drama. There are a number of others which go towards separating Indigenous from mainstream conventional Australian theatre. These make for an originality of theme and content. One is the sense of community, or even the portrayal of family as community. Individuals rarely exist in isolation, but are units in a collective which is constantly emphasised and reinforced at the expense of the individual. This is such a common denominator that it is found in all four texts of Davis and others' *Plays from Black Australia* (1989). Another is that the community rarely exists in isolation; elements of mainstream Australia enter with often-disastrous results, as is found in Eva Johnson's 'Murras' (1989) in which the daughter of the main character is used as a guinea pig in testing a contraceptive which renders her infertile.

But even when the worst has been inflicted, there is the sense of keeping on for the sake of keeping on and most Indigenous plays are filled with a humour which one critic has referred to as the singular capacity to smile even while the figurative hurricane strikes. An example of this humour can be found near the beginning of Merritt's *The Cake Man* where the character, Sweet William, is speaking:

> *(He poses proudly now) See'n I'm a Kuri. The Australian Aborigine, that's who I am and what I am ... made in England. (Pause) Oh! Speakin' of social welfare cheques, y'see that in the paper the other day? (Ponderously) 'The minister said that there is no real evidence to the fact ... that some blackfellers is spendin' their social on likker. They's buyin' booze. (With a sigh) Oh, just like them Red Injuns what ruined 'emselves the same way ... at the firewater all the time. (Sighing, nodding) I know it's a fact. Hang on there. (He nicks offstage and returns with a half flagon of wine. He drinks from it and smiles.) The social cheque came yesterday, thank Christ.*
> (p. 12)

This stance, this self-deprecating humour permeates the dialogue of just about all of the Indigenous plays I have seen or read and so is the presence of alcohol. I refer back to the signifier of Indigenous drama: the pessimistic ending. There is little movement towards a brighter future. Things will always go on in much the same way as they have been going on. This is the same sort of fatalism which may be found in modern dramatic works by such writers as

Samuel Beckett. *Waiting for Godot* could well be staged by Indigenous people as it portrays, in much the same way, the tension found within their dramas. Characters are literally roped together in an uneasy alliance as they wait for outside deliverance which is not forthcoming. Both *Waiting for Godot* and *The Cake Man* use similar symbols of divine intervention. In the former it never comes, whilst in the latter it turns out to be a white man with a box of groceries.

The ending of *The Cake Man* is a fair example of how Aboriginal plays conclude:

> *Two realities (pause) an' I've lost one. (Pause) But I want it back ... I need it back. (Pause) Not yours ... mine.*

Here that aspect of waiting is paramount. There is no movement towards going, getting or retrieving that maban reality, no thought that to capture or recapture that reality involves a mythical heroic quest into Indigenous reality. There is an aspect of cultural paralysis about Indigenous drama which needs to be resolved, that, although the problem has been defined and the quest announced, there is no movement into Indigenality. There is the absence of a hero able to descend into the mythic earth of Indigenality, regain the tjuringas (sacred symbols) of his community and bring these healing symbols back into modern Aboriginal theatre.

It is noteworthy that *Kullark* ends on the same note of pessimism:

> Alec: *Well, here's to us.*
> Jamie: *An' thousands like us.*

But there is a ray of hope when an actor enters to sing a gloomy song, the final stanza of which rings down the curtain:

> With murder, with rape, you marred her skin,
> But you cannot whiten her mind.
> They will remain my children forever,
> The black and the beautiful kind,
> The black and the beautiful kind.

But this hope is nothing but survival; there is nothing of renewal, of rebirth in it. It is only when we see and read *Bran Nue Dae* by Jimmy Chi that we reach a text and a performance which rises above the gloom and presents a celebration of Indigenality and Indigenous people which although it has most of the attributes of the dramas finds the strength to laugh at them. Of course, it is a musical comedy and musical comedies are meant to be happy. This one certainly is and what is more a myriad of influences enter the music to present a happy Indigenality in which people have fun and can be cheeky to the white man and even laugh at such heavy topics as being Indigenous. In fact, although the ending can be read in different ways, when all of the characters discover their Indigenality in a mass discovery, the joy is akin to the joy which might be found at the end of the reconciliation process, though to spoil the celebration the cast exits singing 'Bran Nue Dae' with its message that nothing really has changed and that the Indigenous people of Australia are still waiting for that magical brand new day when reconciliation will truly be achieved.

The message for Indigenous people is similar to the ending of the first version of Kevin Gilbert's *Cherry Pickers*:

> *I am merely trying to tell you that we can't live, nor find a new life by embracing a stone-age culture in this Nuclear Age. We should rightfully be proud of our old culture for what it was—the expression, the cry, the search for beauty by primitive man. This truth we should hold, and advance by, not revert to that cultural age. Man must advance, must mature, and must never, never revert back for life is a constant process of growth.*

But Kevin Gilbert heavily revised his play in 1985 and in the published version of 1988 these lines may not appear. Still, in the foreword to his drama, he explains his play to us:

> The Cherry Pickers *is a play of humanity, of the search for justice, of a return to spirituality. It is an intimate, albeit dramatised, glimpse of the family. It is a communication, a gift that, should your heart glimpse the key, will enable you to understand what is meant when Aboriginals demand integrity as the only basis upon which Blacks can begin to negotiate justice.*

In effect, Kevin Gilbert was seeking to provide a basis to the policy of reconciliation which had not yet been formalised and later, when it had been, became simply another government policy without much going for it. One of the reasons for this is that Indigenous people, like Kevin Gilbert, were excluded from it. Consensus was what the government thought they needed rather than dialogue. In all of his life Kevin was not afraid to postulate solutions. His play also was the first Indigenous drama to be staged, in 1972; then it was rewritten and staged in 1985. Kevin saw his play, as can be seen in the quotation, as a text of healing and understanding. Perhaps it is time for Indigenous theatre to see itself as presenting community rituals of healing and well-being. At the moment, it still seems that, except for *Bran Nue Dae*, we are still in the theatre of misery.

Our Collective Indigenality: Kevin Gilbert, 1933–1993 **11**

An onus is on Aboriginal writers to represent the evidence of our true situation. In attempting to present the evidence we are furiously attacked by white Australians and white converts, whatever their colour, as, 'Going back two hundred years ... the past is finished ...!' Yet, cut off a man's leg, kill his mother, rape his land, psychologically attack and keep him in a powerless position each day—does it not live on in the mind of the victim? Does it not continue to scar and affect his thinking? Deny it, but it still exists.
(Gilbert 1985)

KEVIN GILBERT WAS THE STRONGEST AND TOUGHEST, and yet the gentlest, of the writers of Indigenality. He is gone now, but we will always remember him at our demonstrations and negotiations. It is strange, though not so strange, that an Indigenous man could produce such an important volume of work, whilst still remaining in the forefront of the struggle. Others ascended to sit beside those in power, but Kevin remained with us and documented our survival and struggle. It is rare for a people to have such a person. In newly liberated countries, such men take over the reins of power from the departing colonisers, but in Australia Kevin Gilbert remained at the grassroots level, all but ignored by those in power or by those who aspired to such power as came from being next to those who hold the power. He remained in the struggle and accepted few rewards in his life. His poetry and writings too came under the censuring eyes of the critic.

White critics, with that remarkable objectivity they use on the most passionate of subjects and which in the past has resulted in millions of people being classified and declared unfit and only good for the gas chamber, refuse to come down one way or the other in their assessment of Indigenous writers. Supposedly cognisant of Indigenous history, they may write on Gilbert (Gilbert, the text) as not being familiar with his language—that is, the language of his tribe, the oral traditions of his tribe—and with his failure to list the origins of Indigenous words he does use. What they fail to point out is that Kevin's people on both sides of the colour line have suffered oppression, and that the Wiradjuri people of New South Wales, from the first, had to suffer under a constant pressure which resulted in their language being destroyed except for remnant words.

It is impossible to deal with Indigenous writing in English without an understanding of the history of the Indigenous people and of the assimilation policies which cut the linkage to traditional culture and language. Thus, Indigenous writing in English is precisely Indigenous in English because of that history, rather than of any referral back to tribal roots, and that history is as bleak as the period spent by Gilbert in the prisons of the white man. In these times of text being supreme, and if not the text, the act of reading, the individual act of production by an individual producer is downplayed. One reads the text for the text rather than reading the text for an understanding of the author; though, in some unfashionable areas, it is held that all writing is autobiographical and that what we are confronted with is a continuing dialogue in the writer's mind, 'à la Samuel Beckett', and that simply to rely on the text is to be led astray down the wordy paths of language analysis in which the referent is the referral.

This is important in our approach to Kevin Gilbert in that, through his identification with the black cause, his individuality, as it were, is submerged within the movement, but it must never be forgotten that he, as an individual and as an Indigenous person, is the Indigenous person and that his writings are as much about himself as about his people. His history and his suffering are as much our history and our suffering, as our history and our suffering are his. It is a question of who is speaking, who is writing, which defines the work of Kevin Gilbert. A definition by question which brings into focus the role of the writer, and especially the role of the Indigenous writer trapped in wordplay and structures of genre and composition which he has had no part in forming, and which he often sees as being distant from him.

It is possibly for this reason that many Indigenous writers are free from genre identification and select what the job demands or what tool they feel is useful for the task. Thus Kevin Gilbert is an essayist, a polemist, a poet and a playwright, and none of these. He is even Gilbert the murderer, if occasion and slander demands, or Gilbert the politician, or jailbird, or take your pick. What I am most interested in, as I am approaching Kevin Gilbert through language and texts ascribed to him, is Kevin Gilbert as writer or wordsmith, or Kevin Gilbert as text, for if we have not met the flesh and blood man, all that we may know about him is what we read. He thus becomes a text for us to decipher as much as any other text, which may seem to be very cold for those of us who did know him and shared the struggle with him.

First of all, we may approach his volume of poetry, *People Are Legends* (1978). The cover is dark and sombre, easily blending into the fringe shadows of a secondhand bookshop. The shadows which go to make up the illustration of a child may be easily lost. One eye peers out at us while the child pensively sucks its thumb. In bright yellow uppercase lettering are the words 'PEOPLE' and 'LEGENDS'. Between the two words and of the same size and type font is a white 'ARE', and below in white, though of a smaller size, are the letters spelling out the name: 'KEVIN GILBERT'. The two yellow words stand out and, if you are an Indigenous person, the bright colour reminds you of the yellow sun in our flag, the yellow sun representing the hope of a bright future, and this symbolism is opposed to the meaning of 'legend' which my dictionary says is 'a traditional story, myth, such literature or tradition and thus of the past'. The white 'are' of the title is in the present tense. The verb is a doing word and the colour white reminds us of the Europeans always doing things, either to themselves or to others, and the name, Kevin Gilbert, also in white, is a part of the doing, of that whiteness: it is his book of verse.

We learn little of Kevin Gilbert from the cover, though it is disturbing, and that single eye, that child's eye, appears to have a certain quality of distrust about it. On turning the page, we at last find out that Kevin Gilbert is a poet and a journalist, perhaps poet coupled with journalist to emphasise the commitment of the writer, for we learn that his life's work bears witness to the anguish, the shame and the glory of his stubbornly surviving people, and so the flap notes go on in this vein, and for once the humanity of the fringe is emphasised, but strangely the oppressor is not named. There are no signs displayed that will point to this oppressor and, instead, Kevin Gilbert is constructed as a text individualised, but also identified with people. This long paragraph ends with a signifier, stressed with inverted commas, that Kevin Gilbert's verse is authentic verse, without any recourse to 'culture'. 'Cultured' verse, at least in this reading, is not authentic verse, and 'culture' is modified further by politeness and hypocrisy which are opposed to living, love and humour. The authenticity is emphasised with the phrase: 'without editing'.

We learn little of our text, Kevin Gilbert, in this long paragraph, but in the second paragraph biographical details appear. This gives the necessary signifiers defining Aboriginal writers. He is born, as are most if not all Australian Indigenous people, in Australia and is firmly set in historical existence by being born in 1933. He has the usual primary school education and the work you would expect, a station hand. Then we are informed that he is a murderer and has spent fourteen and a half years behind bars, and five years and seven months of this time in the notorious Grafton 'goal'. This misprint is interesting and even leads on to the next sentence in which he is redeemed by access to books, and so his career as writer—modified by 'Aboriginal'—begins on the backflap where his work is given the seal of approval by the intrusion of a quotation from a person named Stewart Harris who, writing about his previous book, *Because a Whiteman'll Never Do It*, informs us that Kevin Gilbert is a politician (modified by the adjective 'Aboriginal'). The cover note then ends with a direct quotation from Kevin Gilbert in which we are informed that he is working as a nurseryman and art gallery proprietor to gain finance to advertise the Indigenous cause and one day, hopefully, to gain the freedom to further his play writing and art.

Thus Kevin Gilbert as text is constructed for us, and we are made aware that this text has produced the poems, but not just any poems. On the title page we find that we are not being confronted by ordinary poems, but by 'Aboriginal' poems—and what is it that makes them Aboriginal? They are obviously written by an Indigenous person, for we have been told this, and they are about Aborigines and are in the language 'of living Aborigines', and this statement is legitimised by the publisher, University of Queensland Press. What this language is we learn from the contents page. The first poem has the title, 'Baccadul', an Indigenalised English word, tobacco, and all the other poem titles are in English, with the only Indigenous language words being proper nouns. The overall impression we receive from our reading is that the language spoken by living Aborigines is English or dialects of English.

There are sixty-nine poems, a symbolic number, and this may be an example of black humour, an example of the human side of the question, as our flapnote has signified for us. The poems cover the whole gamut of historical Indigenous experience, and the injustice to and the warping of an entire people is laid at the feet of the white man, the oppressor, who has been left out of the preceding notes. The language is terse and bald and bereft of those comforting illusions of simile so beloved by the 'cultured' poet, writing of his own immeasurable personal experiences. 'Baccadul' refers to the slave wages paid to an Indigenous worker. Other titles refer to the dismal handling of Indigenous people at the hands of the white oppressor: 'Soft Sam' has the theme of hunger; 'Fair Swap' refers to an exchange value based on mistrust; 'Maureen' is about white oppression and female suppression; 'Duffed', the same; 'Lover's Lament', the same—and so these poems extend out into a litany of man's inhumanity to man, and man's inhumanity to women. There is little hope, but what hope was there for the buggered black in 1978 when these poems were published?

From the poem 'Birth Control for Blacks', facets of Indigenous life and the conflicts within the community become the subjects of the verses, and again there is the absence of hope. Perhaps from our reading of Kevin Gilbert the text we are entitled to ask: has the experience of prison resulted in a flawed text producing flawed texts, or is it the abysmal reality of Indigenous life in Australia which has led to the production of this poetry, or is it a mixture of both? Could the buggered black produce verses less bitter than these, in which the language flattens, tautens and tenses until the approach is close to the structure of nursery rhymes? We are in the presence of: 'Mirror, mirror on the wall, who is the fairest of them all? Not you, you're black!'

But given the primary school education, the blows of assimilation, the necessity of getting the message across, simplicity of verse structure is perhaps what is needed, not the repetitions and symbolism of traditional Indigenous verse. These are black words on a white page and messages crossing over to black and white. Simplicity, therefore, may not be the result of the lack of education of Indigenous poets as stated by white critics, with the implication being that if only they had been educated in the complexities of Europe, if only they had not been Indigenous, they would produce verse akin to theirs and able to be judged with their own. This protest, this telling it how it is, is not poetry. Thus the inventors of something called a 'prose poem' deny the legitimacy of rhythms and rhymes simple and direct as nursery rhymes, simple and direct as you find in traditional song-types across the world. Not only this but these verses are criticised for not having the rich rhythms of traditional Indigenous society, but where message is more important than form, these rhythms might get in the way, and we might eulogise over the structure without determining the message.

Our text, Kevin Gilbert, as defined for us, is not concerned with inventing new patterns. Intent on the message, he utilises certain traditional rhythmic patterns of Europe that fit his message, and with which his readers are familiar. He is not concerned with the strictures placed on these structures by white critics. The patterns he uses occur and continue to occur and belong to a folk tradition which, although localised in England, still serves as a legitimate form for not only certain Indigenous poets, but for working class poets. The patterns are there to be used, and they are used by people who believe that words are more important than the pattern in which they are placed. Again, from our reading of the text of Kevin Gilbert, we would expect him to use forms with which he is familiar, or which he found in the prison library. Text determines text, and this is what happens in this case, though this Kevin Gilbert is more than a poem.

Kevin Gilbert's books are never prefaced by the words of a seemingly sympathetic white who usually manages to introduce the Indigenous writer as a curiosity of the first variety with a congratulatory slap on the back that at last the Indigenous people are entering the Australian mainstream. Kevin Gilbert has thrust such benevolent, or malevolent, prefaces away, but, as we say, 'push a white man out the front door and, lo and behold, he's knocking at the back door.' It is impossible to escape the convention of 'author', and the writer must be rendered down into a digestible text, must become language in order to set up a discourse.

Already we have seen this in *People Are Legends*; now we turn to *Because a Whiteman'll Never Do It*, which was published about four years before the poems, though the verse was probably written earlier. The cover of the book is plain, in red and gold letters on a black background—the colours of the Indigenous flag—though Kevin's name is in white as on the cover of the verse volume, and, as discussed there, this is because white is a symbolic colour of doing, and Kevin is a doer. His name too is different from his later books. He is 'Kevin J. Gilbert' which perhaps has a nicer ring to it than a straight 'Kevin Gilbert', though it may cause some doubt in a reader's mind as to the identity of the two Gilberts, and if we were to venture an extreme and see each text as different, then this Kevin J. Gilbert is different, though his life is very similar to that of the poet. Our author text is a short publisher's note:

Descended from English/Irish stock on one side and from the tribes of the Kamilaroi and the Wiradjuri in New South Wales, on the other, Kevin J. Gilbert was orphaned at the age of seven—he quickly learnt what it meant to be black and poor in Australia. In 1957 he was sentenced to penal servitude for life for the killing of his European wife. He served fourteen and a half years in Her Majesty's prisons—institutions of which, he says, she is perhaps not as ashamed as she should be. Self-educated in jail, he became an accomplished artist in oils and lino cut, a poet, a dramatist and writer. He has used these abilities to demonstrate to white Australians the injustice and inhumanity that they continue to tolerate toward his black race. Kevin Gilbert sees this book as 'an attempt to make a contribution towards the regeneration of the Aborigine ... in a land that may, one day, at last become big enough to hold a people who have been dispossessed for nearly two hundred years.'

This note sets up the text of Kevin J. Gilbert. It gives him a reality to the reader of the further text. First, we learn that he is a mixture of stock and tribes. Even today this invokes an opposition in that tribes are considered primitive whereas stock is considered civilised. Europeans are not seen as descending from tribes. They have surpassed this primitive stage of human evolution, but other peoples, such as Indigenous people, are descended from primitive tribes. 'Stock' is a signifier of civilised and conjures up the placid nature of Europe, populated by sleek animals bred for a purpose and thus of better quality than the wild. Binary oppositions continue from this first sentence. As we progress, the character is built up for us. We learn that he is poor, an orphan, a black, a murderer, but in opposition to these negativities, these blacknesses, are placed the positive attributes stemming from the civilised stock for, after all, these marks of civilisation are European: accomplished artist, poet, dramatist, writer.

The blackness of his tribal side is downplayed, an accident to be dismissed, and the anger and subject matter of the book belongs to the white stock attribute: 'He has used these abilities to demonstrate to white Australians the injustice and inhumanity that they continue to tolerate toward his black race.' This sentence in itself is interesting in that injustice and inhumanity are tolerated by white Australians, but no mention is made of the inflicting of these inhumanities by white Australians. By adroit use of language, the settlers are rendered guiltless except for a psychological attitude which may be eradicated by education. Here is the danger faced by an Aborigine when playing the publisher's game. By entering the white halls or offices of the publisher, he is leaving himself open to covert manipulation.

A hermeneutic reading makes it possible to divide the publisher's note into binary oppositions:

WHITE US	BLACK THEM
English/Irish Stock	Kamilaroi/Wiradjuri Tribes
	orphan
	black
	poor
European wife	prison
artist/poet/dramatist	murderer
abilities	injustice
toleration	inhumanity

Although this note may compromise Kevin J. Gilbert, or at least construct him as a text for public consumption, the main text is a polemic directed at the injustices inflicted by the European settler on the indigenous people of this country and the result this injustice has had. In opposition to the publisher's note, it is dedicated to those Aboriginal patriots who have refused to sell out, and this is followed by an author's note which acknowledges the compromises made in order to have the book published. This in effect continues the opposition detailed above, but ironically, so that there is a reversal in that, while acknowledging the powerlessness of the Aborigine—and Kevin J. Gilbert is an Aborigine—to change things, a fierce independence is maintained. Again, however, because much has been left out, this in some ways is a sham and exposes the fact that to be published is a compromise and a lack of independence, and this lack of independence is the subject of the book. To be born black in Australia is to be born powerless, to be born into the negativities of blackness as set by the whites.

Kevin's book is the historicity of the Indigenous people in Australia and, as the oppressors hold all power and dominate history, Indigenous accounts are only memories which may be captured on a tape recorder. These are essentially footnotes on the glosses of official white history, though the use of verse at the beginning of the chapters allows the voice of the Indigenous person to be heard. There is an important signification in the use of verse and voice, in that they serve to emphasise the unhistoricity of the powerless. The powerless have no recourse to history. They are not the writers, but the victims, and, unable to construct their own history, they are allowed only their memories passed on as stories whispered in the night or songs singing out protests which may be slurred over in dialect, and as an anthropologist once declared it is a good thing to let the blacks sing, for it shows that they are content in their camps away from the houses of the settlers.

The structure of *Because a Whiteman'll Never Do It*, with the use of poetry and prose, is reminiscent of an English eighteenth century political pamphlet. There is also the device of directly addressing the reader, as in this example:

> *White man, you may well speak to the Aborigine of your 'democracy' and 'justice' and 'Christianity'. But your reality is a little at variance with your theory. The Aborigine snarls his disbelief of your words as he slinks away unmanned.*

There is an immediacy about the book which has not dated. The problems of the sixties are the problems of the nineties and they lie as heavy as the broken promises of the politicians.

Kevin Gilbert's most successful book, which has gone through six editions or reprints, is *Living Black: Blacks Talk to Kevin Gilbert* (1984), in which the position of the author is ambiguous in that the cover both emphasises and denies his authorship. The cover is black and, at the top, large white uppercase letters declare 'LIVING BLACK'. Perhaps the use of the black background has meant the automatic selection of white as the dominant colour, but underneath in orange in much smaller uppercase letters is: 'BLACKS TALK TO KEVIN GILBERT'. Below this is a smiling portrait of Kevin Gilbert, though, as the subtitle refers to his passive role, it may be asked why a group shot of blacks has not been shown, as they are signified to be the true authors of the work. However, on opening the book, we find this reading is in error. It is denied on the first page, where we have Kevin Gilbert as text. This follows what by now we are accustomed to, at least until near the end where, after it is declared that Kevin Gilbert is the first Aboriginal playwright, he is described as a poet, a great talker, an oils artist, and the author of *Because a Whiteman'll Never Do It*, the first major political work by an Aboriginal. And so Kevin Gilbert is fleshed out for us, and we note that he is described as being descended from Aboriginal, Irish, English stock, thus eliminating the racist opposition noted earlier.

The book is completely prose and purports to be tran-scripts of interviews of a large number of Indigenous people by Kevin Gilbert between October 1974 and August 1976. When we examine the interviews, the ambiguity of the writer, or interviewer, is manifest in that the style of the speakers is not the hums and arrhs, the false starts and abrupt transitions of a truly oral style. Their speech has been doctored to give the impression of being oral discourse. This explains the ambiguity of the author as signified on the book cover. This is not to detract from the veracity of the interviewees, but it does create problems of authorship, though the author-as-interviewer does have a prominent part and provides an introduction giving his reasons for writing this book:

> *I have also written this book in order to bring white Australia to some greater compassion through understanding and to enlighten it to its responsibilities in the areas of land and compensation for Aborigines.*
> (p. 3)

It may be argued that this is the purpose of all of Kevin's works and increasingly what has been published are political essays rather than literature. He is a deeply committed writer and a writer of Aboriginality who uses words as tools to get his points across to both blacks and whites. An authenticity of style which Aborigines should strive for is not of interest to him. Language in the main is for communication and not for aesthetics, and being a writer is not an end in itself, but an adjunct to social action. At a recent Commonwealth writers conference attended by African writers, there was some heated discussion on the role of the writer and one suggestion was that he should be a politician. This, Kevin might be in agreement with, for perhaps the rhetoric of his style reflects that of the politician, that the ambiguities of Kevin Gilbert as a writer are really the ambiguities of a politician, and that he is more concerned with the Indigenous situation and the way people feel about it (hence his use of the interview) than in personal creative expression, any personal creative expression being used only to elucidate a programme suitable to eradicate a social evil. Kevin Gilbert is the most socially committed of Aboriginal writers, to the extent of using the device of letting people speak out, and thus bringing into question the role of the writer. In fact, with him the question for whom does the writer write does not arise, because, in *Living Black*, he is to a great extent content to play the part of an individual amidst a community of Indigenous voices, and the writer is a social being engaged in a social act, a voice among other voices with only the authority of the tape recorder to separate him from them.

Kevin Gilbert approached the fatal year of 1988 in which the era of Indigenous activism peaked, and then descended into the days of reconciliation which he was against as being nothing else but a handshake. In that year was published *Inside Black Australia*, an anthology which showed that the politician was still a poet. He followed this up with the publication of the revised text of his play, *The Cherry Pickers*, by his own publishing company. From his deep experience of Indigenous people in Australia and with the renewed interest in a treaty between Indigenous and non-Indigenous Australians, he wrote and published in 1993, *Aboriginal Sovereignty, Justice, the Law and Land*, which set out in detail the terms of the treaty. This draft treaty has all but been ignored by the Council for Aboriginal Reconciliation, though they have spent time and money on trying to find out what Indigenous people want. This is the problem with such government initiatives: a policy is constructed and measures put in place from above without considering the wishes of the Indigenous people which often are to be found in such publications. There have been a number of draft treaties circulating in typescript for some time now, but these are rarely taken into account by such government bodies.

Kevin Gilbert's last book, *Black from the Edge*, was published in a beautiful edition by Hyland House in 1994. In it, Kevin Gilbert returns as an individual poet to show that he has progressed into Indigenality since the publication of his second book of verse. The photographs of Eleanor Williams complement the text and it is perhaps the most professional book of poems and photographs published on Indigenous Australia. In it, Kevin reveals that he was very conscious of his approaching demise and this allows the personal voice of the poet to emerge in a striking originality of style. It is a book which should be looked at and read by every Australian and I end this chapter with one of his poems, which is Kevin saying goodbye in body to us. It reveals a deep Indigenality of spirit.

EPITAPH

Weep not for me Death is
but the vehicle that unites my soul
with the Creative Essence, God.
My spiritual Being, my love, is
still with you, wherever you are
until forever.
You will find me in quiet moments
In the trees, amidst the rocks,
the cloud and beams of sunshine
indeed, everywhere for I, too, am
a part of the total essence of
creation that radiates everywhere
about you, eternally.
Life, after all, is just a
passing phase.

Tiddas' Writing

12

Come inside into my kitchen
and rest your feet and weary mind
you can settle and I will listen
to the problems that you find.
(Tiddas)

IN 1993, THE FIRST NATIONAL INDIGENOUS WOMEN
Writers Conference was held in Brisbane. There, Liz
Flanagan and Cat Felton presented an important paper,
'Institutionalised Feminism: A Tiddas' Perspective', which
argued for the development of a 'Tiddas' manifesto' which
would set guidelines for the development of Indigenous
women's writing. This was an important step in developing
ideas on cooperation and collaboration between Australian
women in general and Indigenous women in particular, and
to develop a fruitful analysis which would in effect end the
casual ripping off by mainstream academics and others who
collaborate in the production of Indigenous women's texts.
At the conference, Indigenous women saw that it was
imperative to assert their position in the production of their
own texts which, in the main, seek to open up the past of
Australia. As Indigenous writer Ruby Langford Ginibi

(1993) states: 'I write truth, and the truth is just to educate people—mostly non-Aboriginal people—about how we really are.' And as white academic Jan Pettman (1992) elaborates and by so doing illustrates the reconciliation process at work:

> *Aboriginal women may write for other Aborigines as part of a process of retrieval and recovery. They also usually write to a white audience, to tell the stories long silenced, to affirm the survival of Aboriginal women and communities against the odds, and to provide positive images of those long stigmatised.*
> (pp. 120–31)

Autobiographical and biographical writings, which I have loosely termed 'lifestories', have formed the bulk of the Tiddas' production. Much of this is written not only for Indigenous readers but for Australian readers in general, though this does raise problems, as pointed out by Indigenous historian, critic and writer Jackie Huggins (1993) who says:

> *Let's face it, there are more whites than blacks who read books out there. So are you looking at a book that's going to be basically written about blacks and called black? Or are you looking at the market which is predominantly white, and in a sense appeasing their conscience about blacks, because that is what they like?*

This is the question which the discussion about a Tiddas' manifesto sought to address, though the discussion failed to raise the issue of Indigenous people within Australia and accepted as a given the position (which must be raised) of Indigenous women within a united Australia. Thus, in Indigenous women's writings wider political issues are usually not discussed, but what is is the empowering of Indigenous women (and men) within the Australian nation. This position received its greatest exposure from Sally Morgan's *My Place* which became a national bestseller. Sally Morgan also contributed to the reconciliation process by designing a poster, and Jackie Huggins (and Marcia Langton) have become members of the Council for Aboriginal Reconciliation which is notable for the exclusion of Indigenous male writers, either through their own choice or that of the government.

Indigenous women's writings on the whole are more successful in the marketplace, noteworthy titles being Morgan's *My Place* (1987), Ward's *Wandering Girl* (1987) and Ginibi's *Don't Take Your Love to Town* (1988) which were collaborations with either named editors or publishers' editors. Needless to say, Indigenality in the main, in language and concepts, is often downplayed in favour of producing a text which will appeal to mainstream readers. These texts are produced, therefore, in a particular genre which the reader will recognise. In this regard it is note-worthy that the first edition of *Don't Take Your Love to Town* has on its cover a simple line—'the ultimate battler's tale'—which sites for the reader the genre in which it is to be placed. This genre identification is added to on the back cover where the text is called 'an autobiography', though there we learn also that she worked with a white woman, Sue Hampton, on the text.

The battler autobiography or biography, in which the emphasis is on the true account of an individual, usually poor and deprived, winning through in spite of her handi-caps of race and social position, is an ideological text, espe-cially when written by an Indigenous person and especially when any criticism of the social and economic structure of Australia is excluded. In effect it supports the Australian dream, which is that any person, including even Indigenous persons, with a bit of guts and determination can come to terms with their lives in the Australian nation without querying the fact that many others do not come to some recognition and never become reconciled to their place. Of course, in this genre, national power relations are often ignored or edited out to keep the narrative flowing.

White academic Joy Hooton (1990), when writing about Indigenous women's literary productions, suggests that she reads most Indigenous 'autobiographies' as directed towards a white readership and tender of 'white suscepti-bilities'. This is backed up by black academic Dr Roberta Sykes' (1988) assertion that, when white people receive a more positive picture of Indigenous people, they will come to respect Indigenous culture. Of course, this might

be challenged in that the 'positive picture' will simply be
what the main Australian readership wants to read and if
they do not get it they will either simply ignore the book,
or pan it. This is not just a matter of conjecture, for we
have the case of what happens when an Indigenous author
in collaboration writes a successful book, then follows it
up with one which is produced (subject to the editorial
policies of the publisher) solely by her own self, that is,
she as joint author becomes the sole authority of her own
work. Ruby Langford Ginibi's *Don't Take Your Love to Town*
(1988) received better-than-average sales and continues to
sell well. Her second book, *Real Deadly* (1992), a collection
of short sketches, did not fare as well. It was reviewed in
the *Weekend Australian* (28–29 March 1992) by Mary Rose
Liverani with the title, 'From Outside, Without Insight',
which concludes:

> *If a white had written this manuscript it would have gone straight
> on to the publisher's reject pile. In publishing* Real Deadly, *Angus
> & Robertson may have opened up a Pandora's box. What if those
> armies of unpublished writers clamouring to be heard start claiming
> Aboriginal ancestry?*

This may, of course, have already happened or, with the
growth of the policy of reconciliation, those who re-identify
as Indigenous or even assert that they are, may end up
being published. This is only one of the many contradictions of the culture industry and the government control of
it in Australia. In fact, the problem is not one of identity as
such, but of Liverani's failure to appreciate any part of the
volume. She feels that Ruby cannot write and, not only
this, she finds the content offensive and immoral. Unlike
Morgan's *My Place*, it does not bring tears to her eyes, but
revulsion to her heart, and by so doing she enters into the
discourse of moral judgement and condemnation which has
gone on since the invasion. If one reads the reports of the
various government departments of Indigenous affairs and
welfare agencies, one will find a blanket condemnation of
Indigenous women as being not only unfit mothers, but
unfit women. This is not what the general readership wants
to read about Indigenous women, so how better to remove

it from view than by having the services of a good editor, who can not only tidy up the style of the manuscript, but also the content as well. In this era of reconciliation the mainstream readership wants their Indigenous people to be either as close to themselves as possible or as further away as possible; that is, to be completely assimilated as to be a darker shade of white, or to be as completely the other and as black as possible. The savage is to be noble, with all that that implies, and even if she isn't, nobleness must be shining through the black.

But what I write here as simple oppositions must not be taken as simple oppositions. What we must be aware of is that there is a reconciliation process which encompasses the assimilated and the unassimilated, that the value of being completely assimilated so as not to be offensive is offset by the value of being completely Indigenous. Both show that the social processes of the Australian nation are working, that those Indigenous people who want to be raised to the level of the general Australian population can be, while those who wish to remain separate, but part of a multicultural Australia, may do so strengthened with the understanding that their culture is accepted as being the foundation of the nation of Australia. Their paintings, their writings, their very beings can be accepted in all their differences. They are not us, but we appreciate their lovely culture and especially the love of our land in which we all should share.

One of the problems with this type of Indigenality, however, is that it is seen as being a singularity. When Indigenous people are written about, it is always from a position of singularity: 'the Aboriginal people of Australia'. And so, instead of a multitude of communities producing texts, we have a singular Indigenous writing or a compilation of Indigenous women's writing, ignoring many of the signs of difference. Thus, if I did stress an Indigenality of women's writing, this would be wrong, as many of these texts show an individuality of style and content which might be as foreign to some Indigenous women as it would be to mainstream women. We see this when we come to examine some of the texts, though we must remember that a succession of government policies has served to give many Indigenous women a singularity of experience and that, in autobiographical writings, this singularity is what is often dealt with rather than an existence outside of it. In effect, writing-as-truth limits the imagination to what has been experienced.

Karobran (1978) is said to be the first novel, or rather biographical text, written by an Indigenous woman, Monica Clare. Instead of a separation between Indigenous and non-Indigenous societies, this urban Koori lived out her life within mainstream Australia and allied to the trade union movement. After her death, the text was edited by her white friends, Jack Horner and Mona Brand, with, as they claim, sensitivity to the author's style and content.

An Aboriginal Mother Tells of the Old and the New (1984) is a rural work written by the Mornington Island woman, Labumore (Elsie Roughsey). It is a completely different work to *Karobran*, with a separation between Indigenous and non-Indigenous, and is a lament for forgotten ways. Labumore managed to escape much of the assimilatory processes as found in the towns, though she did go through the mission dormitory system, and her English is not that of the city, but rather is a Kriol. Kriol, it has been argued, is a language in its own right and differs markedly from standard English; but the text, in order to see publication, was edited by Paul Memmott and Robin Horseman, non-Indigenous people who in an afterword explain their editing process: 'It became apparent that some editing would be required in order for it to be accepted as a commercial publication, and accessible to the average white Australian reader.' It might be asked what would have happened to what is regarded as a masterpiece of modern narrative, *Finnegan's Wake*, if James Joyce had accepted the advice of kindly editors? I doubt that his work would have ever seen the light of day.

What is happening to the Indigenous text? Is it being destroyed in favour of a reconciliatory text likely to be read by a mainstream readership? Are we, given the often silence of the writer at the end of an editing process, engaging in Indigenous strategies (as said by some academics) of constructing a cultural identity as a mode of resistance, or simply being dictated to by the marketplace? These are pertinent questions when we come to examine Indigenous women's texts and those which receive acceptance. These are similar to *My Place* in that they involve a search for identity or a battle for survival. I read Ruby Langford Ginibi's latest book in manuscript and found it exhilarating: the rediscovery of Ginibi's community through a series of journeys, though without the need of a sudden discovery of identity. In manuscript it was a vast sprawl of a work, a container for all of Ginibi's discoveries of the history of her community and a remeeting with old friends and relatives. It was a friendly and an Indigenous discovery of the Bundjalung country and what had happened there. When it was published, I reread her text, *My Bundjalung People* (1994), and found that much had been changed or omitted, that it had been tightened up, though there were still none of the trappings of the battler genre or the discovery of a personal identity. Perhaps, for the mainstream reader, it might read better than the original manuscript; but, for all this editing, it has to a great extent been ignored in favour of *Don't Take Your Love to Town*. Why is this so? I would hazard a guess and say that it is because it is not in an acceptable genre. It lacks the struggle implicit in the battler genre, or the discovery of antecedents as found in the romance. So who would her readers be? I would say those who know and have developed a love for her Bundjalung country and those who have come to know and love Ruby through meeting her and reading her previous work.

There is another strategy employed by Indigenous writers to get their work across: attending literary conferences and making personal appearances. Naturally this is similar to how all writers proceed. It is to get to know your readership and to let the readers get to know you. If this is not done, all that remains is to let the editors have the final word, to let them edit the manuscript in order to make it presentable to, what they regard as, the general readership. In many ways, this is dangerous and assimilationist rather than reconciliationist. What is needed is a two-way process and I will go into what this entails later, through the experiences of Jackie Huggins.

The problem of collaboration, rather than of simple editing, is found in the 1990 book, *Ingelba and the Five Black Matriarchs*, by Patsy Cohen and Margaret Somerville, where the editor enters as co-author. As Somerville writes:

'Hers is the Aboriginal story, the story of her life and the people that go to making her sense of that life. Mine is the process of conducting a written text.' In writing the text she decided to use Aboriginal English which, in a later explanation (1991), she said that Patsy Cohen was against. In other words, Patsy wanted her book to be a written text, whereas Margaret Somerville wanted (and got her way) to produce a written text which had all the signs of orality, or of telling a story. This is laudable if the author or storyteller agrees, and I for one love the Indigenous voice which comes through in oral storytelling. In fact, it may be said that I like it because that was the type of English I spoke as a child and when I write or speak it brings back a sense of community. But still, it is after all the decision of the storyteller what sort of English she wants her story to be written in and I know that, for some Indigenous writers, our way of talking is a lost way. Then again, I know that Indigenous writers know what a book is supposed to be and want their book to be exactly like what they term a 'real' book. There has been continuing debate about this in Indigenous circles and often those living in the cities are alienated from Kriol, or Indigenous English, and must make use of standard English if they decide to express themselves.

But I would say that these are Indigenous concerns and also the concerns of the writer or storyteller. Margaret Somerville in her article, 'Life (Hi)story Writing' (1991), about her collaboration with Patsy Cohen uses what verges on new age feminism to stress that her working on *Ingelba and the Five Black Matriarchs* was for her a journey of self-discovery. Her ideology needs quoting in full, for it is the argument of many new age feminists who seek to find a matriarch within themselves, and it explains why they collaborate and make decisions which in effect take away decision-making from the Indigenous author or storyteller:

> *It was easier to overcome the silences imposed on the written form in the case of finding a voice for Patsy than it was in finding a voice for myself. In traditional histories, the writer herself is absent, a ghost writer. Patsy spoke loud and clear within her own oral discourse. However I still needed to be able to answer the question*

*'Who am I?' in relation to this text. I had not avoided the problem
by writing about Patsy because according to my feminist framework
I could no longer be the conventional 'ghost' writer of life history.
The telling of Patsy's life was created out of the particular context of
our relationship so I needed to be present in the text.*
(p. 107)

But that is how many Indigenous people once saw
European people—as 'ghosts'—and so now we have a
ghost refusing to be a ghost, or denying her ghosthood. 'I
too am human', she cries, and then proceeds to dictate the
terms of her assumption of her humanity. It is her refusal to
be silent, her refusal to let an Indigenous voice speak that
she too asserts her humanity, though perhaps never having
been denied it except by those Indigenous people who
were soon denied theirs by such ghosts. In effect, Margaret
Somerville is asserting an essential universal femininity
which equates her with Indigenous people who have
suffered oppression and a denial of humanity. In effect,
Margaret Somerville in writing her book, in dictating the
terms about what is an authentic Indigenous text, has
found herself and become the 'ghost' matriarch stressing
her claims at the expense of Patsy Cohen.

It is time to turn my attention to a collaborative text by
two black women, mother and daughter, and how the
problems of contradiction, of collaboration, of editing and
publishing were handled. The question here, which I
believe should be raised time and time again, is that, if you
don't know the country and the people, how can you really
write about them, not having the necessary images in the
mind, or the permission to do so. I am talking now about
Auntie Rita, 'Auntie' being a term of respect and love in our
communities, and the emphasis of the text would change
if the title were 'Mother Rita' or 'Mum Rita'. 'Auntie' is a
term that denotes a respect which goes beyond biological
motherhood. If this was not so, Jackie Huggins, the daughter, would not have called her book this. It has a meaning
which goes beyond motherhood and matriarchy, which is
not one of our terms.

I have called Tiddas' writing 'lifestories' in order to
escape the genre of biography or autobiography which

often does not fit this kind of writing. 'Auto' in this sense means 'self' and biography too is concentrated on self, often to the exclusion of community. When we come to *Auntie Rita* (1994), we enter the realm of collaboration; not the collaboration between an Indigenous woman and a European person, but that between a Queensland Murri woman and her daughter. There are two voices at work in the text, explaining and setting Auntie Rita's and Jackie's words down. For Auntie Rita the text tells the story of her life, but for Jackie the project is different, as she explains in the first section 'Writing the Book':

> *The writing of this book was an attempt to reclaim the history of our people. To do this is to encounter a double fold of silence. Each fold is of the same cloth—two centuries of colonisation. There are the acts of violence that attempted to alienate (with varying degrees of success), Black people's access to knowledge of their own culture and its history …*

In doing this, Jackie recovers her own mother's history and situates it within her own experience as a Murri woman. She establishes a continuity which has not been broken and there is the underlying sympathy of the mother–daughter relationship which works beyond the outsider premise found in Morgan's *My Place*. Identity here is not to be recovered, as if it were a thing, but a continuing Murri experience which is unbroken.

I have written elsewhere that structure is just as important as content, and so the structure of the Huggins' narrative reveals how the mother–daughter shared history gives a degree of authenticity not often found, especially in those lifestories or histories written by 'born-again Aborigines'. This authenticity is stressed by Jackie in a 1992 article: 'Yes, I too have lived through every one of those feelings as she related them to me. By virtue of being Rita's daughter, and a close one at that, I possess many of her experiences.'

It has been said that, since the publication of Morgan's *My Place* (1987), there is a market niche for Indigenous women's lifestories; but, once accepted, they are often given low priority, which can have serious implications in that often the lifestories are from elderly Indigenous women who want to see their experiences in print before they die. Furthermore, when the collaborator is working closely with the writer, any elucidations of the material are in danger of being lost. A further point which needs to be clarified is the position of publishers' editors, although this is being redressed by such mainstream publishers as University of Queensland Press and Harper Collins where often the editing seeks to be sensitive to the nuances of Indigenous English, often so much so that Indigenous texts written in standard English are now in danger of becoming Indigenised. Sometimes, even when the editing is done with the best intentions, discrepancies arise, such as I found in Herb Wharton's latest volume of short stories, *Where Ya' Been, Mate?* (1996), where the written style, especially in the introduction and some of the beginnings of his stories, distracts from some of his yarns. In fact, other readers have commented on this with 'That ain't Herb'. One old stockman who read Herb's *Unbranded* (1992) exclaimed: 'Has he ever worked cattle?' This was in response to the substitution of the American 'stampede' for the Australian 'cattle rush'. I quote these two examples because they show that often even the best-intentioned editing can introduce an inauthenticity into the text which is picked up by those readers who are outside the mainstream and who read books when they do because they have had similar experiences.

Jackie Huggins is a product of mainstream education and thus should be able to deal with the vagaries of the publishing process. Yet, she too had to confront the problems inherent in getting published a text that lacks the romantic appeal of similar volumes. This means that an editing process is put into position which shifts Indigenous storytelling from the oral to the written. Jackie was sent repeated requests for footnotes in explanation of Murri exclamations such as 'Look out' and 'Good go'. Jackie says that she tried to explain them, but that they were unexplainable and that there were no accurate standard English translations. In this regard it must be said that sometimes there is an ambiguous area on the borderlines between meanings, much as we see in the poetry of Lionel Fogarty, and this ambiguity threatens those who have a great knowledge of standard English, but not of the dialects which seek to de-establish the concrete meaning which dictionaries and those who compose them seek to give words. This is the case with the Indigenous Englishes which threaten (as do all dialects) the hegemony of a standard English. This is what aware publishing houses seek to address through sensitive editorial help. Jackie Huggins was initially encouraged to put her manuscript into 'acceptable prose'. The editors subsequently travelled to her country to learn more about Murri English and the book was again restructured into mother and daughter talking together. This case illustrates the problems inherent in the editing process if Indigenous writers are expected to conform with non-Indigenous notions of biographical writing.

This story about the publishing of a book with a central concern for authenticity and truth-telling does raise the problem of how this truth is to be presented and the underlying processes which enter into the truth-telling process. But where exactly does the truth lie? I would answer that it lies in both the content and the structure of the story being told; that if we are not careful the demon of genre will enter into the discourse to traumatise the text and produce a volume able to fit into the publishing programmes of those publishers who wish to sell as many books as possible. As a marketing device, genre conformity, especially in autobiography and biography, is successful; but when it is queried and the result is published, visions of the bestseller recede. Publishing is a political process as much as is the structure and content of the product. In a market where the original and the progressive, the contentious and the different, is written out as not conforming to the dictates of a national identity and a reconciliation process all structured and written in a discourse which allows for national self-congratulation rather than national analysis, those books which explore our estrangement rather than add to our good feeling will always be pushed to the periphery. Whether we like it or not, the fringe is still there and it holds those books which do not conform to the national consensus.

Reconciling Our Place 13

THE COMMONWEALTH GOVERNMENT OF AUSTRALIA decided to reconcile the Indigenous people to their place in the nation. The Council for Aboriginal Reconciliation was launched with great fanfare; but Indigenous writers and activists were excluded from the initial deliberations, though when the council was reformed Jackie Huggins and Marcia Langton were given seats. Marcia Langton also was the only writer to contribute to their publications which covered the whole range of Indigenous affairs. I would have thought that Indigenous writers might have been given more of a role in the planning and publishing of such works. This did not happen and they have become reconciled to their place which appears to be outside such government bodies, though reconciliation has been an important theme for many Indigenous writers. The work which has contributed much to this process is Sally Morgan's *My Place* which has sold over 300 000 copies worldwide.

If you ask people in Australia and overseas to name a book written by an Indigenous person, they will respond by naming *My Place*. This does bring into question the author and the authority of a written text and the place in question, though if you ask a person to name an Indigenous artist, he or she will shake their heads, and eventually might say: 'Albert Namatjira', who found a different place indeed, being stripped of his honorary citizenship status and thrust back onto a reserve. He found a place indeed, but then that was some decades ago and things have changed—or have they? Indigenous art also has found a place in Australia, but it seems that the individual artist (perhaps again with the exception of Sally Morgan) has not. This may be in line with the ideology which holds that Indigenous art is 'primitive' and thus without an authorship, except for gallery owners and art connoisseurs, like Jennifer Isaacs. The place of Indigenous art is as much a site of contention as the Indigenous written text. In both, white experts mediate the texts and attempt a reconciliation. Thus, an examination of a written text such as *My Place*, and how it functions and interrelates with particular historical and cultural concerns, I label reconciliation—not only the reconciliation of Indigenous people to the nation of Australia, but the reconciliation of the general population of Australia to the land of Australia. *My Place* is central to these concerns as it traces an individual identity (one identifying with the general Australian settler population) through to an identification with the Indigenous people and thus with the land of Australia. Symbolically, it is a journey which all individuals residing in Australia must make. I am not saying that all Australians must seek out and claim Indigenous ancestry, but that they must become reconciled to being citizens of an independent Australia and thus with the land.

The conscious quest for a national identity for Australia and its citizens achieved one of its peaks in 1988, the bicentenary of the British invasion of Australia and the beginning of the plight of the Indigenous inhabitants. The state and Commonwealth governments at that time provided funding for the celebrations and, though *My*

Place was not a commissioned bicentenary work, Sally Morgan received funds to write her second and less well-known book, with the almost unpronounceable title: *Wanamurraganya*, which was published in 1989 after the celebrations. *My Place* was published in 1987, in time to be caught up in the wave of national reflection sweeping towards 1988. Indigenous culture and its productions were sites of contestation in that they were seen to serve a crucial role in legitimating 200 years of European presence in Australia. The Indigenous communities split on the issue, just as they have split on reconciliation; but there were many takers of bicentennial funding, just as there are many takers of reconciliation funding. Not only this, but there was a counter-celebration of Indigenous people in Sydney which fitted into the discourse of contemporary multicultural Australia. This discourse argues the necessity of all minorities in Australia being allowed to have their say, as long as they do so in a way which does not conflict with the dominant policy of national unity. In fact, in such a discourse, Indigenous protest can be seen as being an acceptable part of Australian nationality, and not threatening at all.

My Place also found a place in the genre of Indigenous women's writing which was then, with some help from the feminist movement, separating from Indigenous writing as a monolithic response to white colonisation. Texts by Indigenous women were placed in the debate that gender comes before Indigenality, and so *My Place* can be compared with Drusilla Modjeska's *Poppy* which deals with similar concerns.

Earlier Indigenous women writers, such as Monica Clare, Shirley Smith, Margaret Tucker and Oodgeroo, were more concerned with their community and how it should advance, rather than with singular searches for identity. These writers along with male writers maintained a strong connection between writing and politics. They in fact were committed writers and active workers in their communities. Sally Morgan, in contrast, was an outsider approaching the Indigenous communities, and from a personal rather than a political space. Her book, with its individual concerns of tracing a family history and thus an Australian identity, reached the world just when many other (often female) Australians were engaging in a similar project of seeking to understand their connection with the land and with the Australian past in general. The newly identified Indigenous woman, Sally Morgan, more rather than less, became the authority on such quests. The structure of her story gave a foundation to this self-reflective site on which the national home could be built. Well-written and edited, and structured around the quest and confessional modes, *My Place* enabled Australians of a similar bent to uncover a similar though not identical 'truth' in their own genealogies, which they knew had always been there. What was more, any politics of difference was downplayed and the Australianness of everyone was emphasised to such an extent that the original British invaders were seen to have Indigenous ancestors, though this 'secret' in the book remains a secret for the astute reader to work out in much the same way as genealogical secrets are worked out. The realm we are in, whether it is understood or not, is that of romance, and perhaps I should extend romance further to call such literature, 'romances of reconciliation', especially when the political is eschewed for the fairytale princess discovering her noble birth. Essentially, the message is 'we are all Aussies, aren't we', and any differences are covered over in a wish for a post-reconciliation republic governed by a benign president.

The late French theorist Michel Foucault, in his paper 'What is an Author' (1979), has this to say about the author: 'The third characteristic of the author function is that it does not develop spontaneously as the attribution of a discourse to an individual. It is, rather, the result of a complex operation which constructs a certain rational being that we call "author"' (p. 150). This is important when we consider the complex Sally-Morgan-as-author and the functions it fulfils. What must be admitted is that Sally Morgan has extended to fill a space and in so doing has become Indigenous-person-as-author. She fulfils this function not only for the person in the street, but also in the colleges and universities where her position is unassailable. This is not to say that her position of authority has not been questioned, but such is the power of the authority that such questionings are easily ignored. In stressing the importance of *My Place* and Sally Morgan, what must not be ignored is the very matrix which enabled the book to be an all-time bestseller.

I have said that Australia was ready for such a work and when it appeared it was readily taken up. It is often said and written that an Indigenous writer (male or female) who writes transforms his or her history, culture and society from an oral to a written form. This is often a statement made by critics; but what happens, we may ask, when the Indigenous writer is not only literate, but is discovering what purports to be her culture? This is one of the sites of contestation between Sally Morgan and literary critics. This is not an Indigenous person writing about her community from a position of knowledge, but an outsider discovering that culture and an identity. Always, we are aware of the individual seeking an identity and in effect resolving the basic split in Australian society: that between invader and Indigenous populations. What this romance effects on the page, the Council for Aboriginal Reconciliation seeks to do on a political and social level.

My Place is a romance. It tells four stories within the boundaries of the author narrative. As a romance it deals with antecedents and the child engaging in a quest to discover her 'true' parentage. This quest for 'truth' continues on when her mother and grandmother are subjected to questions to reveal the secret of her birth. In Chapter 21 she has discovered her Indigenality and is very excited about it. One can see the emotion behind the words and, in my explanation of the success of *My Place*, this is similar to the intense discovery of Australianness which was happening in 1987 and reached a climax in 1988. In fact, there was a veritable crowd of people discovering their long-lost Indigenality, one of whom was the important poet Les Murray who was delighted to find himself with an Indigenous family.

My Place is an Australian text, romance, autobiography, or what you will. What Indigenality is in the text has come from a white readership who at last found an Indigenous text which did not shout at them and in fact mirrored their concerns as to their place in Australia. If we do accept *My*

Place as an Indigenous text, then criticism will always be levelled at this well-written story for not being 'real' enough, as Isabel Tarrago (1993) writes: 'If we are to read the "real" writings of Aboriginal people, then one has to be part of the understanding and to live the life of Aboriginal people.' The problem with such assertions of 'reality' is that there is an educated readership now for what is considered more authentic Indigenous writing and it is this readership which condemns Sally Morgan for not being 'real' enough. This is a problem in itself, as it ignores the fact that the very transcending of 'reality' by the romance genre has made this book accessible to a wide readership.

Murri writer Jackie Huggins (1993) also criticises *My Place*, or rather the author, and declares that it has been Sally Morgan's white readership that has given her the status of 'Aboriginal writer'. I believe that this comes from a confusion of reality and text, although when one writes a 'true' story then the authority who put it together also has a part in the complicity between writer and reader to accept it as 'true' rather than as a 'novel'. By using the word 'novel', I know I am distancing the author from her work; that is, she becomes a storyteller and, instead of receiving her book as 'truth' and accepting or rejecting it on these grounds, I see it as either a good or bad story and judge it accordingly. This is in line with Carole Ferrier's paper (1992) on Indigenous women's narratives:

> *Aboriginal women's narratives have most commonly been cate-gorised as life histories or life writing. This placed them within a particular genre, by implication closer to history than to literature. However, to read them as novels allows them to make an interven-tion in the latter field; allows, for example, the possibility of discussing them as a book.*

Of course, this may seem to be simplistic, but we should be aware that if we do allow such 'true' stories to be read as novels, which I take to mean fictional constructs, then my approach to *My Place* as a romance dealing with the discovery of origins is important in that such a story (whether it is fictional or not) struck a chord in a general readership who were coming to grips with what precisely it meant to shift one's origins from overseas to the land of Australia. *My Place* in this scenario is a text of Australian nationalism and identity, rather than a text of Indigenality, and this explains its great success.

Australianness is where the value of *My Place* lies, not in any assumption of an Indigenality which to give it meaning, anyway, needs to have 'Australian' placed before it. *My Place* might be said to open up the hidden agenda of reconciliation found in more strident texts. In this scenario, instead of seeing reconciliation as being imposed on Indigenous people from above, it would mean that it is truly meeting the aspirations of many Indigenous people to be treated equally and without prejudice in a united Australia. In books like *My Place*, there is no message of any separatism, or really of any political identity of a dynamic nature; rather, we are in the realm of identity for the sake of one's wholeness, a new age phenomenon which seems to suit some. In *My Place*, therefore, identity is or seems to be something waiting to be discovered, and this individual identity to a great extent reflects the popular approach of the assumption of an Australian identity, though one which, on reflection, seems to be made up of any number of warring elements brought together in an uneasy peace, and too often threatening to split apart. What Graeme Turner (1994) writes about Australian nationalism (collective identity) could just as well be applied to individual identity:

> So wide is the field of critique within the humanities and social sciences that resistance to the orthodox definitions of Australianness has become something of a minor orthodoxy in itself. Indeed, Cochrane and Goodman argue that the Bicentenary failed to produce the sense of a unified nation because the very idea of 'nation' is no longer secure in the Australian popular consciousness.

This I would apply to individual identity, especially when it involves a finding of a latent Indigenality. As Marcia Langton (1993) writes: 'Aboriginality is a field of intersubjectivity that is remade over and over again in a process of dialogue, of imagination, of representation and interpretation. Both Aboriginal and non-Aboriginal people create Aboriginalities.' Such a statement more or less puts finis to any essential subjectivity and thus the subject-as-Aboriginal may simply be seen as a fictional construct. This is where literature and *My Place* have such an important place. By questioning and discussing Indigenality, there occurs a displacement in that, instead of discussing Indigenality, we are really discussing what it is to be an Australian.

So, in conclusion, we can see that a literature which was once an ongoing part of the Indigenous struggle for justice and equal rights has shifted its field—from defining and describing an Indigenality, to seeking to have a voice in the ongoing discourse of what it is to be an Australian. Thus it has passed from being confrontational and ignored to being reconciliatory, from being communal-oriented to being individualist. I would argue that this change in direction began with the publication and acceptance of *My Place* in 1987 when conditions were propitious for such a literature of reconciliation. It is from 1988, the bicentenary, that Indigenous art and literature entered the mainstream and the fringe became vacant, except for people who feel left out of the process of reconciliation. As Father Frank Brennan (1995) writes:

> ... *we need to discern the justice of the Aboriginal claims to land, allowing them to speak for country, thereby guaranteeing freedom to those whose ancestors settled and humanised this land tens of thousands of years before Abraham set out for Canaan. We might then discover the full life-sustaining capacity of the land for all Australians. We might live together as the Australian people. We might even design an appropriate flag for this one land, one nation so that all people of goodwill at the 2000 Olympics in Sydney will recognise us, and so Cathy Freeman and her fellow Australians might proudly gather under one flag.*

Appendix:
The Last Interview

(Mudrooroo talks with Janine Little and Carole Ferrier)

cf   When you talk about the novel form and the way it has been used by Aboriginal writers, I am reminded of something that Toni Morrison said in an interview in *Black Women Writers* that, originally, perhaps the most powerful form for African-American artists was music, but that now the novel is the most important and the main one through which the past history is being conveyed. You seem to have rather more reservations about the history of the novel form and what could be done with it than someone like Morrison does.

m   Well, I have a new chapter on what I call 'maban reality', which is a sort of magic realism. It is a return to the magic of Indigenous storytelling.

cf   Are you talking about writers like Sammy Watson?

m   Yes, and myself, of course. A novel is a work of fiction and so you can do more or less what you want with it. Sammy

Watson has done that, and so have I in *Master of the Ghost Dreaming*.

jl   In fact, it's those two novels, along with some of your other works, Muddy, that have proved most popular with readers in France and Holland, while in Australia the ones that could be classified 'realist', or non-fiction, do well. I think it's also interesting that your *Dr Wooreddy* shifts between both generic classifications, and seems to do so outside Australia, as if the historical distancing goes along with the geographical in creating space for that magical element to operate.

cf   That's what Morrison does in *Tar Baby*. It's set in the Caribbean, and she puts in these folk mythological or supernatural or anthropomorphic elements which impinge on magic realism in some ways, but it is still very closely tied into notions of black cultural understanding. This also brings in the question of what label you are putting on a text. It's been suggested that recently there's a shift away from the dominance (particularly in women's writing) of life writing or autobiography, and towards biography, with texts like Ginibi's recent work or *Auntie Rita* or Nugi Garimara/Doris Pilkington's *Follow the Rabbit-proof Fence*. Do you think this is the case and, if so, do you think it is happening with men's writing as well, and why?

m   Well, no, I've always had reservations about autobiography and biography as a genre. Labumore's work is not really autobiography or biography; it's a story of a whole community, rather than self. Sally Morgan's is a prime example of writing about self and so that's more autobiography. But I think the shift in men's writing is towards the novel.

cf   And often more experimental?

m   To a certain extent. In yarning, for example, there is experimental stuff already implicit in that, and so in men's writing, especially old Warrigal Anderson who won the 1995 David Unaipon Award, he uses this as well as writing poetry in Kriol. His work might be classified as a memoir, but I read it as a novel. Actually, with books like his, I am concerned about what happens in the editing process. It's a problem still with black texts, which are too often sanitised; all that invective against white people is edited out to get a nice white text.

cf It is actually in there, but is taken out for publication?

m That's what happens to our black texts. The thing is that now a lot of Aboriginal men's writing, especially, is humorous, though it probably depends on how people read it.

jl That's the issue of storytelling, in essence, isn't it? The inflections so often depend on physically picking up on the delivery. On paper a point can seem quite literal when, in fact, it was maybe ironic or satirical in the oral form.

cf Compared with quite a bit of African-American writing, for instance, there's not a huge amount of violence of language in most Aboriginal writing.

m No, I think that's because it's not allowed. The whole editing and publishing process comes into operation. It's a question of power and representation.

cf Unless it is possible that it's often not there when those particular genres are used?

jl I wouldn't think so. Aboriginal writers of the novel or poetry have the capacity to hold the genre to ransom, rather than the other way round. Do you think that's evident from what you know of any recent texts?

m It is there in Warrigal's book and there was a lot of Ginibi's manuscript which never saw the ink of the printing press.

cf Have you had a lot of stuff chopped out of your books, or have you not put it in?

m My recent *Us Mob* had about one-third chopped out. It depends what you want to do, of course. You can sort of nurse something for ever and ever and ever, or eventually let it go. An eternal struggle against white oppression gets tiring; you want to go back to your country and contemplate other things.

cf Are you saying that what was perceived as excessive language was chopped out, or was it a whole range of things?

m No, I think it was more like theory and so on. Any detailed argumentation and talking about things overlong, as it were. It might have been for the better.

jl I was thinking of the perception that Barbara Christian and Henry Louis Gates had, that when non-white writers started to try and apply some poststructuralist and general French theoretical methods, this was seen to be somehow inappropriate. There's this perception of a clean Aboriginality coming out. I don't know if the editor of *Us Mob* thought that there was much more value in a type of primordial Aboriginality being expressed, than any new sort of taking recourse to what was not Aboriginal or not Aboriginal language.

m   You see, some editors have learnt that there is an Aboriginal style, or so-called Aboriginal style, and so they can use it. The thing is that an Aboriginal does use an Aboriginal style and, although recourse may be made to theories such as are embedded in poststructuralism, well, French theorists rarely talk about the land.

jl   That is what has happened in the relatively recent type of Aboriginal publication; there has been a kind of perception of what is an Aboriginal text that ignores the fact that the text is highly mediated.

m   I blame myself for being one of the causes of it. There's an Aboriginal style, as we find in Ginibi's texts: the change of tenses and things like that, and also a different type of grammar. Any editor with a bit of experience can pick these up.

cf   That specific issue of what's perceived as violent or excessive is interesting because there is a kind of long-time historical construction of Aboriginal people, compared with a lot of other races, as relatively placid. Until very recently, the history of the actual physical resistance that did occur, despite the incomparability of the weapons, was almost entirely unwritten. But even perhaps a lot of Aboriginal people have been saying, well, Aboriginal people compared with Islanders, say, are quite placid. Has it got something to do with that, what might be quite a soothing construction for white Australia to put on the notion of the Aboriginal person, but something that would get challenged by a lot of explicitly violent language, such as you find in some African-American texts?

m   This came out in the 1988 demo in Sydney when they were talking about Aboriginal people as being prone to violence, and I was saying, no, they're not. But there's a contradiction here: on the one side, they're seen as excessively violent; on the other, they're excessively placid. The whole domestic violence issue amongst Aboriginal communities is one of the things that underlies that. The idea that if they could go back to their culture, or whatever, they wouldn't be like this. It is a reading based on those sorts of binary oppositions. It's more a new age notion of the noble savage than an actuality of Indigenality.

jl   That is what I meant by the primordial Aboriginality aspect. There is a perception of primordiality that's been built up through the recent publication history of Aboriginal texts, and that might come through in some ways when you are negotiating publication.

cf   They have found what they can sell, even if they can't necessarily endlessly sell more of the same. Something that does happen if you read a lot of it is that you do think, well, I've pretty well read that already. But presumably there is a new audience that hasn't read the other ones, so there is still space.

jl   That's why you've got to be careful about someone who runs an argument about seeing autobiography as transferring over to biography, because in some ways it can be seen as endorsing that type of collaborative ethic.

m   And there is a problem there, anyway: is *Auntie Rita* biography, or autobiography, or is it both? Once you start using these genre labels, that's where the problem arises and that's one of the reasons why I have used 'lifestory' instead of 'autobiography' or 'biography'. I think that would-be Indigenous writers must learn that, instead of striving for a truth-effect, they must also remember their readers. If I find a book boring, I switch off and so do a lot of readers, I think.

cf   In a lot of recent writing about genre, the term 'lifestory' tends to be used for something that's pretty close to oral history, that supposedly hasn't had much done to it. There's a notion that autobiography or biography has been more gone over.

m   Oscar Lewis is one who I think might write life history rather than lifestory. His *Children of Sanchez* was cleaned up; it was a bestseller and it reads really nicely. It is a bit like *My Place*, you know, readable.

cf   I agree overall with your comments about modern Western criticism and that there's a whole process of exclusion and of canons and so on. But I also think that, in a fairly substantial way, a lot of space has been opened up not just for non-Anglo-Celtic writing or gay writing or women's writing, but also for non-white writing. There was this fairly widespread shift, in some universities, right away from canonicity and value that produced some changes of taste and of ideas about other cultures being as interesting as British ones or whatever. It was not all terrific, but there was a quite substantial push from a minority of people to shift the climate and context, and it was remarkably successful through the seventies and early eighties. Though now what you've got with types of, say, postcolonial approaches is a certain demobilisation of some of that earlier, often explicitly political kind of demand for space and room and different ways of reading, trying to generate different ways of reading.

m   I think my argument was that we're in this sort of postmodern period and that, as the grand Western narrative fragmented, it allowed room for other voices to be heard. One of the reasons it occurred was because of economic conditions and a shifting in power centres in the world. Having a Western canon didn't fit the postmodern reality anymore.

jl   So you are saying that it is more of a reactive response from that small Western critical circle that tried to expand ... ?

m   I think it was reactive to everything. It wasn't because it was forced on them.

cf   Another thing that struck me in rereading *Writing from the Fringe* was that you're very generous towards anthropologists. You say that their role was comparatively positive historically compared with various other people. That's fairly controversial.

jl   It might be controversial if there's an idea of a hierarchy of kindness in the acquisition thing, do you think?

m   It's most likely controversial now because they were the only ones that collected the song cycles; in that way it's positive. Basically my argument is literature-based; a couple of anthropologists went to Indigenous people and saw literature there.

cf   There seems to be a bit of a feud going on between the historians and the anthropologists. James Weiner's recent article, 'The Secret of the Ngarrindjeri', passionately defends anthropology as the superior mode of knowledge;

oral history is considered a really inferior mode. It is a very anxious article, as well as quite aggressive. There is clearly something going on in relation to who gives the most accurate representation of a culture, which methodology is best. I don't think you necessarily have to pick one or another, and exclude what can be used in the others.

m   I don't think either gives an accurate representation. It's all a whole lot of white shit, anyway. It's only that sometimes we have a use for it.

jl   It gets really interesting when you also start thinking about boundaries around cultures, too, and who's crossing them, who's invading and who's being voyeuristic. It's all voyeurism, to a certain extent.

cf   I felt in that very passing comment that you were implying that anthropology had some sort of preferred status for you.

m   I came and I looked, eh? God, who cares about anthropology. Sitting on the verandah of some station and staring at the blacks. Strehlow who was in a privileged position castigated them. He said that they had theories, spent six weeks or so in the field collecting information, and went back and wrote it all up as if they knew everything. Strehlow could whinge like this because his father was a missionary, and because he played with black children and all the rest of it, so he felt that he was superior to any anthropologist.

cf   Instead of saying that something is a more useful or superior mode of discourse for certain kinds of purposes, a much more valuable activity is taking what you want from different disciplines. And then, when they come into conflict, this becomes an interesting issue because why is that happening? This gets lost if you go along with those particular constructed boundaries between different disciplinary knowledges.

m   In the Northern Territory Land Rights Act of 1976, which was passed by the Fraser Liberal government, the evidence which had to be supplied in regard to Indigenous ownership of land rested on anthropological data. The blacks couldn't be trusted, you see. Now, after Mabo and with the Native Title Act, continuing relationship to the land must have a historical basis. So there has been a shift from anthropological evidence to historical.

cf   The argument seems to be that anthropologists actually live with the cultures they are giving evidence about, whereas historians tend not to. That is not entirely true of all historians, but they probably don't immerse themselves in the same way.

m   Usually the anthropologists don't do that either.

cf   One of the things you did in *Writing from the Fringe* was give some sort of attention to the various ways you can reproduce knowledge of the past, or try to understand the past. There's these labels for it, like history or literature or anthropology or whatever—all with certain sets of dominant practices, and institutions they circulate within, that by and large have been very much dominated by the colonising culture. How far is it a constraint on your use of those different modes of knowledge that they are labelled and compartmentalised, or is it possible that a certain mode of inquiry has a certain set of concerns that are really important? Like, for example, the concern of a lot of literature with the aesthetic, or the supposed concern of history with truth, or the concern of anthropology with everyday behaviour that has certain kinds of social effects. Do you see those assumptions perhaps triggering off the possibility of thinking differently, or do they constrain an Aboriginal aesthetic? Are they things that you have to battle with because you are battling already with an alien mode of discourse?

m   With Aboriginal history, and with anthropology, you end up using white documentation, anyway. In literature you can do whatever you want to; you don't have to use historical or anthropological sources if you don't want to. We're talking about the freedom of the arts, of the imagination.

cf   You say several things about how you might describe or understand Aboriginality. You say it is 'the cultural system structured within the writing' at one point, then that 'Aboriginal reality is an expandable reality akin to the dreaming life'. You do that interesting analogy with surrealism, and then later on that Aboriginality is 'a metatext' in a lot of recent white criticism of not necessarily literature in particular but discursive constructions of Aboriginality. There is a whole dispute about whether this produces a fixed, essential notion of race. Does it tend to paralyse things in a more or less nostalgic mode? Some people will even say: how then, writing now, can we even use the term 'Aboriginality'? Then there are others saying, well, something that might sound essentialist is in fact tactical (Spivak uses the term 'strategic essentialism'). It is useful in various kinds of struggles for that to be constructed.

jl   When you have other critics also reading Aboriginal literatures for what has been called 'negotiated identity', where Kevin Gilbert's famous statement that 'You're either Aboriginal or you're not' gently slides into obscurity, I don't think working boundaries apply, do you?

m   I think there is a real problem involved with the term 'Aboriginality', and that's why I use say 'maban reality' or 'Indigenality', hoping to start the process again. There's lots of problems with constructing terms, they get taken over. The trickster character is in our maban reality to keep the boundaries fluid.

cf   So for literature, or writing in particular, it is an aspect of the economic base of that activity, perhaps? Aboriginality has to be reproduced in order to insist on a measure of economic power, which is actually enormously unequal. But if there hadn't been various kinds of tactical or strategic constructions of Aboriginality operating, say, in areas like landrights, then other constructions of it would have been different across the board.

jl   But look at what's happened to those strategies now. You find the very traditional, derogatory connotations of Aboriginality being turned against the landrights struggle, starting from attacks on the services, like the Aboriginal Legal Service, which are launched by individuals who could be constructed as fitting those tired stereotypes. I think literature becomes a crucial medium in a climate like this.

m   The thing is, if there is no Indigenality, you don't have an Indigenous literature. You have an Australian literature and a common culture. Indigenality is the basis of Indigenous culture, without that we have nothing.

cf   But perhaps then you would have a lot more in common with the rest of the Australian population?

m   Perhaps, and this is really what the Council for Aboriginal Reconciliation is seeking to do, putting across the idea that

'Aboriginal people are just like us'. It wipes out any difference, rather than promoting any sense of diverse cultural
difference.

jl   The Council, on one level, has to try and reconcile what is
happening interracially in the country, but then there is a
complete ambiguity about what 'race' actually is, and this
is why it comes back to an anti-racist type of argument. Is
race anything more or less than racism, and what is racism?
There seems to be a dire lack of understanding of what
race is.

cf   I think it is really useful to distinguish between race and
ethnicity, not just in Australia and not just for tactical
reasons, in relation to the Aboriginal community. I suppose
there are also kinds of class dimensions, where you have a
much more explicit class division that has maintained itself
in that you have still got enormous differentials in terms of
economic power between the Indigenous and other populations in general.

m   Well, race has always been a white thing, and blacks get
sucked into it. Indigenality and culture are the most important things. We exist as a distinct entity because of them.
There are even blacks now saying that we get too much.
We don't get too much.

jl   Does that go back to what you were saying before about
the Aboriginality of the city and the Aboriginality of the
country?

m   It does. A lot of Aboriginal people I know have nothing
except a tree to sleep under and people say we're all growing fat, we should all pull back, you've given us too much
money. This is how Indigenality is reported, that
Aboriginal people come up and say these things, when a
lot of Aboriginal people haven't got landrights or anything.

jl   Remember Kevin Gilbert, when he refused to take his
Human Rights Award because of the shocking state of
Aboriginal health and living conditions? Then you've got
the situation where more Aboriginal men are dying in
custody now than before the Royal Commission.

cf   Is it possible that your use of 'Indigenous', rather than
'Aboriginal', is an over-response that might ultimately not
be politically helpful for struggles in general? If people
stop using the term Aboriginality in literature and critical

theory, is it backing off from something that has still got strategic use, and does it also possibly incorporate the Torres Strait Islander population, in particular, in ways that aren't being given representation in your account as an Aboriginal person of particular aspects of Aboriginal cultural production?

m   The thing is that the whites have taken over our identity and they debate it with terms like 'essentialism'. Indigenality is very simple: if you have Aboriginal ancestry, Indigenous ancestry, Torres Strait or anything else, then you belong to Australia and you have your Indigenality. It doesn't matter how it functions, you are still an Indigenous person and there is no reason at all to debate it.

cf   Except that, since there are gigantic differences between the two Indigenous cultures, is that a problem for this construction? There is the common cause that's been made, with varying success, in terms of struggling with the gubbament, as Ruby calls it. But there's also a big gulf that opens up if you are dealing mainly with literary or cultural production, that's obscured if you use 'Indigenous' rather than 'Aboriginal'.

jl   Muddy, is your Indigenality now a pan-Indigenality in a similar way to Aboriginality being a pan-Aboriginality?

m   I believe in pan-Indigenality, otherwise communities are picked off one by one, as happens. If you are an Indigenous person, then you have to connect up with other Indigenous people across the world. Nations within nations. Indigenality means you come from a land, and you've been here for thousands of years and trace your descent back.

cf   I suppose, on one level, the construction of the Australian nation requires the appropriation or incorporation, or at least the presence, of various Indigenous manifestations. In 1988, there was wild running around throwing money at them so they could be seen.

m   This is where *My Place* comes into it, that the whole of the Drake-Brockmans have Aboriginal descent, that Sally Morgan belongs to their family and all the rest of it. And a lot of old English families, British families, can claim they are Indigenous. You have that strangeness happening, and

My Place has really cemented it in. I was amazed how many books there are in that bloody library at the University of Queensland, but the only Aboriginal author who has made it is Sally Morgan. So you have to ask why and one of the things, I think, is because she traces her descent back to an old English family as much as to an Aboriginal family, saying well, we belong to that sort of thing too, we're Indigenous. So you set up the whole genre of nationalism which does exclude migrants, anyway.

jl So *My Place* has reconciled two histories, a very short one and a very long one.

cf In *Writing from the Fringe*, you take up the 'personal success story' in relation to some Aboriginal women's writing. If you have these success stories of individual oppressed Aboriginal women, they give the white community reason to believe it is actually redressing the injustices of the past, and that's a problem. But you also comment on bleakness, lack of hope, in other Aboriginal writing, that you say you also have a problem with. It is too bleak, it is doing a construction of Aboriginal people as victims.

m Ruby Langford Ginibi and Herb Wharton are prime examples of that.

cf I think it was more the personal success story as embodied in the literary text rather than the individual.

jl Do you mean where somebody makes a 'grim' discovery and then they rise above it?

cf Yes, they somehow get on in Australian society and become moderately accepted or, at least, economically viable.

m In *Through My Eyes*, Ella Simon personifies that, but there are very few Aboriginal men who do it. At the end of *Wandering Girl*, Glenyse Ward postulates that everything is over and now everyone is going to be happy, my children are going to grow up to be doctors and lawyers and all that. The only problem is that she still lives in a caravan, last time I heard.

cf And all Australians can be doctors and lawyers, black or white.

jl Doesn't this sound familiar, a bit like the American Dream, à la the Cosby Show, where success is measured by changes of colourful pullovers and which Ivy League institution to go to—the agony of choice?

m   It's Kevin Gilbert who critiques that.

cf That was a false future; but then you said there was also some problem in saying there is no future, how can we get on, or do anything. It is a dialectical kind of complication.

m   The whole trouble is that the Reconciliation Council through government intervention has more or less made assimilation inevitable. Reconciliation means you assimilate, so all the government policies are towards educating black people into white society, and just about all the welfare programs, Abstudy, and all the rest of it are not used for Aboriginal people but to produce white people with brown skins. Instead of reconciliation, I prefer the term cooperation.

jl Different names, same old story.

cf You talk positively about access to the educational system of the colonisers, even though that is problematic in terms of its real tendency to wipe out Indigenous culture. But without access to the coloniser's culture, is the power available to challenge it?

m   It is, for Indigenous culture now. City Indigenous people have no formal Indigenous culture. Because of this they are at risk, in that they are told that the way forward is to become assimilated. Indigenality is a hindrance and should be got rid of. Once they have found some goals in life, they will stop drinking, get a job and become like all the rest of the city dwellers. In the country, the position of the Indigenous person is different. He or she is supposed to retain his or her culture and bring it into the Australia of the cities as a relic of the true Australia. It has been city people who have given an importance to Indigenous culture. It seems to be that it is because they feel that Australia needs Aboriginal culture to give it some sort of spirituality, and so Indigenous people who are in rural areas shouldn't be contaminated, but be allowed to remain as the spiritual guides of the whole continent.

jl But capitalism has already destroyed it, so Aboriginal people are asked to redress all of what capitalism has destroyed.

m   You write off urban Indigenous people as not having anything of value and so might as well assimilate, but you have to preserve rural Indigenous culture, or what is constructed as Indigenous culture. You even have Indigenous people aspiring to remain in their culture, like John Tatten with his boomerangs. He has that Indigenality coming in culturally, but then he is more than a city black. He has lived in Alice Springs and acquired the knowledge and the skills. Indigenous artists and writers are like this, they can dive deep into Indigenous culture and come back with cultural treasure. Lin Onus is another one who has done that.

jl   You commented earlier that once capitalism has destroyed everything else, all people have is to go back into their own familial groups. Do you think that this can be racialised in any way, or is it a symptom of capitalism, for everybody, given that there's been as much non-Aboriginal biography and family writing, and personal narrative, introspective narrative?

m   I was saying that Indigenous men don't write family histories, Indigenous women do. I haven't yet read a Sal Morgan.

jl   So it is gendered?

m   It is. Warrigal Anderson writes of his adventures rather than his family. It is really nice reading.

jl   When I spoke to some Aboriginal women about this, and why there is so much domestic violence, the way the conversation went was that the issue of domestic violence was attached to literary production because Aboriginal women produce always in an environment of being involved with every other issue as well. They said it was because colonisation has taken the strength out of Aboriginal males and they have no power any more.

cf   That's almost a cliché of African-American culture, isn't it?

m   Really, you would have to look at what the Indigenous family was. It was a completely different set-up. Women are more or less custodians of genealogy, and now the problem is that in Indigenous genealogy it's a mother which you know for certain bears a child, never the father. The father is more or less accidental. In Nyungar society, a man hasn't got much responsibility for his children at all; you have the grandmothers and all the rest. Then, if the whole system's in place, when the male kids reach 9 or 12, they would be taken away and put through initiation to become men. Now, how do you put the European system among that, especially in areas where people are not used to it?

jl   I think that the idea of chronicling your life, or a family history, being a symptom of what capitalism has done through imperialism, is interesting. But then there seems to be quite a strong bourgeois obsession with doing it as well.

m   In Indigenous cultures I know of, the genealogist is usually a granny, and they sit around and work out who belongs to whom. One thing is that they don't write books.

jl   I am reminded of a comment by an elderly family friend who said that being taken away from their family and put in an institution was the best thing that ever happened to them, that without that institutionalisation their lives would have been much worse, that they would have been much more in danger had they been left where they were.

cf   So that's where we get back to people like the missionaries and their whole dialectical role as well. On the one hand, as purveyors of the oppressive white culture and then, on the other hand, as the preservers. You are actually soft on the missionaries in *Writing from the Fringe*, about their offering a type of education that might have been useful.

m   Well, many Indigenous people had some kind of education from them, and it shouldn't be forgotten that some of us are descended from them on the father's side. All in all, we did receive some education, for which we're thankful.

jl   So where do you think that comments like: 'I would have been much worse off if I hadn't been put in a mission' come from?

m   They come from that whole mission thing that Indigenous people are dirty and naked and hanging around out there, and who knows what they are doing; they've got to be civilised. You had the mission compound where people were put, and those that conformed were seen as good. Then you had the other people camping around it, just being Indigenous, and this caused a split: mission boy and maid, and the others looking at the new Jackies and Marys. Those who could handle it, handled it.

jl   Talking about the differences in experience between Aboriginal women and men, has the law had an influence on the male community more than on the women's community, so that the heavy impact of being incarcerated has been felt primarily by the men?

m   No, this is getting back into an outlaw thing, where you get a warrant and you split.

cf   Except you could say that it was more oppressive to be the person looking after everybody than the one doing the interesting thing, being in jail or something.

jl   Ruby said that in *Nobby's Story*.

cf   And possibly less psychologically taxing. If you are actually doing something, you are being active; if you're the one picking up all the pieces and holding everybody together, that's a horrible role.

m   Unfortunately, that is the role Indigenous women are placed in. At least in Nyungar society to a great extent, unless the men have a job that gives some sort of security, you tend to have them going off all the time. This comes through very strongly in the male Indigenous texts. You don't have to hang around, you can always go, you have that sort of freedom which is part of the Australian myth.

cf   The definitions of political seem to be complicated here, because there is a lot of political interest in, if you like, gender politics or strong women getting to survive, whatever you read in *Don't Take Your Love to Town*.

m   I just see it as a white wank, to tell you the truth. I think *My Bundjalung People* is a much better book because it is more community; she goes back to community and establishes those links and it is a very strong woman's text.

cf   Relatively public issues for the community rather than private?

m   No, not private, because it is community which is most important in Indigenous culture; this is what she set up and so it's one of the reasons why her book is being ignored. *Don't Take Your Love to Town* was in the battler genre. Here's a woman by herself doing all that, who goes back and finds that other women have been doing the same thing, and meets all her mates and so on. It is completely ignored because it is not the white way, and also because it has been edited. Once, it was a huge manuscript.

jl   Are you saying that, while Ruby was seen to be doing something similar to Sally Morgan, that was okay and she would be accepted because she was an individual, but as soon as she started to establish some sort of collectivity …?

m   Yeah, it was wiped out. Once you start going beyond perhaps your first book and do things like that, it's ignored.

cf   It's possible there was also a very strong reception for *Don't Take Your Love to Town* from a (mainly white) women's movement that was much more political in the seventies and eighties, but now can't necessarily engage on a more widespread scale with Ruby attempting to move into what you might say were more public concerns, that a lot of Aboriginal women before that hadn't engaged with publicly or written.

m   *Nobby's Story* comes out of it, Ruby engaging with her son.

jl   You get that classic part where she writes to Nobby and says: 'Don't you think you're the only one involved in this, because when you go to jail we all go to jail with you.'

m   So all those things are really important, but the whole white movement is individuals doing things; that's the most important thing. You have Drusilla Modjeska's *Poppy*, writing about her mum and coming through as an individual. Ruby is doing the same thing, coming against her life and coming through.

cf   But Drusilla had a rather more comfortable time with it perhaps than Ruby did.

m   But we are talking about genre here, not about the content. They are very similar, much like Sally Morgan, she had the same upbringing, that's where all the problems arise, apart from the fact she almost destroyed her family in writing the book. If somebody says don't do that, you don't do it because the story must be told.

cf   Probably writers often destroy their families if they write books, don't they?

m   But Sally Morgan isn't exactly a writer. You have that thing that must be told, but who is it to be told to? If your grandmother or your mother says, well, I don't want to tell that, you don't do it.

jl   That was what Jackie was doing with *Auntie Rita*, she was saying a lot of the things that Rita didn't want to talk about.

cf   But you said it was more interesting if it also talked about Jackie as well as Rita. Jackie said to me that, at one point, Rita didn't want Jackie in the book at all. She just wanted her to be the oral historian that she had been trained to be, to say exactly what Rita wanted told without even asking a question.

m   Jackie does that, doesn't she? That's the difference.

cf   To a certain extent. I think beyond that she couldn't because of family pressure that's probably more on a woman than a man.

m   It is in most Indigenous books. Kevin Gilbert might be the only one that escapes that.

cf   Can I come back to your use of 'Indigenality' instead of 'Aboriginality'? I think on one level the primary difficulty in using 'Indigenality' is that you lose the politically powerful term 'Aboriginal', as well as having a lot of confusion potentially produced by your having to speak about, or for, the other Indigenous race.

m   I don't see any problem with that. It means Indigenous people of Australia will have to go and find out what indigenous people elsewhere are doing.

jl   There's not a difficulty that by imposing this term you're excising an indigenous population out of Australia?

m   The British came here and they established something called Australia which is an artificial construct, and they have by force imposed everything on us.

cf   Of course, but it still seems to me there could be a problem with removing the term Aboriginality, because it is so pervasively current as generally representing certain kinds of things.

m   That's the whole point about doing it, isn't it?

jl   Are you saying that's why you want to remove it because it becomes such an expedient type of thing, and it's not a term that was chosen by the Indigenous people?

m   It's like Mudrooroo and Colin Johnson. So put Aboriginality in brackets after Indigenality, and so you have a whole discourse continuing.

cf   The only thing is you would really have to explore the political effects of moving into another paradigm. It may be much easier said than done.

m   Unfortunately ATSIC has done it already. They haven't explored the potential effects, but they have moved towards it and so have a whole lot of Indigenous people now.

cf   What I was trying to focus on is the way *Writing from the Fringe* gets rewritten, and it will be quite influential. (This copy from the library is scribbled all over, dozens of people have been reading it.) To completely occlude the differences is problematic, I think. Politically there are united interests, but if you are trying to talk in subtle sorts of ways about cultural traditions or beliefs, they are vastly opposed. … Coming back to the notion of the aesthetic, one critic says about Aboriginal writing: 'By keeping in mind the contingent and performative act of story-telling we can avoid depoliticising and aestheticising these stories.' What they seem to be saying is that, as soon as you take on any notion of aesthetics (whether bourgeois or Western or whatever), you simply cannot apply any criterion of quality or the politics go. That seems to me fairly crude, but one wouldn't necessarily want to completely reject a notion of aesthetics. In *Writing from the Fringe* you suggested that there could be an alternative aesthetics, evolved out of an Aboriginal world-view, one resting on different central criteria?

m   Yes. There is an aesthetic effect in Indigenous English and I think a lot of Indigenous writers like Jack Davis use it so that our people can recognise it. The whole point is, what is aesthetics? As far as I know, if you receive pleasure from a text, that is aesthetics and if I gain pleasure from an Indigenous text, then there is an aesthetics there.

jl   There is a lot of bloody awful writing, regardless of whether it is Aboriginal or not, and to run an argument about remembering that it is contingently performative, and don't depoliticise it by demanding an aesthetic from it, is like, well, don't demand any quality from an Aboriginal writer because, let's face it, they are just Aboriginal. You could run a counter-argument that it is not anti-racist at all, that it is actually quite complexly racist to say that.

m   My 'Giant Debbil Dingo' poem, for example, which is very aesthetic, consciously uses Indigenous English so that people can appreciate the flow of words and then listen to the message if they want to. Is this aesthetics? Appreciating the flow of words, and how it is written? My argument against a lot of these bloody lifestories is that editors have got to them and made them really boring. It's just flat prose without much aesthetical value.

cf   One of the things that you are moving towards doing in *Writing from the Fringe*, but you haven't developed it, is saying what sorts of aesthetic quality or pleasure could be produced by different kinds of texts. One doesn't have to be constrained by different genres, because it can become most interesting when they merge. There are types of writing within a particular genre that have got aesthetic quality in terms of the way they are performing that particular genre. But there's been a tendency to go back to the 'fifties kind of thing—if it has got heavy politics in it, it has got no quality.

jl   This has been the argument of some Aboriginal critics, like Jackie Huggins who has said: 'Don't patronise us by not engaging with us as writers, by engaging with us like we are sort of poor blackfellas and you should make allowances for us because we are just poor blackfellas.' And Bobbi Sykes found the way Margaret Somerville had rendered Patsy Cohen's Aboriginal English in *Ingelba* patronising. Then you find other critics that say: 'Well, what's being produced is really contingent and really political', but they don't ever specify how. They don't articulate what this aesthetic form is—is it a bourgeois aesthetic, is it a working class aesthetic, is it a non-dominant racial position aesthetic? Just some kind of spurious undefined aesthetic.

cf   I don't think you have to hand any term over to the other side, allow them to own aesthetics or anything else. You say, well, that is your notion, but I have another one …

m   I read Herb Wharton as saying that, and so it is there.

jl   There seem to be a lot of non-Aboriginal critics who want to fix a stage of Aboriginal studies at a point where it is not autobiography anymore, it is biography, and you don't read it to say that it is aesthetically bad, you read it to say: when it is performed it's okay, we can listen to it, and kind of fix it at a point where it is all right, we can engage with this stuff even though we are not black.

m   But aesthetics are very, very important in storytelling. You always look around the audience to see their reactions. This is the aesthetic effect, the whole process of telling. I do have a problem in taking performance away from the arena and placing it in a book.

jl   Would you say that that's missing from Herb's book? When Herb performs a story there is a direct engagement because he has that storytelling thing happening with his audience. In this book it's been edited and mediated, it's gone.

m   When Herb is not allowed to do that, it becomes written and the aesthetics lies down on the page and dies an unnatural death. Herb finds his inspiration in the yarn, from oral literature; Sammy Watson gets his from the ancestors. And so you go either to Indigenous culture or Indigenous storytelling. You go to our side of the fence and that's why there are problems in how these books are received.

jl   So when you say 'the Fringe'...?

m   I don't any more, the term came from those fringe settlements around some country towns. It is when we move into the town that our territory changes. It is the same with our culture; when our art pieces started being placed in art galleries instead of museums, things started to change. Indigenous culture and its products have achieved an importance in Australia, which is the most important thing that has happened to Indigenous people in the last 200 years. It seems that we have now arrived, but we still have to work hard and keep this place, a place after all where we belong as the Indigenous people of Australia. It is our land and we have never given up our sovereignty.

jl   You've actually left that term behind now and your new edition refers to Milli Milli Wangka or 'Papertalk'.

m   Yes, to acknowledge that there are Indigenous writers. We have arrived and claim our sovereignty of the page. We have proved our worth and claim our paper rights.

Carole Ferrier is an Associate Professor in the University of Queensland. She is also an activist and writer in socialist and women's liberation areas. She is the founding editor of Hecate: A Women's Interdisciplinary Journal *which she has continued to edit since 1975.*

    Janine Little is a former journalist who has worked on several newspapers in Australia and the United Kingdom. She has published a number of articles on black writers and has taught Aboriginal and Torres Strait Islander courses.

Select Bibliography

Andrews, L.V. *Crystal Woman, The Sisters of the Dreamtime*. New York: Warner Books, 1987.

Astley, T. *Vanishing Points*. Melbourne: Heinemann, 1992.

Baker, S. 'Binarisms and duality: magic realism and postcolonialism', *Span*, 36, October 1993.

Barnes, J. (ed) *The Writer in Australia: A Collection of Literary Documents 1856 to 1964*. Melbourne: Oxford University Press, 1969.

Barthes, R. *Image-Music-Text*. Glasgow: Fontana, 1977.

Beckett, S. *Waiting for Godot*. London: Faber, 1956.

Bennell, E. 'My Spiritual Dreaming', play performed at Perth Festival, 1992 (unpublished).

Benterrak, K., Muecke, S. & Roe, P. *Reading the Country: Introduction to Nomadology*. Fremantle: Fremantle Arts Centre Press, 1984.

Berndt, C. 'A drama of north-eastern Arnhem Land', *Oceania*, 22(3), 1952.

Berndt, R.M. *Kunapipi*. New York: International Universities Press, 1951.

—— *Djanggawul*. Melbourne: Cheshire, 1952.

—— *Love Songs of Arnhem Land*. Melbourne: Nelson, 1976.

—— *Three Faces of Love*. Melbourne: Nelson, 1976.

Berndt, R.M. & Berndt, C.H. *Arnhem Land: Its History and People*. Melbourne: Cheshire, 1954.

—— *The Speaking Land: Myth and Story in Aboriginal Australia*. Ringwood, Vic: Penguin Books, 1989.

Bird, D. & Haskell, D. *Whose Place? A Study of Sally Morgan's* My Place. Sydney: Angus & Robertson, 1992.

Brandenstein, C.G. von. *Tatura: Aboriginal Song Poetry from the Pilbara*. Adelaide: Rigby, 1974.

Brennan, F. *One Land, One Nation: Mabo—Towards 2001*. St Lucia: UQP, 1995.

Bropho, R. *Fringedweller*. Chippendale, NSW: Alternative Publishing, 1980.

—— 'The great journey of the Aboriginal teenagers', in J. Davis, S. Muecke et al (eds), *Paperbark*. St Lucia: UQP, 1990.

Chatwin, B. *The Songlines*. London: J. Cape, 1987.

Chesson, K. (ed) *Jack Davis: A Life-story*. Melbourne: Dent, 1988.

Chi, J. & Kuckles. *Bran Nue Dae*. Sydney: Currency Press, 1991.

Clare, M. *Karobran: The Story of an Aboriginal Girl*. Chippendale, NSW: Alternative Publishing, 1978.

Cochrane, K. *Oodgeroo*. St Lucia: UQP, 1994.

Cohen, P. & Somerville, M. *Ingelba and the Five Black Matriarchs*. Sydney: Allen & Unwin, 1990.

Coloured Stone. *Konibba Rock*. Alice Springs: Imparja Records, 1984.

—— *Island of Greed*. Alice Springs: Imparja Records, 1985.

Cornwall, G. 'Evaluating protest fiction', *English in Africa*, 7(1), 1980.

Cox, L. *Kimberley Legend*. Perth: Abmusic, n.d.

Davidson, J. Interview with Kath Walker, *Meanjin* (Aboriginal issue), 36(4), 1977, pp. 428–41.

Davis, J. *Jagardoo*. Sydney: Methuen, 1978.

—— *Kullark* and *The Dreamers*. Sydney: Currency Press, 1982.

—— *The First-born and Other Poems*. Melbourne: Dent, 1983 (1st edn 1970).

—— *No Sugar*. Sydney: Currency Press, 1986.

—— *John Pat and Other Poems*. Melbourne: Dent, 1988.

—— *Barungin (Smell the Wind)*. Sydney: Currency Press, 1989.

—— *A Boy's Life*. Broome: Magabala Books, 1991.

—— *Black Life, Poems*. St Lucia: UQP, 1992.

Davis, J., Johnson, E., Walley, R. & Maza, B. *Plays from Black Australia*. Sydney: Currency Press, 1989.

Davis, J., Muecke, S. et al (eds) *Paperbark: A Collection of Black Australian Writings*. St Lucia: UQP, 1990.

Delany, S.R. *Triton*. London: Grafton, 1992.

Dixon, G. *Holocaust Island*. St Lucia: UQP, 1990.

Dixon, R.M.W. & Duwell, M. *The Honey-ant Men's Love Song and Other Aboriginal Song Poems*. St Lucia: UQP, 1990.

—— *Little Eva at Moonlight Creek and Other Aboriginal Song Poems*. St Lucia: UQP, 1994.

Doobov, R. 'The new Dreamtime: Kath Walker in Australian literature', *Australian Literary Studies*, 6(1), 1973.

Egan, T. *Ted Egan Presents the Kimberley*. Alice Springs: The Artist, n.d.

Fanon, F. *The Wretched of the Earth*. Harmondsworth: Penguin Books, 1973.

Ferrier, C. 'Aboriginal women's narratives', in C. Ferrier (ed), *Gender, Politics and Fiction*. St Lucia: UQP, 1992.

—— '"Written out of the text?" The reception of Aboriginal women's writing', in L. Rowen & J. McNamee (eds), *Voices of a Margin*. Rockhampton: Central Queensland University Press, 1995.

Fogarty, L. *Kargun*. Coominya, Qld: C. Buchanan, 1980.

—— *Yoogum Yoogum*. Ringwood, Vic: Penguin Books, 1982.

—— *Kudjela*. Coominya, Qld: C. Buchanan, 1983.

—— *Ngutji*. Brisbane: C. Buchanan, 1984.

—— *Jagera*. Coominya, Qld: C. Buchanan, 1989?

—— *New and Selected Poems: Munaldjali, Mutuerjaraera*. Melbourne: Hyland House, 1995.

Foucault, M. 'What is an author?' (trs J. Harari), in J. Harari (ed), *Textual Strategies: Perspectives in Post-Structuralist Criticism*. London: Methuen, 1979, pp. 141–600.

Gilbert, K. *Because a White Man'll Never Do It*. Sydney: Angus & Robertson, 1973/94.

—— *Living Black: Blacks Talk to Kevin Gilbert*. Ringwood, Vic: Penguin Books, 1984.

—— *People Are Legends*. St Lucia: UQP, 1978.

—— 'Black policies', in J. Davis & B. Hodge (eds), *Aboriginal Writing Today*. Canberra: Aboriginal Studies Press, 1985.

—— *Inside Black Australia. An Anthology of Aboriginal Poetry*. Ringwood, Vic: Penguin Books, 1988.

—— *The Cherry Pickers*. Canberra: Burrambinga Books, 1988.

—— *The Blackside: People Are Legends and Other Poems*. Melbourne: Hyland House, 1990.

—— *Aboriginal Sovereignty, Justice, the Law and Land*. Canberra: Burrambinga Books, 1993.

—— *Black from the Edge*. Melbourne: Hyland House, 1994.

Ginibi, Ruby Langford. *Don't Take Your Love to Town*. Ringwood, Vic: Penguin Books, 1988.

—— *Real Deadly*. Sydney: Angus & Robertson, 1992.

—— 'Ruby records her history', interview by Sonya Sandham, *Sydney Morning Herald*, 26 June 1993, p. 13.

—— *My Bundjalung People*. St Lucia: UQP, 1994.

Grotowski, J. *Towards a Poor Theatre*. London: Eyre Methuen, 1975.

Hegel, G.W.F. *The Philosophy of Fine Art*. New York: Hacker Art Books, 1975.

Herbert, X. *Capricornia*. Sydney: Publicist, 1937.

—— *Poor Fellow My Country*. Sydney: Collins, 1975.

Hercus, L. & Sutton, P. *This Is What Happened: Historical Narratives by Aborigines*. Canberra: Aboriginal Studies Press, 1986.

Hodge, R. & Mishra, V. *Dark Side of the Dream*. Sydney: Allen & Unwin, 1990.

Homer. *The Odyssey* (trs R. Fitzgerald). London: Panther, 1965.

Hooton, Joy. *Stories of Herself When Young: Autobiographies of Childhood by Australian Women*. Melbourne: Oxford University Press, 1990.

Howitt, A.W. 'Native songs and song makers', *Journal of the Anthropological Institute*, 13 (1884), pp. 185–97.

Huggins, J. 'Writing my mother's life', *Hecate*, 17(1), 1991.

—— 'A contemporary view of Aboriginal women's relationship to the white women's movement', in S. Hawthorne, J. Huggins, L.C. Johnson et al (eds), *A Woman's Place in Australia*. Geelong: Deakin University, 1992.

—— 'Always was always will be', *Australian Historical Studies*, 100, 1993.

Huggins, R. & Huggins, J. *Auntie Rita*. Canberra: Aboriginal Studies Press, 1994.

Hunter, R. *Thoughts Within*. Melbourne: White Records, 1994.

Identity (Aboriginal and Islander Identity). Sydney, Perth, Canberra: Aboriginal Publications Foundation, 1972–82.

Johnson, Eva. 'Murras', in J. Davis, E. Johnson, R. Walley & B. Maza, *Plays from Black Australia*. Sydney: Currency Press, 1989.

Kelleher, V. *Wintering*. St Lucia: UQP, 1990.

Keneally, T. *The Chant of Jimmie Blacksmith*. Sydney: Angus & Robertson, 1972.

Labumore (Elsie Roughsey). *An Aboriginal Mother Tells of the Old and the New*. Fitzroy, Vic: McPhee Gribble, 1984.

Langton, M. *'Well, I Heard It on the Radio and Saw It on the Television': An Essay for the Australian Film Commission on the Politics and Aesthetics of Filmmaking by and about Aboriginal People and Things.* North Sydney: Australian Film Commission, 1993.

Laseur, C. '"beDevil": colonial images, Aboriginal memories', *Span*, 37, December, 1993.

Little, J. '"Tiddas in struggle": a consultative project with Murri, Koori and Nyoongah women', *Span*, 37, December, 1993.

—— 'Placing authority in Aboriginal women's prose', in L. Rowen & J. McNamee (eds), *Voices of a Margin*. Rockhampton: Central Queensland University Press, 1995.

Macartney, F.W. *Australian Literary Essays*. Sydney: Angus & Robertson, 1957.

McGrath, A. *Born in the Saddle*. Sydney: Allen & Unwin, 1987.

McGuinness, B. & Walker, D. 'The politics of Aboriginal literature', in J. Davis & B. Hodge (eds), *Aboriginal Writing Today*. Canberra: Aboriginal Studies Press, 1985.

McKellar, H. *Matya-Mundi: a History of the Aboriginal People of South West Queensland*. Cunnamulla, Qld: Australian Native Welfare Association, 1984.

McLaren, P. *Sweet Water—Stolen Land*. St Lucia: UQP, 1993.

Malouf, D. 'The only speaker of his tongue', in *Antipodes*. London: Chatto & Windus, 1985.

Manning, N. *Close to the Bone*. Sydney: Currency Press, 1994.

Maris, H. & Borg, S. *Women of the Sun*. Sydney: Currency Press, 1983.

Marshall-Stoneking, Billy. 'Epic trek's characters lost in the telling', *Australian Weekend Review*, 6–7 April 1996.

Mattingley, C. & Hampton, K. (eds) *Survival in Our Own Land: 'Aboriginal' Experiences in 'South Australia' since 1836, told by Nungas and Others*. Adelaide: Wakefield Press, 1988.

Merritt, R.J. *The Cake Man*. Sydney: Currency Press, 1978/1983.

—— 'Eora Corroboree' (video text), *Impact*, ABC, 13 September, 1986.

Miller, J. *Koori: A Will To Win*. Sydney: Angus & Robertson, 1985.

Mirritji, J. *My People's Life*. Millingimbi, NT: Literature Production Centre, 1983.

Mixed Relations. *Aboriginal Woman*. Sydney: Red Eye Records/Polydor, 1993.

Modjeska, D. *Poppy*. Melbourne: McPhee Gribble, 1990.

Morgan, M. *Mutant Message Down Under*. New York: HarperCollins, 1994.

Morgan, S. *My Place*. Fremantle: Fremantle Arts Centre Press, 1987.

—— *Wanamurraganya: The Story of Jack McPhee*. Fremantle: Fremantle Arts Centre Press, 1989.

Mudrooroo. *Dr Wooreddy's Prescription for Enduring the Ending of the World*. Melbourne: Hyland House, 1983.

—— *The Song Circle of Jacky and Selected Poems*. Melbourne: Hyland House, 1986.

—— 'Mutjingabba', play workshopped at Second Aboriginal Dramatists Conference, Sydney, 1989 (unpublished).

—— *Writing from the Fringe*. Melbourne: Hyland House, 1990.

—— *The Master of the Ghost Dreaming*. Sydney: Angus & Robertson, 1991.

—— *Us Mob*. Sydney: Angus & Robertson, 1995.

Murray, Les. *The New Oxford Book of Australian Verse*. Melbourne: Oxford University Press, 1986.

Nangan, J. *Joe Nangan's Dreaming: Aboriginal Legends of the North-West*. Melbourne: Nelson, 1976.

Neidjie, B. *Story about Feeling*. Broome: Magabala Books, 1989.

No Fixed Address. *From My Eyes*. Melbourne: Rough Diamond Records, 1982. Reissued on CD Mushroom Records, 1992/3.

Nowra, L. *Crow*. Sydney: Currency Press, 1994.

Nugi Garimara/Doris Pilkington. *Follow the Rabbit-proof Fence*. St Lucia: UQP, 1996.

Oodgeroo (Noonuccal)/Walker, Kath. *We Are Going*. Brisbane: Jacaranda, 1964.

—— *The Dawn Is at Hand*. Brisbane: Jacaranda, 1966.

—— *My People*. Brisbane: Jacaranda, 1970.

—— *Stradbroke Dreamtime*. Sydney: Angus & Robertson, 1972/1992.

—— 'Custodians of the land', speech delivered at Griffith University, 22 April 1989 (published in Cochrane 1994).

Pettman, J. 'Gendered knowledges: Aboriginal women and the politics of feminism', in B. Attwood & J. Arnold (eds), *Power, Knowledge and Aborigines*. Special edn of *Journal of Australian Studies*, 35, 1992.

Prichard, K.S. *Coonardoo*. London: Cape, 1929 (reprinted 1964, 1990).

Rabinow, P. (ed) *The Foucault Reader*. London: Penguin Books, 1984.

Randall, B. *Bob Randall*. Alice Springs: Imparja Records, n.d.

Riffaterre, M. *Semiotics of Poetry*. London: Methuen, 1980.

Roach, A. *Charcoal Lane*. Melbourne: Aurora Records, 1990.

—— *You Have the Power*. Sydney: Angus & Robertson, 1994.

Roe, P. *Gularabulu* (ed. S. Muecke). Fremantle: Fremantle Arts Centre Press, 1983.

Roheim, Geza. *The Eternal Ones of the Dream: A Psycho-analytical Interpretation of Australian Myth and Ritual*. New York: International Universities Press, 1945.

Rowley, C.D. *The Politics of Aboriginal Reform*. Ringwood, Vic: Penguin Books, 1986.

—— *The Remote Aborigines*. Ringwood, Vic: Penguin Books, 1970.

Rutherford, A. (ed) *Aboriginal Culture Today*. Sydney: Dangaroo Press/Kunapipi, 1988.

Sachs, W. *The Development Dictionary: A Guide to Knowledge and Power*. London: Zed, 1992.

Said, E.W. *Orientalism*. London: Penguin Books, 1987.

Sellin, E. *The Dramatic Concepts of Antonin Artaud*. Chicago: Chicago University Press, 1975.

Shaw, B. (ed) *Countrymen: The Life Histories of Four Aboriginal Men*. Canberra: Aboriginal Studies Press, 1986.

Shoemaker, A. *Black Words, White Page: Aboriginal Literature 1929–1988*. St Lucia: UQP, 1989.

—— *Oodgeroo, A Tribute*. St Lucia: UQP, 1994.

—— 'Selling Yothu Yindi', in G. Papaellinas (ed), *RePublica*. Sydney: Angus & Robertson, 1994.

Skipper, P. *The Pushman*. Fitzroy Crossing, WA: SIL, 198?

Smith, Shirley & Sykes, Bobby. *Mum Shirl*. Richmond, Vic: Heinemann Educational, 1981 (2nd edn 1987).

Somerville, M. 'Life (h)istory writing: the relationship between talk and text', *Hecate*, 17(1), 1991.

Spencer, W.B. & Gillen, F.J. *The Northern Tribes of Central Australia*. London: Macmillan, 1904.

Strehlow, T.G.H. *Aranda Traditions*. Melbourne: Melbourne University Press, 1947.

—— *Songs of Central Australia*. Sydney: Angus & Robertson, 1971.

Sykes, R. *Love Poems and Other Revolutionary Actions*, 2nd ed. St Lucia: UQP, 1988.

Tarrago, I. 'Response to Sally Morgan and the construction of Aboriginality', *Australian Historical Studies*, 100, 1993.

Taylor, 'A review of *The Dawn Is At Hand* by Kath Walker', *Overland*, 36, May 1967.

Thomas, W. Papers, Set 214, uncatalogued mss. Sydney: Mitchell Library.

Thompson, J. *Reaching Back: Queensland Aboriginal People Recall Early Days at Yarrabah Mission*. Canberra: Aboriginal Studies Press, 1989.

Tiddas. *Inside My Kitchen*. Sydney: Blackheart Music, 1992.

Turner, G. 'Breaking the frame: the representation of Aborigines in Australian film', in A. Rutherford (ed), *Aboriginal Culture Today*. Sydney: Dangaroo Press/Kunapipi, 1988.

—— *Making It Natural: Nationalism and Australian Popular Culture*. St Leonards, NSW: Allen & Unwin, 1994.

Unaipon, D. Legendary Tales of the Australian Aborigines, unpublished ms. Sydney: Mitchell Library, ?1929.

Walker, Kath (see Oodgeroo)

Walley, R. 'Coordah', in J. Davis, E. Johnson, R. Walley & B. Maza, *Plays from Black Australia*. Sydney: Currency Press, 1989.

Ward, G. *Wandering Girl*. Broome: Magabala Books, 1987.

Watego, C. 'Aboriginal poetry and white criticism', in J. Davis & R. Hodge (eds), *Aboriginal Writing Today*. Canberra: Aboriginal Studies Press, 1985.

Watson, S. *The Kadaitcha Sung*. Ringwood, Vic: Penguin Books, 1990.

Webb, H. 'Conning popular music: up against the wall', *Australian Journal of Cultural Studies*, 21, 1984.

Wellek, R. & Warren, A. *Theory of Literature*. Harmondsworth: Penguin Books, 1973.

Weller, A. *Day of the Dog*. Sydney: Pan Books, 1981.

—— *Going Home*. Sydney: Allen & Unwin, 1986.

West, I. *Pride Against Prejudice: Reminiscences of a Tasmanian Aborigine*. Canberra: Aboriginal Studies Press, 1984.

Wharton, H. *Unbranded*. St Lucia: UQP, 1992.

—— *Where Ya' Been, Mate?* St Lucia: UQP, 1996.

Willett, J. (trs and ed) *Brecht on Theatre*. London: Methuen, 1964.

Willmot, E. *Pemulwuy, the Rainbow Warrior*. McMahons Point, NSW: Weldon, 1987.

Yothu Yindi. *Homeland Movement*. Sydney: Mushroom Records, 1989.

—— *Tribal Voice*. Sydney: Mushroom Records, 1991.

—— *Freedom*. Sydney: Mushroom Records, 1993.

Index